360
DEGREES
LONGITUDE

360 DEGREES LONGITUDE

JOHN HIGHAM

One Family's Journey
Around the World

PROSPECTA PRESS

To the wonderful people of Lushoto, Tanzania.
May I someday be able to return the favor.

CONTENTS

Author's Note • *ix*

AUTHOR'S NOTE

Travel can change a person, and it can change the world. That's a bold statement, and I believe it.

As we look beyond our borders, it is easy to see how *different* people are, *over there.* It is a lot harder to see how *similar* they are. I'm convinced that you have go and spend time *over there* to accomplish that. It can be hard to do, which is why I wrote this book: to take you to distant lands and meet the people who live *over there* to show that, at the end of the day, humankind in all its wonderful weirdness is the same all over the planet.

A large part of this story is contained within the pages of this book, but there is more than what you are holding in your hands. Whenever you see the Google Earth logo 🌏 there is more waiting for you online. The Google Earth companion layer that is available online contains the "Director's Cut" of anecdotes, photos, video, and stories that couldn't be presented on mere paper. Google Earth is free and is probably the coolest piece of software developed by humankind. The extra features add a dimension to the manuscript that will connect you to the places around the globe in a way previously impossible. There is a quick tutorial in the appendix that explains what you need to know to use these features.

The Appendix of How To is chock-full of details about how one would go about planning their own around-the-world adventure, from basics on budgeting, to homeschooling children on the road, to getting immunizations. Even more information can be found at www.360degreeslongitude.com. If there is anything you want to know about world travel in general or about this story in particular that isn't in this book or on our Web site, send me an e-mail at john@360degreeslongitude.com.

0.

Countdown

"You're awake, I can tell. What are you thinking about?"

It was my wife, September. I really didn't want to be talking about this, as we had already discussed everything there was to discuss. "Same thing as you."

"I've been looking forward to this trip for over ten years," she said. "Now that we're just weeks away from leaving, I'm afraid."

"It's just nerves. Once we're on the road, we'll get into a rhythm, and it'll be fine."

"Then why are you awake?"

"I can't turn my brain off. You know. EBS." EBS is shorthand for Energizer Bunny Syndrome—my brain just keeps going and going. As an engineer, I am duty-bound to reduce everything to three-letter acronyms. September just accepts it.

As it applies in this case, EBS meant going over and over scenarios about what could go wrong during our 52 weeks abroad. I had a pit in the bottom of my stomach.

www.360degreeslongitude.com/concept3d/360degreeslongitude.kmz

How is it that Obi-Wan Kenobi made us toss and turn at night? Use Google Earth and the *360 Degrees Longitude* layer to find out.

. . .

Urban legend has it that rocket scientists are smart, but I can be pretty clueless. It was that cluelessness that led to my meeting September. After finishing graduate school I accepted a job offer in the San Francisco Bay Area from a commercial aerospace company. I moved far from my small-town roots and shared an apartment with a couple of other guys who were also relatively new in town. We set about the difficult task of meeting girls who would actually still talk to us after they found out we were engineers. Despite our geekiness we were able to build up a decent network of acquaintances, and so one day when I locked myself out of my apartment (see *clueless* above), I wasn't completely without options.

As my roommates wouldn't be home until late that evening, I searched my brain for phone numbers. I had gone out a couple of times with a girl named Biz, so I called her with hopes of spending some quality time with her, or at least helping myself to her bread and peanut butter.

Biz wasn't home. This was a solid decade before the blessed arrival of the personal digital assistant (aka electronic brain). For reasons I can't recall nearly two decades later, the only other phone number I remembered was for Biz's friend, September. But remembering those seven digits may be one of the most brilliant things I have ever done.

September not only provided bread and peanut butter; she had jelly, too. Plus, she was a smart blonde with a knockout figure and had a cool mountain bike. She must have seen some quality in me to counterbalance my cluelessness, because we soon became inseparable.

On the face of it, September and I were an unlikely match. Though I had a few nerdy interests, I owned one of those high-powered Japanese bullet-bikes that your mother warned you about. I wore racing leathers during my daily commute. At night I listened to Pink Floyd on speakers that were as tall as I was. September couldn't have picked Roger Waters from Johnny Carson in a lineup, and she played violin in a local symphony.

September hooked me with the gorgeous and smart thing, and after several trips to the symphony I grudgingly learned to distinguish a melody in a minor key ("bad guy music") from a melody in a major one. She learned to appreciate tearing up mountain roads on the back of a motorcycle, and I pretended not to fall asleep during films with subtitles.

Before earning my graduate degree, I had spent a lot of time wandering the western United States on my motorcycle, while September had been doing a significant amount of wandering of her own. Shortly before we met she spent a month backpacking around West Africa. "Why Africa?" I asked.

She shrugged her shoulders, "Dunno. Sounded fun."

September had also spent six months on the island of Tonga during her senior year of college, doing anthropology fieldwork. "I loved my experience in Tonga," she explained to me. "I came home a changed person. The airlines lost my luggage, and I arrived with just a notebook, a camera, and the clothes on my back. Five months went by before I saw my luggage and in that time I learned that all I needed to be happy was something to eat, something to wear, and somewhere to sleep. But it wasn't all as romantic as it sounds. Not long before I came home island fever had set in, and I gradually came to realize that what I really wanted to do with my life was to go home and get a job in high-tech. That's how I got into computer software."

I was in love. Here was a woman who was five years younger than me, and, despite the fact that she had a degree in anthropology, one of those "soft" disciplines that engineers love to diss, she was making more money than I was. I asked her to marry me.

We had been married two years when a career opportunity presented itself. My company was looking for someone with my exact qualifications to go to Japan for twelve months. I had 24 hours to make a decision, and we would have to leave for Japan in three weeks.

I called September at work. "How would you like to move to Japan in three weeks?" I asked. Her reaction was strong and without hesitation. "OKAY! Sounds like fun!" And although it wasn't actually per plan, it was in Japan that September and I started our family.

Our time in Japan was the genesis of the idea of traveling around the world with our kids, although we didn't recognize it as such then. Being away from everything we knew forced us to rely solely on each other, and brought us so close that we knew we wanted to recreate the experience with our kids—when we had them.

September returned to the United States when she was eight months pregnant with our daughter Katrina. One month later my yearlong contract in Japan was over and I flew home. September met me at baggage claim and said, "Can we go to the hospital after this? I think I'm in labor." Katrina joined our family and when our son Jordan arrived three years later, we already knew that in eight or nine years we would leave the comforts of home in order to travel around the world with them.

In the interest of conditioning the children for our around-the-world trip, we started traveling with Katrina and Jordan when they were in diapers, visiting such varied destinations as Maui, Mexico, and New Zealand. Jordan was just learning to talk when he heard of our future yearlong trip. When referring to it, the words "World-the-Round Trip" came tumbling out of his mouth; the name stuck.

As the kids grew older, the abstract discussions about this future trip started to come into focus. Three years before we left we took an ambitious month-long test trip to the most expensive places we could think of, Switzerland and Austria. This was to help us gauge our budget, but it was also to test ourselves.

That trip cemented our resolve to execute the plan. Although we had been setting money aside for several years already, suddenly we put a rigid savings plan into place with a specific date in mind. We placed a gigantic map on a wall of our house. A favorite family pastime became placing Post-it notes near locations we would like to visit, describing activities there, climate patterns and so on. About a year before departure our research expanded to include airfares, equipment, online bill paying, and homeschooling Katrina and Jordan while on the road. The months remaining whittled down to weeks and the number of items on our to-do list seemed more numerous than the days remaining. We drew up our wills. We rented our house. September's parents offered to maintain our domestic affairs at home, like receiving our mail and managing the house. As our departure date neared, the tempo increased and so did our anxiety level.

What made us want to leave home, pull our kids out of school, then risk life, limb, and career to travel? September and I had learned how travel can shape one's thinking; we wanted to give this to our children. Living in an affluent country it is easy to think of luxuries such as a manicured lawn and flashy car as things we "need" and that all we have to do to obtain them is buy them. When we embarked on our adventure, Katrina was eleven, and Jordan was eight. Our plan was to help Katrina and Jordan distinguish between wants and needs and to experience first hand that all we really *need* is something to eat, something to wear, and somewhere to sleep.

We also realized there would be an additional benefit. Living in modern suburbia came with many well-intentioned interests, ranging from Little League to the PTA, all gnawing away at our family time. Our plan to get away from it all so that we could have quality family time while our kids were still young became such a priority that the casual observer would have thought that's all we were doing. Friends, family, and coworkers started a betting pool over whether or not we would ever return.

Katrina's Journal, June 1
In merely five hours me, my brother, my mom, and my dad leave for the airport for an adventure of a lifetime. This isn't your normal two-week trip; it's a full twelve months, 52 weeks, 365 days of freedom.

Twelve years ago, a year before I was born, this very glorious idea found its way into my parents' heads while they were living in Japan: to travel for a whole year and see the world.

Now, the world is a big place, and we can't see all of it. But we are seeing a pretty big portion of it in my mind. First we're going Iceland, but only for a couple days. Then we'll fly to London. Once there, my dad will put our bikes together, for they can be taken apart to be packed. From London we'll bike all over Europe on tandems, my mom and me on one, my brother and dad on the other. Our things will be packed in bike panniers. After five months we'll arrive in Istanbul, Turkey, ready to hop on a plane to Tanzania, where we'll go on an animal safari. Then we'll go to an island off the coast of Africa called Mauritius. From Mauritius we'll go to Singapore, then Japan, China, and Thailand, where we'll spend Christmas. Granny is going to visit us for Christmas. Our last stops will be in Central and South America.

Getting on that first plane to Iceland was a lot like looking over the edge of a cliff, closing our eyes, and then jumping. We couldn't know it at the time, but every worry that kept us awake before we left home pretty much came to pass, from broken bones to being stranded in the middle of nowhere. In spite of (or because of) it all, we not only survived, we thrived. This is a story about coping with those challenges, but it's more than that. It is a story about discovering how people all over the world are similar, yet different in profoundly subtle ways, and how because of those very differences we were always able to find something to eat, something to wear, and somewhere to sleep.

www.360degreeslongitude.com/concept3d/360degreeslongitude.kmz

How could a chocolate-covered malt ball scuttle an around-the-world trip? Use Google Earth and the *360 Degrees Longitude* layer to find out.

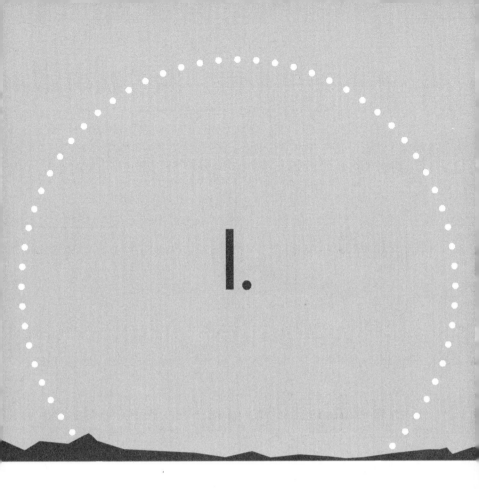

I.

SPLAT

1.

Geothermal Sludge and a Good Advertising Agency

June 1–June 4
Iceland

I don't remember stepping off the plane in Iceland. After more than a decade of planning, we were finally on our way. My head was buzzing.

I do remember tumbling out of the airport. Our family of four hauled our four massive bicycle cases containing our two tandems plus eight bicycle panniers (special bags designed to attach to a bicycle) that contained all our gear. We were anything but inconspicuous with our small mountain of equipment. As we proceeded to our rental car, one person was compelled to inform us of the merits of traveling light.

"Why on earth would you need that much stuff on vacation?" our new friend asked. "Are you preparing for the end of the world?"

I live for moments like this. "We aren't on vacation. We are cycling from here to Istanbul," I replied, "and then continuing on around the world. What you are looking at is our bicycles."

I kept walking without breaking my stride, listening to his response trail off as the distance between us grew. "Cycling? From here? With two kids?"

Not really, but Mr. Smarty-Pants didn't need to know that. While we were planning on cycling from London to Istanbul, the remainder of our journey around the world was either going to be with or without our tandems, all depending on who you asked—me, or September. The funny thing is, despite what it looked like, we were traveling light. Sure we had two tandems, but we also had schoolbooks, first-aid supplies, a well-stocked bicycle tool-kit, and even a tent and sleeping bags. Personal items, such as clothes, seemed like an afterthought. And all of it had to fit into our panniers.

We also had September's treasured wilderness survival saw. We'd spent our last day in the United States trying to get everything in the "to take on the trip" box to fit in our bicycle panniers. Each of our piles of underwear and socks were reduced by 25 percent. Towels got cut in half with scissors. We agonized over whether we should bring just rectangular Band-Aids, or square ones, too. I removed the saw, but September was adamant.

"We might need that! Put it back!"

"What on earth are we going to do with a saw?"

September takes being prepared much more seriously than your average Boy Scout. I thought of our earthquake kit at home with the two 50-gallon barrels of water. If a wire embedded with teeth was going to make her feel secure, I was willing to give in; it was nothing compared to the electronic brain ("e.brain") I relied upon for *my* security blanket.

We maneuvered our great heap of belongings to our rental car. Arriving at the appointed spot, we discovered a Toyota Yaris subcompact occupying the space. "This stuff will never fit," I said.

"I didn't marry an engineer for nothing," September countered.

September and I frequently challenge, test, and even play pranks on each other. While it may seem somewhat contrarian, this style has kept our relationship as fresh as the day we met. I accepted the challenge without a second thought. After a moment of luggage Tetris, I felt guilty having eight-year-old Jordan's face wedged between some luggage and the roof of the car, but it all fit. Pulling out of the parking lot I called, "Little Dude! You okay back there? Can you breathe like that?" Hitting one good pothole would stamp the likeness of Jordan's face permanently into the ceiling.

"Shur! Diz iz fun, Dad!" came his muffled reply. Everything is an adventure for a kid.

One of the few accommodations we pre-arranged before leaving California was at a hostel in Reykjavík simply because we would arrive in the afternoon on a red-eye flight and would need a place to sleep right away. With me acting as navigator, September maneuvered the Yaris straight to the hostel. I dislodged the kids and the luggage from the back of the car while September checked us in. A moment later the kids and I started bringing our luggage into the lobby of the well-kept hostel. September was picking up our keys from the manager.

"Any problems?" I asked.

"Nope," September replied. "They were expecting us."

"You were speaking to him in English," Katrina noted. "I heard you. I thought you would have to speak Iceland."

"The language here is Icelandic," September corrected. "Iceland is part of Scandinavia, and the percentage of the population who speaks English is high throughout Scandinavia."

"In fact," I interjected, "many people here speak three languages, Icelandic, Danish, and English. Especially the younger generation, because all three are taught in school. What do you think of that?"

Katrina considered that question for a moment, and her response caught us off guard. "How come we don't do that back home?"

• • •

Our arrival in Iceland was just three weeks shy of the summer solstice. Even after the sun officially set, the sky would turn a silvery shade, never turning black. When we got to the room, it was 9:00 p.m. and still light out. I closed the windows, drew the shades, and hoped for sleep. Immediately, the temperature in the room spiked. "Uuuggghh! Let's keep the window open. It must be 90 degrees in here!" September moaned.

One of the things that endears September to me is her ability to keep me *somewhat* in line, but not *too* in line. The need to be kept in line comes with the territory of being clueless, but I had twenty pounds of jet lag and wasn't in the mood to be reprimanded. "You know I can't sleep unless it's dark," I protested. "It's noonlike outside. We need to shut out some light so we can sleep."

But the room *was* steaming. The root of this dilemma, we later found, is that Iceland has all the hot water it wants, compliments of geothermal activity. The hot water circulating through the radiators in our hostel seemed to have but one setting, calibrated for mid-January.

"We can't sleep in this oven—*please* open the window."

We all have our little "thing" that we like to have a certain way, and mine is a dark room to sleep in. The simple fact was that the four of us were going to become well acquainted with one another's "things" in the next 52 weeks. As I tossed and turned in our not-dark-enough room, I reminded myself that September's special "thing" was her need to have a pristine bar of soap in the shower, whereas I like to optimize and conserve, so I'll take soap scraps and mold them together to form one piece.

The next morning before September went to take her shower I was feeling mischievously petty from the lack of sleep. I found a scrap of soap and molded it into another bar. "Katrina," I said, "trade this for the bar in Mom's soap case."

"No way, Dad. I know what you're up to."

Katrina is encumbered with being the family's moral compass, but ever since Jordan was old enough to toddle, he has been fascinated with being just mischievous enough to elicit a reaction, but not enough to get in any real trouble. "I'll do it!" Jordan enthusiastically offered.

Jordan swapped the bars for me. As I made my way to the shower with the bar that had been in September's case, I smiled, knowing what her reaction would be. Luckily for me, September would know it was my way of being just mischievous enough to elicit a reaction, but not enough to get in any real trouble.

• • •

Ask any grade school student what they know about Iceland, and you will get the same answer.

"The Vikings named the country 'Iceland' to confuse other would-be settlers. The Vikings wanted people to think the country was icy and cold so they could have the place to themselves. The Vikings named the really cold and desolate land they found 'Greenland' to throw people off in the wrong direction."

Rarely does lore seep so deeply into a culture. Being a devout contrarian, I'm highly skeptical of almost anything held as "common knowledge," such as the playground folklore of a human's mouth having more germs than a dog's rear end.

We didn't touch our tandems during our stay in Iceland; with only three days in the country, there was little point in doing anything with them. We took our rental car out to the countryside, more or less looking for evidence of a tree or patch of green. We headed for Pingvellir National Park, where we learned from the visitors' center that the legend behind the name "Iceland" is, in fact, true.

Pingvellir is a giant gash in the ground in the midst of a barren, rocky plain. What makes it special is that on one side of the gash is the Eurasian continental plate, and on the other is the North American plate. It's also roughly the Icelandic equivalent of Plymouth Rock; the original Scandinavian settlers gathered here in 930 A.D., conspiring to call their new home "Iceland" and the *really* bleak place "Greenland."

There are no trees in Pingvellir, but there are a lot of rocks. We decided to walk on the wild side and took the nature trail into the rift between the two continents. A well-worn trail, wide enough for a small car, leads down into a gash in the earth. As the trail descended, jagged granite walls rose on either side; in places it seemed narrow enough to touch both sides with outstretched arms. Ever since the upper deck of the Bay Bridge collapsed during the Loma Prieta earthquake back home in the San Francisco Bay Area, I hadn't been able to look at a bridge in exactly the same way. Whenever traffic slows near one, I make darn sure that if I have to stop, it is not *under* the bridge. So forgive me if walking between two continental plates gave me the same queasy feeling as stopping under a bridge. But I always say if you're going to tempt fate, you may as well do it in a way that will get you a flashy epitaph on your tombstone. I called out to Katrina, "Come here. Put one hand here, and the other there. Then push with all your might." 🌐

"This is a trick, isn't it?"

"No! I just want to get your picture!"

She wouldn't do it. So I stretched out my arms and placed my right hand on Europe and my left on North America and pushed with all my might. I am confident that somewhere, someone felt the Earth move. It was me.

All of the literature we read before we arrived described Iceland as a land of "fire and ice" due to the occasional volcano and the ubiquitous glaciers and geothermal activity. We visited icy waterfalls and hot geysers but found that the best way to appreciate the geothermal activity in Iceland is to visit the Blue Lagoon, about a forty-five-minute drive from the capital of Reykjavík.

Adjacent to a massive geothermal power plant used to generate electricity, the Blue Lagoon is one of the "must-see" attractions of Iceland. After the steam is used to power the generators, the effluent is collected in an enormous pool. Naturally occurring minerals in the effluent give the water a milky color and texture, and algae give it an unnatural bluish tint. Stated in another way, the famous Blue Lagoon is a basin full of industrial waste water.

Yet people flock to the Blue Lagoon from around the globe to soak in the warm water, experience its legendary healing powers, and to scrape the muck up off of the bottom and smear it on their faces. Fortunately, the muck is just a mix of minerals and biological sludge that probably won't kill them. I do have a suspicion, however, that if you put it under a microscope, it wouldn't look terribly different from what you would find on your average barn floor. You can even buy the stuff at the gift shop in dainty bottles.

• • •

After a few 24-hour cycles of constant daylight, it was time to haul our mountain of equipment back to the airport and head for London. Iceland happened so fast it almost shouldn't count as a stop. But the purpose of our brief layover was more to take advantage of an Icelandair special and to ease us into the Brits' time zone than it was to see the country. The reality was, however, that September and I sported rings under our eyes, while Katrina and Jordan proved immune to jet lag and capable of sleeping under a sun lamp. Still, we were excited to start the real first leg of our journey—cycling from London to Istanbul.

www.360degreeslongitude.com/concept3d/360degreeslongitude.kmz

Behold the marketing genius that gets otherwise intelligent adults to willingly part with their cash to smear essence of Petri dish on their faces.

2.

Home Is Where Your Stuff Is

June 4–June 22
England

The surest way to put me in a good mood is to get me on a bike. There's nothing quite like pedaling across the Golden Gate Bridge on a sunny day with a cool sea breeze to get me doing my Julie Andrews impression from the opening scene of *The Sound of Music*. Not that we would be crossing the Golden Gate in England, but we were going to ride. And in not too many weeks we'd be passing the same mountain in Austria that had inspired that famous scene. I was in a good mood.

But to get started we first needed to get to the starting gate. That would be at the home of some dear friends, whom we had never met, in Leighton Buzzard, a suburb somewhat north of London.

A few months before our departure, September went on a business trip and met a gentleman named Wayne on the plane. Unlike me, September makes friends instantly. I wasn't even there but I know exactly what happened. Before the plane even left the tarmac, Wayne knew our life story and knew about our upcoming trip and our plans to cycle across Europe on tandems with our children.

Small world that it is, Wayne had friends in England who have been cycling across Europe on their tandems with their kids for years. Wayne introduced us to his friends, David and Carolyn, via e-mail. In no time David and Carolyn became our lifeline. They were generous beyond imagination and offered a fountain of cycling information. Plus, they offered us, complete strangers, their home as a starting point.

You have to be extremely dedicated to cycling on a tandem to schlep one of them around the world. You must be certifiable to schlep two. This wasn't the first time we had taken the tandems out of the country, but we had yet to discover any method of moving two disassembled tandems from point A to point B other than brute force and awkwardness. Lucky me, I am the only one in the family strong enough to pick up one of the tandem cases—of which there are four. The Great Tandem Schlep goes something like this:

September takes some of our bicycle panniers about twenty yards from point A toward a distant point B. I then carry two of the tandem cases the same distance while Katrina and Jordan stay behind to guard the remaining pile of tandem cases and panniers. I then leave the two tandem cases with September while I go back for another load. After ferrying stuff back and forth between September's base and the kids' base, I do it all over again and move another twenty yards toward our destination.

In this fashion we made our way out of Heathrow International Airport to the London Underground, onto the train, through the long corridors of a connecting station, onto the train again, and then finally up to street level and to our hostel several blocks away. Getting four tandem cases, eight panniers, and a family of four off the London Underground during a twenty-second stop while a wall of human flesh is trying to carry all of you in opposing directions is a lot like being a goldfish in a blender.

September had been to London before, but this was the first time the rest of the family had been outside of Heathrow, so we arranged to see the sights of London for a few days before making our way to David and Carolyn's in Leighton Buzzard. On our first morning in London, Katrina was using the computer in the hostel lobby to e-mail her friends back home. I sat in a lounge chair waiting, reading a current *Time* magazine. At least that's what it looked like to the casual observer. September walked over and asked, "Anything happen in the world in the last week?"

"Well, we haven't invaded Canada yet, if that's what you mean," I replied, hoping she would not investigate my reading material any further.

As part of the plan for the kids' education, we had brought with us a bunch of children's books on British history. Mind you, it isn't as though prepubescent literature targeted for double-X chromosomes is normally on my reading list, but the book I was reading was more interesting than current world events. I had Katrina's copy of *Beware, Princess Elizabeth* stuffed inside the *Time* magazine, as I wasn't about to be caught in public reading a book about a princess.

The names "Bloody Mary" and "Elizabeth I" were familiar to me, but it wasn't until I started reading Katrina's preteen princess books that I learned that they were sisters, albeit in an "are-you-sure-what-you're-eating-isn't-poisoned" sort of way. All the underhanded cloak and dagger stuff caught my imagination.

We went to Westminster Abbey full of anticipation. I wanted to see where archrivals Mary and Elizabeth were buried, side by side, no less. Plus, I had learned that Sir Isaac Newton's final resting place was in Westminster Abbey and wanted to pay my respects to Mr. Gravity. If it weren't for him, I'd be out of a job.

As I stood in line at the abbey, I noted September's eyes were fixed on a sign adjacent to a counter. "It's almost a hundred dollars to get the four of us inside," she said.

"To visit a *church?* What if I have the urge to absolve myself of some naughtiness, and I'm short of funds? Do they have some sort of frequent sinner program, so we could use the same pass here and at some of the other sites we want to visit?"

"No," September replied. "For example, if we want to see where Anne Boleyn took her last steps on the way to the chopping block at the Tower of London, it will be another hundred."

Planning a yearlong trip around the world isn't like planning a two-week vacation, where every activity for every day can be planned and budgeted well in advance. In the months before we left, we made plans only in the general sense. For example, we knew what regions of the world we wanted to see and in what season, so most of our intercontinental airfare was prepurchased. Conversely, all overland transportation and day-to-day activities were left completely open. As one person wisely summed up long-term travel, "Why plan anything? The first day something could happen which changes everything." We were committed to our budget, but when standing outside Westminster Abbey the budget suddenly seemed just plain rude. It was immediately clear that if our funds were to last the entire fifty-two weeks of our trip, we couldn't do everything we wanted to do.

"According to our guidebook, the British museums are completely free," September commented hopefully. "Even for Americans."

So that is where we spent our time in London. These vaunted institutions are fascinating resources to explore if you ever doubted the breadth and depth of how the British looted their colonies.

· · ·

When I was a kid, the litmus test of whether or not your town had arrived in the Major Leagues was if there was a McDonald's. When a McDonald's opened in my hometown, it was quite an event. We boasted with pride, "Logan, Utah now has a McDonald's!" Kids on the school playground would discuss in awed tones the fact that the sign in front of the McDonald's had changed from "100 Million Served" to "200 Million" and ultimately "Billions and Billions." It was big news.

We hadn't been in the U.K. very long before we learned they have a not-too-dissimilar litmus test. A city isn't a city unless it has a university.

We also learned that there are specific qualifications for whether a village is a town or a town is a village, but we could never remember what those qualifications were. I don't know how many times we were corrected by a well-meaning local that the next town was actually a *village*, or the village we were in was in fact a *town*, thank you very much.

After a few days in London it was time to make our way to David and Carolyn's in the town of Leighton Buzzard. The towns (pardon me, did I say towns? I meant villages) in England have these terribly funny names. Leighton Buzzard is one of the more prosaic. How about Piccadilly Circus? Or there is Spital Tongues. Somewhere there must be a Toenail Fungus, England. I looked on a map but couldn't find it. Someone a very long time ago had a great sense of humor.

Leighton Buzzard is about 40 kilometers north of London, and its calm neighborhoods and well-trimmed hedges contrasted dramatically against the insanity of London. I was grateful to have quiet streets to start pedaling on. David and Carolyn were gracious hosts and accomplished cooks. They served superb meals for September, Katrina, and me, and humored Jordan with a mac and cheese food substitute from a box. We were going to have to work on Jordan's picky eating habits, but that was a battle for another day.

I assembled the tandems and we tested our ability to ride on the left-hand side of the road. David offered to keep the tandem cases at his house until such time and place that we sent for them. The night before we departed we stayed up much later than we should have, discussing world affairs, where we would find campgrounds in southern England, and most importantly, the merits and drawbacks of various types of fenders on touring bicycles.

Katrina's Journal, June 10
Today was the day! After packing up everything, we loaded the panniers on the bikes and left. David rode with us on his own bike for a distance, and then headed back home. England seems very hilly.

Not too far from our starting point in Leighton Buzzard is the tiny village of Eydon where my fifth great-grandfather was born. I don't think Eydon has changed since he left in 1855 and probably not even since 1555. Houses are made of stone and have thatched roofs. The paths are impossibly narrow for cars and perfect for cyclists. We found a church with a graveyard that contained several Higham graves, but none that were familiar to us. As a bonus, and a complete surprise, our map showed us that a short hop from Eydon was Cold Higham, an even tinier village.

After a full day of cycling, we approached the town (village?) of Islip, where David had told us we'd find a campground.

After arriving at the campground, I went into the office to secure a site, but quickly learned the awful truth—they were full. The Fickle Finger of Fate had brought us to Islip on the very day of the one thousandth birthday of Islip's most famous son, Edward the Confessor. Of course I knew who he was. In addition to reading Katrina's teen-princess series of books, I had also been reading Jordan's *Horrible Histories—England*.

Horrible Histories is a series of books for reluctant readers ages eight through twelve published in the U.K., mixing history with the details that kids might actually find interesting, such as methods of torture, gory diseases, bloody battles, rodent infestations, and even medieval bathroom logistics.

Edward the Confessor was the guy who lost to William the Conqueror, who invaded England in 1066, united the disparate fiefdoms in the land, and became England's first king.

Hello!

Why were these people celebrating the one thousandth birthday of the loser? I have a hard time visualizing a celebration in New Rumley, Ohio on December 5, 2839, for George Armstrong Custer, loser of the battle of Little Bighorn. Then again, I can't see the British getting all cheery over William the Conqueror's birthday, either. He was *French*. Let's imagine for a moment that the United States lost the Revolutionary War in 1783. Would we celebrate King George's birthday? I think not.

I went back to September and the kids to break the news. "They're full—someone turned a thousand years old today." Jordan had spied the pool and was virtually wet already; he looked pained at this news. "Oxford is only a few miles down the road. We should get going."

"We aren't giving up so easily, are we?" September asked. "Can you go back and ask again?"

"You know I'm no good interfacing with people in these situations."

"That's because, dear," September said patting me on the shoulder, "*people* don't interface. Only engineers do that. We're ready to camp here. Jordan, come with me. Try to look pathetic." And with that September roughed up Jordan's hair so it looked like the kid had been dragged behind the bikes rather than propelling them.

A few minutes later September came back. "We're in pitch number three—I had to promise one night only."

"One is enough. What did you say to make them decide the place wasn't so full?"

"I just told them how fabulously beautiful the countryside was and how we couldn't believe our good luck to have arrived in town on such a historic day, what with us unfortunate Americans having no king of our own whose birthday we can celebrate. Having Jordan as a visual aid didn't hurt, either."

Later we pitched our tent and crawled into it. We had, of course, camped in our tent before, but that night I slept with Katrina's elbow in my back all night, thinking, "*What have we done?!*" Camping was the only way we could stay on budget in Europe. We had roughly 18 weeks and 2,500 miles ahead of us to Istanbul. It was looking as if it would be a long road.

By morning, September's key-chain thermometer sported a reading of 34°F. We weren't ready for that—we had brought thin, tropical-weight sleeping bags. I checked the date; it was still mid-June.

Jordan woke up sporting a 101.4° fever. We weren't ready for that, either. Since we were welcome in our campground for exactly one night, we guiltily pumped Jordan full of Tylenol, worked with the kids on their homework, broke camp, and rode into Oxford.

Oxford, located on the Thames River, is home to England's oldest and arguably most prestigious university. Americans know it as the place where Bill didn't inhale.

Speaking of Bill, there isn't a day that goes by that I don't thank his dear friend Al for inventing the Internet. Such a wonderful thing. But lately I had been wishing Al had invented Wi-Fi, too.

The particular e.brain I had chosen to accompany me on our yearlong journey was a kind of electronic Swiss Army knife, as it did just about everything, including connecting to the Internet wirelessly via Wi-Fi. Ever since 9/11 I'd had a compulsion to get the news, and found myself going online and reading the latest headlines frequently. With full connectivity my e.brain was my lifeline to the outside world. I *loved* it.

As with all things loved, it occasionally made me crazy. I had been certain that I would be able to take it with me on our trip and find a Wi-Fi network just about anywhere. This proved to be a much more frustrating task than I'd originally anticipated. That isn't to say that I couldn't find Wi-Fi networks, I just couldn't get into them. For example, while in Oxford, I ended up wandering all over the university campus looking for a department that left its network unguarded so I could check e-mail and get a quick news fix.

Despite its being overly informed about network security, Oxford became our favorite city in England (I can say "city" here because, you guessed it: Oxford has a university). The Oxford city council has chosen to keep its city pedestrian and cyclist friendly. Lacking the frenzied pace of London, Oxford can be easily managed on foot, or more importantly to us, by bicycle. For example, the Museum of the History of Science, Gutenberg's Bible, Martyr's Memorial, and many of Oxford's colleges are all easily accessible on foot from the market square.

One of the most popular pastimes in Oxford is punting, which has nothing to do with kicking a pigskin on fourth down. A punt is not too dissimilar from a canoe, but with its flat bottom, it's much more stable, and it's propelled by using a pole to push off of the bottom of the river. Our punting experience had us starting just past Christ Church

Meadow in the Botanical Gardens, where we looked for hobbits near Tolkien's Tree named for the famed author who received much of his inspiration there. Despite its popularity, once past the immediate vicinity of the pier and rental shop, punting is a quiet, rural experience.

We also found Oxford almost impossible to leave. Cycling out of town, every time we turned around to see a sign posting how many miles back, it read the same thing.

> *Katrina's Journal, June 13*
> *. . . After riding for about ten miles, we realized we'd practically gone in a circle. Great. That was but the first wrong turn. Next, after riding for about three or four miles, we found the road we were looking for. This road was supposed to take us several miles down to a bridge that crossed a small river, and shortly after crossing the bridge, we would find our campsite. After a long time of riding downhill, Mom said something like, "Sometimes I have this strange feeling that this road is just a path to someone's farm." Just a tiny bit after she said that, we came to a dead end. In front of us was a river, only about twenty feet wide. But where was the bridge? On the other side of the river was a pub, with a deck and tables and chairs and people and plenty of boats. On our side, there were no boats. We called to people on the other side and begged them to come and get us in a boat, but they didn't own the boats.*

Our map showed a bridge where we were standing, but if there was a bridge, it was doing a great job of hiding. Talking to the locals who were lurking on the other side confirmed that there *used* to be a bridge, but the owners of the land nearby didn't like the through traffic and, well, somehow the bridge had been damaged beyond repair and torn down.

We had no choice but to go back and take the long way around. About three hours and more than twenty miles later we were on the other side of the river, and only twenty yards farther down the road.

Some members of my family have the irritating quality of seeing the humor and adventure in situations like the bridge being out. Later that night as we pitched the tent, Jordan and I plotted against Team Estrogen for their high spirits and good nature. We snuck another two pieces of soap that had been squished into one bar into September's soap case.

A few days later we arrived in Salisbury to see our first UNESCO (United Nations Education, Scientific and Cultural Organization) World Heritage site: Stonehenge.

The only thing I knew about Stonehenge was from the movie *This Is Spinal Tap*, so we got the obligatory headphones for the self-guided tour. We learned that Stonehenge was already ancient history when the Romans ruled England and that the stone pillars were built by . . . nobody really knows.

We would have good and bad experiences with UNESCO sites as our year unfolded, but Stonehenge reminded us of what we already knew; Katrina and Jordan experienced culture and history much differently than September and I did.

We walked along the path encircling the stone columns that have been enshrined on screensavers around the globe. Jordan paused, and looking at one of the columns noted, "They sell hot dogs here. And there is a gift shop."

Katrina, always budget conscious, retorted, "We have food in our panniers, and we can only get one souvenir per continent." Then, adjusting the headphones of her audio guide, she added without taking a breath, "These headphones hurt my ears."

Summer solstice was only a week or so away. If we waited, a large gathering of people who hadn't found proper homes since Woodstock would be arriving to visit Stonehenge to feel its vibes. I could feel the vibes before summer solstice—it was the traffic thundering past only a few hundred yards away on the A303. It was so loud it was as though someone had turned up the volume all the way to eleven.

•   •   •

On a tandem you have a captain (the person in front) and a stoker. The stoker gets his name from the bygone era of steam trains when a person tended, or "stoked," a fire. The hotter the fire burned the more steam was produced for the engine and the faster the train went. On a tandem the stoker's job is similar—to provide power.

Jordan and I had a lot of miles under our belts before we arrived in England. We had cycled across Austria before Jordan was in kindergarten, and it was while cycling the backside of Maui that we learned the hard way that you can't eat or drink a computer.

Even without a computer weighing us down, I knew that Jordan wasn't much for pedaling. I had hopes of conditioning him because Katrina, at eight, had been a great asset as a stoker. As hard as it was for me to admit it, part of Jordan's problem was me. I tried to ask for "pedal power" as nicely as I could but under the strain of huffing up a hill, my words could easily be interpreted as a bark to an eight-year-old. In those early days cycling in England, Jordan was starting to withdraw.

I was also having a hard time finding "my groove." In the days before we left California, some friends asked me if I thought we were in shape to cycle such a vast distance. I quipped, "Well, let me just state that I don't think *my* physical condition is going to be our limiting factor!" I now realized that my *mental* condition was at risk of being a limitation.

David and Carolyn had warned us that finding camping spots in Southern England that are a comfortable day's ride apart might be difficult. I regretted pontificating on the virtues of camping, as many times I was shamed by Katrina's tenacity to cycle farther than planned in search of a campground. The nights we actually found refuge in a campground were a treat, even in a drenching rain. The night we had to make do in a farmer's field, I woke up the next morning with Jordan's sore throat and fever.

Then there was the matter of our load. Despite the time we spent economizing the "to take" pile, we still had to carry food and water, schoolbooks for the kids, clothes for everyone, a tent, four sleeping bags and mattress pads, rain gear, a first-aid kit, a camera, three PDAs, a cell phone, and enough bike tools to stock a small repair shop. And three pairs of shoes for September? What was with the hair dryer?

Clothespins? Matching socks? And, since I was the strongest rider, Jordan and I had the "heavy stuff."

Team Estrogen, however, was thriving, and due to all those fashion choices, was quite stunning.

John's Journal, June 18

The British Postal Service was kind enough to sell me an international calling card that has free calls to the United States on every Saturday in June. So, as I have on every Saturday for the previous twenty-odd years, I called my mommy.

I ended up talking to her about Jordan, who has been acting very surly. I've been wondering if this trip is doing him more harm than good, and told her I was thinking about bringing him home—not seriously thinking about it, at least not yet. She was kind enough to remind me that Jordan was acting normally for eight years of age. I think her exact words were, "Well, if you can't remember what you were like when you were eight years old, then let me do it for you!" Above all else, she convinced me that Jordan was fine, and that I should forget about pampering him, let alone bringing him back home. For once it was good to be told that his behavior was hardwired in his DNA.

September is much better at personal relationships than I am, so I turned to her for advice. "I need help getting Jordan to provide some power for going uphill," I said.

"Don't ask Jordan," September said. "Spider-Man is the person you need to talk to."

Jordan was first introduced to his alter ego when he was four. We were on everybody's mailing list; buy a couple of things mail order, a few more online, and suddenly you're getting five pounds of mail every day. Jordan would watch for the postman every afternoon, and then run to the mailbox looking for toy catalogs. He would then study them as a starving person would a menu. When he found the sleek Spider-Man costume, he found his soul mate.

At the tender age of four Jordan had never seen Spider-Man before—
not the movie, the comic book, nothing. But as soon as he saw the advertisement for a Halloween costume, he knew! He knew Spider-Man was
bad to the bone. When Jordan finally got a Spider-Man costume of his
very own, he wouldn't take it off and would do all sorts of things he
knew were taboo.

September would say, "Jordan! You know better than that!"

"I'm not Jordan anymore! I'm Spider-Man!"

"Well, Spider-Man would never pinch his sister. Spider-Man is
good!"

"NO! Spider-Man is baaaaaad!"

During the intervening four years Spider-Man had been Jordan's
alter ego. A year or so earlier I saw Jordan "shooting a web" at the ball
during a basketball game in an effort to steal it. So, I wisely followed
September's advice to have Jordan get in touch with his inner Spider-
Man. Not insignificantly, we also started to lighten the load by abandoning anything from that extra pair of sneakers to hand towels. You
could map our progress by the stuff we left behind at various campsites.
Katrina and Jordan caught on quickly and lobbied to abandon their
math workbooks.

Cycling from Salisbury to Fordingbridge via a route that goes
through the New Forest and Godshill was the best cycling we did in
England. The scenery was green, the traffic was light, the sun was shining, and for a stretch the road was even flat.

Jordan and I pulled off to the shoulder for a moment. We were on
a long straight road and the trees formed a perfect canopy overhead;
September and Katrina were little more than a dot in the distance.
As they approached us, I made small talk with Jordan about our next
move. "I think those Spider-Man turbo boosts up the hills are really
helping. If I didn't know any better I'd think Spidey was shooting a web
and just pulling us up those hills today."

Jordan gave a noncommittal grunt.

"Do you think you have a couple of more miles in those legs? Our
map shows that there's a campground around here, but if we could

get farther down the road, it will just make the ride that much shorter tomorrow."

I could see the wheels turning in that little head. "Why?" Jordan asked. "What's happening tomorrow?"

"We're trying to reach a place called Poole, where we can catch a ferry to France. France is where they make French bread." I had to make the goal of getting to France personal for Jordan. Along with Kraft Macaroni & Cheese, French bread slathered in Nutella was one of his half dozen or so dietary staples.

Jordan and I commiserated for a moment while we waited for September and Katrina. I whined about the lack of burritos in my diet—Jordan, the lack of French bread and Nutella. When September and Katrina pulled up a few moments later, we started to discuss our options: find a place to stay now, or continue down the road a bit more. We pulled out a map to investigate our options. The English are among the most friendly on the planet. We found that standing on the side of the road perusing a map was all that was required to obtain assistance.

As if on cue, Mr. and Mrs. English-Person in the Ford Anglia pulled over to ask if they could help us. "So, where is home for you?" they asked.

"Well, for the next year or so, home is where our stuff is," I told them. "We're trying to decide where we want to call home for the night. Is there a campground nearby?"

"Why, there's a very nice campground just a mile or so down this road. Sandy Balls. 🐚 You can't miss it."

I tried to stifle a laugh, but there was too much momentum behind it. Trying to keep it in would have resulted in my eyeballs popping out or something equally nasty happening. "That sounds like someone had an accident at the beach!" But something was lost in translation, as they just gave me a blank stare.

Just like that our mantra was born: *Home is where your stuff is.* And with a name like Sandy Balls, how could we pass up the chance to call it home for the night?

• • •

Southern England seemed to be landscaped by committee—the hedges were all trimmed to regulation and the flower beds all had a Photoshop quality to them. As we pressed south, we stayed on the back roads that a century earlier served horse-drawn carriages. Homes with thatched roofs came to the very edge of the narrow lane, and if I closed my eyes I could imagine a hitching post to serve the travelers' horses passing through. Every village came with a High Street, which back home would be Main Street.

As we made our way from village to village, we would roll in on High Street, park our bikes in the center of the roundabout, and look for lunch. Villages take great pride in the roundabout on High Street, and it would invariably be outfitted with benches, an arbor, and of course the regulation landscaping. Lunch, however, proved maddeningly elusive some days. We had a difficult time remembering the English definition of a village or town. Our definition, however, was easy to remember: A village does not have grocery stores or ATMs. Towns do.

Ten days after we left the suburbs of London we arrived in the port city of Poole, where we could catch a ferry to France. It was a major mental milestone.

> *John's Journal, June 21*
> *. . . that isn't to say the kids haven't been getting on my nerves. Yesterday was a good example. We came straight down from Fordingbridge to Christchurch, and then cut over to Poole, which meant leaving the quiet roads for fifteen miles of cycling on two heavily loaded tandems through bustling city traffic. We got lost so many times as we crossed town and every time we stopped to look at a map the kids would start to play this game where each would try to touch the other one, without being touched in return. Aarrgghh! It is difficult enough to have a conversation with September over the roar of traffic, and hold up a tandem all while under the stress of not getting clipped by a bus, but when you add a stupid, silly "touching" game and a spasmodic stoker,*

*it was tough not to scream at the kids. But cycling through a city
the way we did today isn't much fun, especially for the kids, so I
didn't yell at them for playing it. That's a start, isn't it?*

*We decided we needed a P-Day (Preparation Day) to do
laundry, write letters, and just do something fun. And no museums or cathedrals allowed.*

Starting out meant getting adjusted to our new surroundings, our new
routine, and to being together all the time. Things weren't always as we
had imagined—sunshine, smiling faces, and deeply introspective family discussions on just about any topic.

The next morning we got up at 5:00, broke camp, and cycled down to
the dock, where we boarded a ferry for a 6:30 sailing across the English
Channel. ● We were going to get French bread!

www.360degreeslongitude.com/concept3d/360degreeslongitude.kmz

Now where did I put that bridge? Being lost and going in circles
is frustrating when you are powered by dead dinosaurs, but when
you are self-propelled it can put a sane person into a murderous
rage. I knew it was time to find my happy spot when I started to
consider swimming across the river with the tandems in tow.

3.

Egad! Cowboys and Croissants!

June 22–July 8
France

've never been to Texas. I hear Texans wear cowboy boots and talk funny. My presumption is that if I ever dared enter the People's Republic of Texas wearing my Birkenstocks I wouldn't get service at restaurants.

I was apprehensive about entering France for the first time, because I'd heard they dressed and talked funny, just like in Texas. I was already aware of France's redeeming qualities, such as Euro Disney and really good croissants, but everyone knows the stereotypical Frenchman is someone who has perfected the art of sneering, and can speak good English, but not to you.

Try as we did, we never found this person.

To a family of four pedaling through the countryside on two tandems, the French were warm and kind, often going far out of their way to help us. Never did September's rusty high school French receive a sneer. However, we found other French quirks to test us. It was in France that I started a mental inventory of the differences between "us" and "them."

Brittany Ferries dropped us off in Cherbourg, on the Normandy coast of France. After we rolled off of the boat we contemplated our next move. September pointed out, "We only have a couple of apples and 'English' bread in our panniers. We should ride into town while we're here and buy groceries."

The Normandy coast had been on my list of places to ride for a long time and I was anxious to get moving. Cycling is somewhat of a religion in France and I had been tortured by stories of the great cycling along the Normandy coast for long enough by otherwise good friends. I had also been fascinated by the D-Day invasion since a reading assignment in a high school history class, and Utah and Omaha Beach were just down the road. "Do we really want to do that?" I replied. "We just had breakfast on the boat and we have a little to tide us over."

Without panniers, my bike was like a Ferrari—fast and nimble. But when packed for self-contained touring, it was more like a Peterbilt. The thought of cycling a couple of miles into town to scout out a grocery store, only to have to re-pedal those same couple of miles back out was not on my top ten list, especially when the open road beckoned.

"Remember what David and Carolyn told us," September cautioned.

I recalled them saying, "As much as we love France, you will find your number one irritation will be business hours in the French countryside. 9:00 a.m. to 11:00 a.m. and then 3:00 p.m. until 6:00 p.m., Tuesday through Saturday, closed Sunday and Monday. Forget this fact, and you go hungry."

"We'll be cycling along a main road," I pointed out. "Surely some entrepreneurial type will want to feed us."

September reluctantly agreed and without fanfare we cycled past a column of cars that had recently been disgorged from the ferry, crawling at a snail's pace. We came to a roundabout and cycled right past the exit for the town of Cherbourg, opting for the open road that would take us to Barfleur. The cycling gods smiled upon us immediately. English rain turned to French sunshine, and we could cycle on the correct side of the road without being reminded by a lorry bearing down on us. Suddenly, everything was brand new once again.

The Normandy coast was everything we had hoped it would be. The traffic was well behaved, and with idyllic green pastures on our right, blue surf on our left, and the wind to our backs, who could ask for anything more? When lunchtime came, we found a small market along the main road.

September peeked in the window. "There's not a soul in there."

"Not to worry," I said. "I'm sure there'll be plenty more."

And there were. Every few miles we came to another market or restaurant, all shuttered for the afternoon siesta. "These business hours are highly irritating," I remarked after striking out three times in a row.

Taking it in stride, September asked, "Who wants an apple sandwich?"

Attempting to rewrite history I replied, "If you would have only listened, we could have picked something up in Cherbourg while we had the chance."

"Dad can have the apple core," Katrina suggested.

• • •

The French are dedicated vacationers. We found a campground in virtually every town, no matter how tiny, and the anxiety we'd experienced in England over finding places to camp for the night simply melted away. Yet campgrounds are where we got acquainted with Irritating French Quirk number two: You are expected to carry your own toilet paper and soap into a public restroom. And many public toilets, um, how to put this delicately . . . do not have seats. You are expected to squat without making physical contact.

September came out of the facilities clearly irked.

"What's the matter?" I asked.

"No T.P., no soap, and no toilet seats! Did these people just move out of caves?" I was somewhat taken aback at September's indignation; she is usually much more charitable.

It took us a few days to determine that no soap or T.P. and seatless toilets were a bona fide trend. If we wanted to be hygienic in France, we would have to carry our own supplies, and . . . well, you don't really want to know. There is such a thing as too much information:

> *TMI; (noun.)* Acronym *Too Much Information. 1. The dissem-*
> *ination of information that is unwanted by the recipient; may*
> *be intentional or unintentional. Etymology: originated among*
> *groups of people living in close quarters, such as tents, for extended*
> *periods. Ex.: "I have a severe rash and an itch right where . . . "*
> "*ACK! TMI! I don't want to know where your itch is!*"

Two weeks after leaving David and Carolyn's, we were finally working into a routine. Our days started with an hour of math every morning before we hit the road. September and I traded off teaching duties with the duties of breaking camp and packing up. On a good day we were pedaling by 11:00 a.m.

As each day progressed, we were sure to find a local Co-Op (a budget grocery store) before it closed for the afternoon. The utilitarian ham sandwich became our dietary staple since ham doesn't spoil easily. We then spread out our tent footprint in a park or a roundabout and dined on warm ham sandwiches on squished bread that had been fermenting for a day at the bottom of a pannier.

At night we simply reversed the morning procedure; either September or I would set up camp while the other acted as teacher, covering the history of the area we were going through. This usually meant having the kids read a book about the area, and then talking about it. After writing in our journals, it was off to bed.

A few days' cycling from Cherbourg brought us to the D-Day beaches of Normandy. I recalled the first time I had read about the Allied invasion for a high school history class, feeling as if all the air had been squeezed out of my lungs and struggling to breathe. Since that time I had read many such accounts, and that feeling never changed.

From the commanding heights on top of the cliffs, we had the perspective of the Germans looking out over the water. We had been reading about the 1944 invasion as part of the kids' homework, but there was a difference between holding a book in your hand and walking in and through the bunkers, foxholes and decrepit equipment. Even though more than six decades had passed, somehow there was an echo of the thundering bombs and a whiff of gunpowder that was palpable in the otherwise serene landscape.

Later, as we explored the American Cemetery, I was astounded that even after multiple generations, there were still personal connections powerful enough to have people travel 5,000 miles to lay flowers at the grave of a loved one. 🐟 The very existence of a German cemetery came to me as a surprise, since they were the enemy, but there was a beautifully kept cemetery honoring them as well. I was hoping that our experience at the D-Day memorials and battle sites, complete with leftover military equipment and foxholes, would help the kids understand the horrors of war and the human cost of the freedom they enjoyed. However, as is often said, education is wasted on the young.

Jordan's journal, June 27
> *Today we went to Omaha Beach. It is a D-Day beach. I climbed on some wrecked ships. Then we went to a cemetery. Then we went to a place that has lots of holes in the ground. Katrina and I loved to run into them and then play hide-and-seek from Mom and Dad. Then we went to our campsite. I found a Star Wars light saber in my cereal box!*

Home base during our stay in the Normandy invasion area was the city of Bayeux, home of the Bayeux Tapestry. (It's okay, we hadn't heard of it, either.) Before we left the area, we paid the tapestry a visit. The Bayeux Tapestry is a 76-yard-long embroidered cloth that hangs on a wall of a museum. It tells the story of William, Duke of Normandy, kicking English butt in the year 1066. It seemed ironic that both the English and French revere the guy. The French seem to love to remind the world that Billy the C. was French. The English seem all too happy to overlook the simple fact that their first king was from across the Channel. On the other hand, they also seem happy to overlook the simple fact that their current monarch is German.

The Bayeux Tapestry marked the beginning of a long learning curve for us, when we realized that not only could we not see and do everything, but more importantly, we didn't *want* to see and do everything.

"What did you guys learn?" I asked as we left the museum.

Katrina screwed up her face. "The French weren't very nice, and the arrow through that one guy's eye was gory."

Jordan was more succinct. "There's an amusement park nearby." Grasped in his stubby little fingers was a brochure for Festyland in Caen, our next destination. I sighed in defeat. The kid had a radar that I was sure some government agency would like to duplicate. He could find any high-adrenaline entertainment within 50 miles.

Cycling out of Bayeux the following day, Jordan heard the word "Caen" used in the same sentence as "next destination."

"Isn't that where Festyland is?" he asked.

"Yes, Jordan. Festyland is in Caen." I could immediately feel Jordan's pace quicken, as the pedals on a tandem are linked together.

Folks in those quaint English villages (towns?) would look at us oddly as we passed through on our bikes; the French, in contrast, would roll down their car windows, and give us a huge thumbs-up and shouts of encouragement. Of course, for all I knew, they could have been swearing at us for slowing down traffic, but I didn't think so.

By the time we got to the heart of Caen, it was the peak of the afternoon and very hot. We'd been following hot and smoky buses through traffic that was jack rabbit fast sometimes and turtle slow at others, only to find ourselves gazing at half-completed apartment buildings where the Caen campground had once been.

"It's time to splurge," September declared. "Let's find a hostel."

France being the way it is, by the time we were settled in our hostel all of the stores were closed. Dinner became leftovers from lunch, and breakfast held all the promise of the vending machines in the lobby. But the hostel held a reward.

Unless you have been cycling all day, it is hard to understand the lure of a nice shower. Long before we got to Caen we began rating campgrounds solely by the quality of this three-minute experience. There is the drippy shower, more of a leaky faucet than a proper shower. There is also the one-size-fits-all shower, which has a non adjustable water temperature. Last, but not least, is the dreaded timed shower, operating off a token whose timing is unpredictable. These three types can be combined, but the nadir shower experience is the insult-to-injury shower: a combination of all three where you get to pay for a token, and get no water pressure or heat in return, only to have what water flow there is cut off while you have shampoo in your hair.

Our hostel in Caen had showers in which we could actually adjust the temperature to whatever we liked. Is that a novel concept, or what? To top it off, we could let the water run as long as we wanted. To clinch the experience, the hostel had chairs *right there in our room.* Sheer decadence.

• • •

I thought the French were all beside themselves with disgust at the thought of a theme park with mouse ears. As we entered Festyland we saw that its theme was William the Conqueror and the events of the year 1066!

"What's with the Viking war ships and weapons?" I asked September. "I thought the French were pacifists."

"And I thought the theme of the park was the Battle of Hastings in 1066. Last time I checked, there weren't any Vikings there."

The gears in my brain jammed at that comment; I would need to consult Wikipedia to drink from the fountain of knowledge.

Later that night at an Internet café I learned there *is* a Viking connection with the year 1066. My spin on it is that Festyland was purposely built by the French to torment the English. One of the most brutal chapters in English history came to a close on September 25, 1066, when a king of one of the many disparate fiefdoms in England defeated the occupying Vikings once and for all at the Battle of Stamford Bridge. Exactly nineteen days later was the Battle of Hastings when William the Conqueror (who was French, remember) defeated the English and became what modern Britons call their first king.

So, just about the time the picnics were winding down in celebration of the end of centuries of tyranny and Viking oppression, the French showed up and one of them declared himself king. A thousand years later, they still haven't left. Festyland, with its half-Viking, half-William the Conqueror theme, is France's way of reminding the world that the British have had only nineteen days of sovereignty in the last millennium.

> *John's Journal, June 29*
> *Jordan and Katrina have become the very best of friends. They were close before we left, but now that they have no one else they have become very tight.*
>
> *Anyway, the old saying is that what doesn't kill you makes you stronger. I guess that applies to relationships, too. All this togetherness could tear us apart, but so far, it hasn't. That can only be a good thing, right?*
>
> *Speaking of family togetherness, one of the problems with all this quality time is that there are no opportunities to get away from each other. This was, of course, known beforehand. But it becomes more "personal" when there really isn't an opportunity for two consenting adults, to, well, consent. Before we embarked on this endeavor, September and I talked about this very problem, and didn't come up with a satisfying solution. We hoped something, or some opportunity, would present itself. It hasn't. The best idea we have come up with so far is to send the kids to the shower to get ready for bed and then quickly move the tent before they get back. We haven't resorted to that—yet. But it is starting to look like our best option.*

Most people go to Paris to see the Louvre or the Eiffel Tower, or to people watch at trendy streetside cafes. We were off to Paris to pick up our mail; the Louvre and the Eiffel Tower were mere perks.

In the months prior to leaving California, using our general route as a guide, September researched the places we were going to visit and had amassed a mound of books about two feet high and three feet in diameter. These books were age-appropriate reading material about the places we were to visit, and formed part of the kids' homeschool plan. September's mother agreed to send us a package of books and fresh math homework every month so long as we supplied an address. We took care of the first shipment ourselves. The day before we left California, we had placed our first installment into the U.S. mail bound for Paris and now we were going to pick it up.

Katrina and Jordan had already polished off all the books we had brought with us, as well as an extra infusion we had picked up in the U.K. September, tired of the preteen genre, bought a copy of *The Da Vinci Code*, and then placed it in *my* front right pannier.

We had been advised that Versailles was a better base than Paris proper, as it was easier to approach and maneuver by bicycle. We planned to stay in Versailles to be tourists for a few days, leaving our bikes locked up at the campground and traveling into Paris using the Metro.

We settled into a five-star campground near the Palais de Versailles that soon enough would be seared into our memory as the Campground of Shame: the worst of the worst and the one by which to judge all others.

The morning following our arrival we made preparations to go into Paris. September returned to our tent from the shower. "How was it?" I asked.

"Awful. It's the insult-to-injury type. And in a five-star campground, no less." The Campground of Shame still had more to offer, but we wouldn't discover that until later. With no real agenda except to spend the day in Paris, we soon found ourselves sitting on a bench along the Champs-Elysées.

In our party of four we were rarely more than an arm's length from another and the kids wanted to be part of everything. As a consequence, no conversation was too trivial or too private to interrupt. We ate our lunch (yet another ham sandwich!) and watched a mind-boggling number of people rush past us. "Six billion is a really big number," I muttered to myself more than to anyone else. It seemed a planet's worth of people was pushing past us at that very moment.

"What!?" the children demanded. "What are you guys talking about!?" It was as though the fate of the world hinged on every syllable we spoke; everything became a four-way conversation. We did find a solution for about an hour when we got to the Eiffel Tower.

"Race you to the top!"

I gave it my all for about two flights of stairs, then happily abandoned the lead to Katrina and Jordan. We paid about thirty dollars for the privilege of climbing halfway up the Eiffel Tower, only to find that it cost another thirty dollars to complete the journey by elevator to the top. In the interest of sticking to our budget we sent Katrina and Jordan into a hopelessly long queue to wait to go up to the top by themselves. They felt very grown up, and we were free to enjoy a conversation without its being punctuated by "Huh? What did you say?" If only they'd had a room for rent on the first deck.

• • •

When we'd first arrived at the Campground of Shame, we had the place virtually to ourselves. We set up our tent and had a nice chat with a father-daughter pair from Oklahoma who were cycling roughly the same route we were.

However, the population of the campground exploded while we were in the city. "It looks," I said, casting my eyes about, "as though the six billion people we saw along the Champs-Elysées followed us . . . "

" . . . here." September had noticed the same thing I had and completed my sentence. Everyone was under the age of twenty-five and sporting a ring or stud on the odd body part. "There must be some sort of festival or something."

It was the *or something*. Live 8, a rock concert devoted to raising awareness of the upcoming G8 meeting, was scheduled at locations around the world with people gathering planetwide for music and demonstrations. One of those places just happened to be at the Palais de Versailles, within shouting distance of our tent.

It's not that I don't like The Cure, but I don't like them rattling my fillings loose at 2:00 a.m.

. . .

"Okay guys, today we're going to visit two important places. One is the Louvre, probably the most famous art museum in the world." There was a collective groan from my audience of two. I needed to work on my intro.

"The second place is the Palais de Versailles, where . . . "

"Hey, Dad!" Jordan cut me off. "Isn't that the place where the queen with the big hair used to get mad at the men because they would pee in a corner because there weren't enough places to go to the bathroom?"

"Yes, Jordan. Marie Antoinette." Jordan was clearly retaining what he was reading in his *Horrible Histories* books. Seeing where men would pee in the corner of the palace in defiance to the queen was worthy of a visit in a kid's eyes.

Unfortunately, when we arrived at Versailles we found it had recently closed for renovation, so we made our way to the Louvre.

The Louvre happens to be free of charge one day a month and we happened to arrive on the very day. We stood in line with all 6 billion people who had been following us around Paris, inching past François Mitterrand's now (in)famous glass pyramid that doesn't have 666 glass tiles. It has 673, but that just doesn't elicit the proper emotion for the conspiracy theorists, so the urban myth endures. But counting them gave us something to keep our mind off of the searing sun until we finally crossed the threshold into the Louvre and blessed climate control.

"Okay, we could spend a week here and just scratch the surface, so we need to prioritize," September advised, "or else we run the risk of attention spans expiring before we see what we came here to see."

I gave September a blank stare. "So, like, what did we come here to see?" It isn't as if I'm a great patron of the arts. I knew that the *Mona Lisa* was lurking about, but that was all. "I are an engineer. I don't know nothing about art," I said, summing up the situation succinctly.

September smiled and gave me a little pat on the shoulder. "It is *your* short attention span that we need to be careful that we don't exceed, *not* the kids'." With that we made it our mission to see the *Mona Lisa*, which took another forty-five minutes. Half the population of Japan was queuing to have their picture taken in front of the famous painting. We hopped into the queue and another forty-five minutes later we had our few milliseconds next to it.

"So, why is that painting so famous?" Katrina asked.

"That's why we have Google and Wikipedia. Between the two of them they know everything."

"I thought you said *you* knew everything," Katrina said coyly.

"Well, I had to tell someone in case I forgot some detail, such as why the *Mona Lisa* is famous. See how it works? By the way, isn't it time to be going?"

September cast one of her looks in my direction that let me know I was about to be given a lecture in art appreciation. "You know," she said, "the French make fun of Americans for this very reason."

I feigned stupidity. "Because we look up stuff on Google?"

"*Non!* We just got here. The French accuse Americans of being monosyllabic mouth breathers because they rush into the Louvre, see the *Mona Lisa,* then scurry away. By leaving now you are proving them right."

I shrugged my shoulders. "I'm okay with that. They make fun of us for our two-week vacations, too. But I know if I go to my corner Super Wal-Mart at 3:00 a.m. to buy the Brady Bunch-size pack of Twinkies, that Wal-Mart will be *open.* And if I stop in to use the facilities, hey, I don't have to worry that I left my personal bar of soap at home." I gave my dear wife the most heartfelt smile I could muster, batting my eyelashes for added effect.

Standing in line for the *Mona Lisa* followed by all this rumination had generated basic needs. September made a dash to use the facilities. She came out of the restroom with big news.

"Dan Brown has clearly never been to the restroom at the Louvre, or anywhere else in France for that matter; Robert Langdon could not have escaped like he did." September explained that Robert Langdon, the main character in *The Da Vinci Code,* evades the French police in the Louvre by finding the tracking device planted in his pocket and embedding it into a bar of soap from the ladies' restroom and throwing it out the window. "That could never happen, because there is no soap in any restroom in France. The book is a fraud."

"Does this mean we can go now?"

"*Non!*"

. . .

We wanted to retrieve our shipment of books, part of the kids' school curriculum, before we left Paris. We had mailed them to friends from home, the Bennions, who had been living in Paris. We had hoped to visit the Bennions in Paris but unfortunately events transpired that brought them back to the States before we even arrived. Our package of books would be forwarded to friends of the Bennions who would hold them for us. We had been checking with them daily, but unfortunately, we made the mistake of entrusting the package of books with the U.S. Postal Service and six weeks was not long enough to get it across the big water. I had mixed emotions about this, because after the whole family had read a book, we would often leave it behind. I was now quite a bit lighter than when we had set out, and if we got a new shipment of books they would land in my right front pannier.

On the other hand, the times when the kids were reading were those rare moments when it was quiet enough to think. I grudgingly had to admit that we needed books. We could no longer wait for our package from home. We found an English bookstore near the Louvre and bought another month's supply of reading material.

Jordan's Journal, July 3

Today we went to the Louvre. It was really crowded and we saw the Mona Lisa. It took a long time. Then the best thing happened! We found a bookstore that sells books in English! Dad got grumpy because all of the books we wanted were too heavy. The bookstore was really fun. I got Harry Potter and the Philosopher's Stone in English.

• • •

With the help of the TGV, France's version of the bullet train, we crossed the Alps and were cycling onward toward Evian, of bottled water fame. Evian is on the shores of Lake Geneva, known in the French-speaking world as Lac Leman.

The road that follows the shores of Lac Leman is narrow, with no shoulder. Large trucks carrying bottled water to stores around the world roared past us. Not only were large trucks roaring past, but American Steel. We were enjoying a lunch of, you guessed it, ham sandwiches on the side of the road, when a bunch of big guys on Harleys, carrying, of all things, fresh baguettes and a picnic lunch, thundered into the same roadside rest area.

Harleys? In France? The Harley riders were large burly men decked out in black leather and—egad!—cowboy boots! If I hadn't known any better I would have thought I was in Texas … except that when I spoke to the Harley riders, they had the cutest Inspector Clouseau accents.

I was having trouble holding onto my stereotypes of Frenchmen, Harley riders, and Texans. The Harley crowd wanted to know about us and we wanted to know about them, which after all, is the *raison d'être* of travel.

September used her high school French and the French cowboys their best high school English, and after exchanging stories we bid our new friends and their cowboy boots *adieu* and continued eastward. Within a few kilometers, we were in Switzerland.

www.360degreeslongitude.com/concept3d/360degreeslongitude.kmz

Bouveret, Switzerland, on the shore of Lake Geneva, is breathtaking. The prices, I mean are breathtaking. The scenery isn't too bad, either. Bouveret is also home to a campground and a waterpark. If only I had a crystal ball, I would've avoided a summer-long guilt trip.

4.

Cyclus Interruptus

June 8–July 20
Switzerland

Three years prior to the World-the-Round Trip, we had brought our tandems on a cycling trip across Switzerland and Austria. One purpose of that trip, other than to simply ride our bikes in the Alps, was to learn how we coped with longer duration trips than we had previously done. That trip took on a mythical quality for the entire family.

One of the things we enjoyed was taking a gondola to the top of Männlichen, of World Cup fame, and hike down to the small town of Grindelwald. The hike was several hours long, and we stopped for a picnic lunch partway down the mountain, looking over the entire valley. Per Katrina's pleading, we took the seeds from an apple and planted them.

Nearly every day for the past three years when I would walk Katrina and Jordan to school the conversation was nearly identical:

"Do you think the seeds will grow, Dad?"

"Absolutely!"

"You remember where we planted them, right?"

"Yes. We wrote it down, and took a picture."

"And when we go on the World-the-Round Trip we'll go back to visit, right?"

"Without fail."

"How big do you think the apple tree will be?"

"I suspect about a foot high."

The apple tree had become the stuff of legends in our kids' minds. Visiting it was a top priority for the World-the-Round Trip.

As we cycled across the Swiss border everything changed; the road widened, we were presented with our own cycle path signposted all the way to our next destination, and most important, the Evian trucks were not allowed on the cycle path.

You gotta love the Swiss. It's as though their national pastime is being smug about how beautiful their country is and then being out in it. The country is very well set up for doing just the sort of thing we were doing. There are nine national cycle ways, as well as numerous regional cycle ways and endless numbers of hiking trails, all of which are clearly signposted with travel times and distances. I credit all the outdoor activity with keeping the Swiss slim, even in the face of the ice cream stands and specialty chocolate boutiques that seem to adorn every street corner.

I found that when you tell someone that your favorite place to cycle is Switzerland, you instantly get a little respect. But here is a little secret— four of those national cycle ways are along rivers, lakes, and valley floors. You cycle *between* the Alps, not over them. And if you come to a mountain pass, you can throw your bike on the train; they are ubiquitous.

Slowly, we were chipping away at our route to Istanbul. The Rhone River route was to be our companion for several days, then we would connect to another route that would take us to Lake Constance where Switzerland, Germany, and Austria come together. From Lake Constance we would follow the Romantic Road into Germany and the Danube River. The Danube would take us all the way to the Black Sea. The shores of the Black Sea would take us right to Istanbul.

Our first night in Switzerland was spent in Bouveret, camping where the Rhone River flowed into Lake Geneva. Looking up river we could see the narrow Rhone River valley with cliffs towering above the clouds. But it was the sailboats with their gleaming white sails set against the blue sky and blue lake that spoke to my wanderlust. Where were these boats' captains, and why weren't they taking us out on the lake? Even though we didn't go sailing, I couldn't imagine a more beautiful place. ◕ The following day we put Bouveret behind us and entered the narrow valley that was cut by the Rhone.

In the near term we were heading for Zermatt, about three days' ride from Bouveret. High in the Alps near the Italian border, Zermatt wasn't exactly along the Rhone River cycling route, but it wasn't too far afield. We would simply follow the Rhone River cycle path to the city of Visp, then take a cog-wheel train up to Zermatt for a few days' diversion. Then we would continue on to our apple tree and beyond.

Jordan's Journal, July 8
   Today we rode our bikes for a long time. We didn't mean to ride our bikes for so long, but we were looking for a campsite. We had a map and a guidebook that told us where some camp-sites were, but when we got there, they weren't there anymore. We were so sad. Then we found a campsite with miniature golf. I hit Mom in the face with a golf club accidentally. Dad says her blackeye looks "smashing."

Our guidebooks, maps, and well-meaning but misinformed people sent us off to no fewer than six campgrounds that had recently closed. As sunset approached, I said in desperation, "I vote we go into Martigny-Ville and look for a campground. If we can't find one, let's grab a hotel." September wouldn't have been hard to convince but the kids were another matter. To them, sleeping indoors was a cop-out, and they were infused with a fervent penny-pinching zeal. In an effort to sabotage a whine-fest about sleeping indoors I mumbled in their direction, "I am at the end of my rope." After six weeks of togetherness, this was a code they now knew only too well.

A grandfatherly gentleman with two young children was cycling along the same path we were. They pulled up beside us just as I was planting the hotel seed in the kids' minds. He spoke very little English, which complemented September's very little French so that we could communicate very little.

He nonetheless patiently communicated that Martigny-Ville did indeed have a campground, and it was on the far side of town. That was the most we could understand. As we prepared to go our way, to our surprise he followed us. As dusk approached he dropped off his grandchildren near what we presumed was their home and led us about seven miles through town and to the campground. Eternally grateful, we said good-bye to our new friend as he made his way back home in the dark.

This was another example of a complete stranger helping us in a pinch, but it was significant for another reason. It had been a long and tiring day. The promise of a place to stay had been dashed time after time, often after we'd gone veering down side roads, only to find a dead end with no place to camp. Through it all the kids complained not once. It was a breakthrough. I recorded in my journal later that night:

John's Journal, July 8
We knew there would be hard days when we started. Maybe we underestimated just how hard. But we have been able to clear each and every hurdle thrown at us. Katrina and Jordan have started to see the adventure in every little thing. Jordan has changed the most in the last six weeks. For example, when we were in England, if I asked him to help pedal up a hill, I couldn't tell that he was helping at all. He is now a very good stoker. He is starting to thrive in this environment.

The Rhone River was our constant companion over the next few days, sometimes on our left, and sometimes on our right. We were riding upstream but it was impossible to discern a change in elevation. We had the wind to our backs; I noted that the trees were bent over with resolve against the prevailing wind. The valley we were going through was at times broad and other times so narrow that I thought someone with a good arm could throw a baseball from one side to the other.

Perhaps it was because the conditions were so favorable, or perhaps because we were finally starting to click together as a team, but for the first time, Istanbul wasn't looking so far away.

• • •

"Why don't we cycle to Zermatt?" Katrina asked.

We had arrived in Visp and were preparing to hop on a train. "Big hill," I replied. "We'll ride down, though. It's supposed to be one of the best downhills there is." I had been waiting a long time to ride the road from Zermatt to Visp. It is one of the bicycling world's "must-do" routes and Zermatt itself is world renowned for scenery and outdoor activities. Yet, if we had known what was waiting for us there we would have skipped the side trip and just kept on going.

Precisely at 24 minutes past the hour the train to Zermatt comes to the end of the line. Its cog-wheel design enables it to get up the steep incline from Visp. Once at the final station the two groups who frequent Zermatt pour out of the train—the privileged and the tight-pursed thrill seekers.

The privileged come for the afternoon or maybe a day or two to browse the trendy shops, but never really stray too far beyond the town's main square. Walking through Zermatt, you would be forgiven for wondering who goes on holiday to shop for expensive timepieces, as there is a Rolex dealer every other door along the main street. Towering above that main street at the end of this high alpine valley is the full-sized Matterhorn, looking as though Walt had the whole place purpose-built. I was ready to queue up and get my E-ticket for the Bobsled.

We pulled our tandems off the train and went straight to the local Co-Op. Katrina and I watched the bikes as September and Jordan procured lunch. Moments later they emerged from the store with our standard lunch fare of ham, cheese, and a baguette. "Shoot me now," was all I could say.

"If you can think of something else that we can afford, packs easily, doesn't require cooking, and the kids will eat, I'm all ears," September countered. She was as weary as I was of the standard lunch fare, but I did enough complaining for the both of us. The lack of variety didn't seem to affect Katrina, and blandness suited Jordan.

After eating lunch in a park, we rode our bikes a few blocks to the local campground and settled in for a couple of days with the rest of the tight-pursed thrill seekers.

Our campground in Zermatt was different from the ones we had gotten used to in previous weeks, where more often than not we were the only people in tents. Other campers throughout Europe were in RVs or campervans and had settled in for a week, a month, or even the entire summer.

In Zermatt's campground, all were in tents. Since it's not possible to drive to Zermatt, we saw exactly zero RVs or campervans. All private traffic is stopped in Täsch, about three miles short of Zermatt. Only Zermatt residents can continue on, and then only as far as the garage where they are compelled to park their cars. In the Zermatt campground I found an unsecure wireless network, courtesy of the adjacent hotel. Bliss.

As we set up our tent we talked to a climber who had scaled the Matterhorn the previous day. I thought he was nuts. Of course he thought the same of me for attempting to pedal from London to Istanbul with two kids under the age of twelve.

We soon got to the business of seeing what Zermatt had to offer in the way of excursions. We learned to stay alert so we could keep our toes out of the trajectory of the predatory golf carts the locals use to get around town. Passing through town, we were drawn to the back of the valley, toward the Matterhorn, where we found a dirt path; the trail offered a perfect opportunity for our lack of an agenda. We followed the path, which paralleled a river that raged with fury as it carried glacier melt down to the Rhone, eventually flowing to Lake Geneva. The trail then worked its way up steeply toward the Matterhorn.

We hiked along for the better part of an hour, with no particular destination. It was, really, the perfect Higham outing—beautiful surroundings, warm sunshine, and no particular place to go.

Above Zermatt there are several tiny mountain villages with no more than two or three dwellings and a restaurant for the wandering hiker. One village was Blatten, and we arrived purely by chance. Nestled in with the two or three dwellings and the restaurant was a playground. We had gotten used to the weird juxtaposition of playground equipment at or near the tree line on our previous trip through Switzerland.

We stopped at the playground to let the kids run free. September and I treasured moments like these because it meant we could have a quiet conversation. The playground had tall grass filled with grasshoppers practically begging to be caught by a kid with no agenda. The centerpiece of the playground was a massive boulder about the height of a two-story house. Permanently affixed to the top of the boulder were ropes to assist anyone who wanted to climb to the top. 🖎 One side of the boulder had a modest slope that you could climb, even without one of the ropes. The other side of the boulder was a vertical face.

We let the kids play, climb, and catch grasshoppers. Before long, the shadow of the Matterhorn fell across the playground and it was time to head back to our campground.

For the next few days we enjoyed taking trams up the mountainsides, then hiking down while sunshine splashed across the mountains and valleys. You never know what you'll find while hiking in Switzerland. We found curious items along the trail, such as long slides, zip lines, swings, and outdoor chess sets that were so big that a person could choose to be one of the pieces.

The morning came for us to leave Zermatt, cycle down the mountain to Visp, and continue our journey toward Istanbul. The sun shone brilliantly. "We're not in a hurry," I said. "Is there anything we want to do before we take off?"

"Yes!" exclaimed the kids with one voice. "We want to go back to that boulder to climb it again."

I hadn't planned on anything quite that involved, as the excursion would be at least three hours round trip. I glanced at September. She gave me the one-eyebrow-raised-other-eyebrow-furrowed look, which I interpreted as approval. "Okay, let's go climb that boulder!"

An hour later we were once again in the high mountain village of Blatten. September and I let the kids use the ropes to climb the boulder as we sat in the shade of one of the three dwellings that comprised the village.

We sat there for a long time. Eventually Jordan came and sat by us and I decided it was time to get going. Katrina was nowhere in sight. "Little Dude. Where's your sister?" I asked.

"I don't know. She was climbing the boulder, but I was chasing grasshoppers."

I looked over at the boulder she was climbing. At the age of eleven, Katrina had had a fair amount of climbing practice, with a climbing wall in the basement of our house six thousand miles away. I couldn't see her from where I was. "Jordan, go tell Katrina we need to be going."

But Jordan was busy trying to gross out September with the grasshopper he had caught, and pretended he didn't hear me. "Want to hold this one, Mom?"

One of the three dwellings that made up Blatten also housed a restaurant. People were sitting on the porch, enjoying the alpine air.

September, Jordan, and I sat in the shade for several more minutes. I was starting to get annoyed. Katrina knew we had to get going soon. I started to look around for her a little harder, letting my eyes do the work; I was still committed to sitting in the shade.

It was then that I noticed a little boy. He was in front of the porch full of people devoted to their lunchtime conversations. He kept looking at me in earnest, and then pointing to the sheer face of the boulder that was blocked from my view.

I walked over to where the boy had been pointing and found Katrina standing on one leg and leaning against the boulder. "What are you doing?" I asked.

"Nothing."

"Well, we have to get going if we're going to cycle off this mountain before the sun sets." I turned and started to walk away.

"I can't," she said.

I turned to face her. "Why not?"

"I can't walk."

"Why?"

"I was rappelling down this side of the boulder and the rope broke," she answered matter-of-factly. "My leg hurts when I try to put any weight on it."

I looked up. Sure enough, about fifteen feet up hung a frayed rope end flapping in the breeze; at her feet lay the other half of the rope. The hair on the back of my neck stood up, and my mind started cranking out questions faster than my mouth could form them.

"How far did you fall? How long have you been standing here? Have you tried to put any weight on your leg?"

Katrina replied conversationally, "I fell about ten minutes ago, and I'm not sure how far I fell. I've tried to put weight on my leg, but it hurts too much."

Only someone who knows Katrina would understand. She has ignored away every injury she has ever sustained. At the age of three if she bumped into something or fell down, we could see the pain in her face, but her words and actions would pretend any injury away. By the age of five she had learned to conceal any look of pain and flatly refused to acknowledge anything that might have hurt her.

I picked Katrina up in my arms and carried her back to where Jordan and September sat. I also took the coil of rope that had fallen to the ground. I put Katrina down gently beside September where we retold the story.

"Well, there isn't any swelling or bruising," September said, carefully examining Katrina's leg. "It's probably just a bad sprain. Let's see if we can get some ice to put on it."

I wasn't so sure. The ice sounded like a good idea, but the location where Katrina was indicating pain wasn't a joint. You can't exactly get a sprain in the middle of your shin. "Little One, where does it hurt exactly?"

"Oh, I don't know. Sort of all over."

September walked over to the restaurant and came back with a bag of ice. "The people over at the restaurant want to know how she is. Apparently a few of them saw it happen."

"Nice of them to let us in on it," I said through clenched teeth.

After a few minutes, it was clear the ice wasn't going to make Katrina magically walk again. "With all the backpackers and hikers who go along these mountain trails, you know this sort of thing has happened before," September said. "There has to be a way to get her off the mountain."

"I agree. Did you notice on the way up here there were a few tractors and trucks harvesting hay? If they can get up here, some sort of rescue vehicle can. Worst case, maybe a farmer will take us down on his tractor."

I scooped Katrina up in my arms and we all walked over to the restaurant, where I was able to get the attention of the owner.

"My daughter hurt her leg climbing down the boulder face when the rope snapped." I handed the frayed coil of rope over for dramatic effect. "She can't walk, and I'm afraid her leg might be broken. Is there someone you can call to take us down the mountain?"

"There is a helicopter, but it is quite expensive," he answered. "It also usually takes an hour or two to get one to respond. You could carry her down before one arrives."

"How about a four-wheel-drive vehicle from town?"

"They are not allowed to come up here."

"I saw tractors and trucks on the way up here. What about them? How come they're allowed to drive up here?"

"They have a special permit for harvesting, and that is all. They are not licensed to take passengers."

The Swiss and their freaking rules. "What about a horse then? If I can't get a car or truck up here, what about a horse?"

"Sorry. No horses. You carry her yourself or I can call a helicopter for you. It is $5,000 U.S. and it will be here in an hour or two."

As if it would suddenly change the situation, he offered his advice. "Your daughter just took a little fall on my playground. Her leg is not broken. It may hurt, but it is not broken."

"So you are a doctor, then?" All pretense of civility evaporated. "You can diagnose a broken leg without looking at an X-ray?"

"I have been a guide in these mountains all my life and have had a lot of experience with broken legs. There is bruising and swelling. It causes a grown man to cry out in pain. She has neither bruising nor swelling and makes no cry of pain."

I couldn't help but wonder if his lack of conviction for the seriousness had any influence on whether a horse or four-wheel drive could come to the rescue. Fuming, I turned on the spot and while walking out the door said, "A mountain guide inspects his ropes daily. You should, too."

I started to carry Katrina down the steep trail, trying my best not to slip on the gravel. It wasn't long before my knees ached, and the helicopter option wasn't looking too bad. "Maybe our insurance will cover the helicopter."

"Maybe," September said. "There's only one way to find out. I can go back to the restaurant and call the insurance company."

A long time passed before she returned from the restaurant shaking her head. "They don't have a proper phone, just a radio."

I knew any amateur radio operator worth his salt could patch into the telephone network. I interpreted the situation as an unwillingness to help. Without a word, I picked up Katrina and proceeded down the mountain.

It was a long way down, but we took it one step at a time. About two hours later we arrived at the edge of town. "Now what do we do?" I was asking this question of myself more than of anyone else.

"No idea. I guess we go to Tourist Information," September replied.

Just then a woman walked up to us. It was easy to tell we were in a bind, since I was carrying an eleven-year-old girl around, talking frantically, and looking bewildered. She asked in English, "Can I help you?"

The Swiss speak four languages in their country, and English isn't one of them. Many in the tourist industry speak English, but it is unusual for someone from the general population. We were grateful once again for the help of a stranger.

After a brief review of the facts, our new friend explained, "There is always a local doctor on call for emergencies." She hailed us one of the infernal golf-cart cabs that we had grown to loathe and asked the driver to take us to Dr. Julen.

Dr. Julen immediately recognized us. "You are the tandem family," he said in perfect English. "I saw you a few days ago in the park. You were eating lunch, I think."

I remembered him from the park as well. He was eating what looked like a burrito. Being burrito deprived can be a dangerous thing for a California boy, especially when fed a steady stream of plain ham sandwiches. I had wanted to mug him and steal the burrito, but now I was grateful that I had suppressed the urge.

By this time Katrina had grudgingly given up some other information. Her wrist hurt as well, and she couldn't move it.

"Her leg does not appear to be broken," Dr. Julen said, "as there is no swelling, but to be sure, we should x-ray both her wrist and her leg."

Doctor Julen disappeared with Katrina, and after what seemed like an eternity, he came back into the waiting area and announced, "It is broken."

September and I looked at each other for several seconds, the silence thundering in our ears. After a decade of anticipation, our once-in-a-lifetime journey was doing a serious Ctrl-Alt-Delete maneuver.

Jordan walked into the x-ray room and hopped up onto the examining table next to his sister. Katrina's face was unreadable. Dr. Julen held up the X-ray for us to see. Katrina turned her head from the X-ray as if denial would make it all go away. Katrina's leg was broken below the knee, and not just broken, but to my eyes, her tibia looked shattered. There was, however, no sign of a break in her wrist; it was only sprained.

"With this kind of break, it is very important to immobilize the leg at the knee," explained Dr. Julen.

"But doctor," I said, "the break is *below* the knee."

He merely repeated what he had just said, and then as if he was reading my mind, "No cycling until her cast is removed. No swimming or getting the cast wet, either."

I stood there with my mouth moving, but no sound coming out, like a fish out of water gasping for breath. September came to my rescue. "And how long will that be?" she asked.

"At least six weeks. For a break this bad, possibly eight." The good doctor was kind as he spoke these words, but he didn't sugarcoat his diagnosis.

Later, after Katrina's cast was in place, a nurse brought a set of crutches. Katrina tried them, but it was impossible for her to use them with her wrist in its current condition.

Dr. Julen asked, "When do you go home? I would like to see Katrina in 24 hours, and she needs to have a follow-up visit in seven days." Of course we had planned on leaving Zermatt that very day. After some explanation about our situation, we got Dr. Julen to consent to a visit in twenty-four hours and again in four days.

Walking out of the office, I looked down the street and noted the only car I ever saw in Zermatt—a rugged red four-wheel drive with a red cross on it and EMERGENCY RESCUE written in German, French, and Italian on the door.

. . .

It was late afternoon when we returned to our campground; our tandems were where we had left them, all packed and ready to go. The spot of grass where our tent had been that morning was still flattened. I looked around feeling helpless. Jordan broke the silence. "I'm hungry."

It had been a long time since breakfast and reality was just now starting to come crashing down. September and I wanted to sit down and feel sorry for ourselves, but there was nowhere to sit. Katrina could not stand for long and as she couldn't sit cross-legged with her cast, she just lay down in the grass for want of a proper chair.

The simple task of going to get some dinner was on the verge of overwhelming us. It was then I noted September looking at Katrina lying in the grass, crutches by her side and a cast up to her thigh. Katrina had been stoic all day—she hadn't once complained about pain and had not shed a single tear. Reality had just hit hard and she was now lying in the grass, her little body uncontrollably wracked with sobs; not from physical pain, but from the heartbreak over the plans that would not be fulfilled.

September turned her gaze from Katrina to me and said, "Is this the best we can do for our child? We drag her halfway around the world to make her lie in the grass, homeless, with a broken leg?"

Well, we didn't actually *drag* her. Last I checked Katrina was pretty enthusiastic about the whole World-the-Round Trip thing, but this was hardly the time to argue the finer point.

I set our tent back up and carried Katrina inside. Actually, it is impossible to *carry* a person through a three-foot-high doorway. I sort of pulled her in and thought, "Okay, now I *am* dragging my child." An upgrade in our accommodations was a top priority, but it would have to wait.

In my professional life I had spent my career dealing with crises in one way or another. I had spent hundreds, if not thousands, of hours writing procedures for various spacecraft-related contingencies. The previous several years I had been on call twenty-four hours a day as part of an "On-Orbit Help Desk" and had dealt with all kinds of emergencies. I was used to bad things happening, but this was a lot more personal. My mind raced with how to cope with our immediate needs as well as the longer-range problems that we now faced.

As with every contingency I had ever worked through in my professional life, there were a lot more questions than answers at this early stage of our recovery. We simply prioritized issues into what had to be done and ignored everything else for the time being. In this situation, that meant Jordan and I walked into town and picked up something to eat and brought it back. We didn't get ham sandwiches.

. . .

Morning dawned with a beautiful blue sky and sunshine. During the night September realized we had another priority besides an upgrade in accommodations—a wheelchair.

Where the heck do you get a wheelchair in a small resort town? I left September and the kids at the campground and began my quest. Zermatt doesn't have a hospital. After a lot of asking around town and pantomiming a wheelchair I found one at a nursing home. The receptionist scribbled my name on a yellow Post-it note and smiled as I wheeled the chair out the door.

We spent the remainder of the day pushing Katrina in her wheelchair, going about town looking at apartments. We quickly learned what every disabled person knows.

"There isn't a single place on our list we can access with a wheelchair," September exclaimed after several hours of searching.

Zermatt is a hilly town with lots and lots of stairs and steep paths. Even the town's youth hostel was unreachable because of the long stairways that had to be negotiated to reach the grounds.

We were still without a better place to stay than the local campground when we returned to Dr. Julen that afternoon for Katrina's follow-up appointment. We explained our predicament to Dr. Julen's receptionist, who happened to also be Mrs. Dr. Julen. "The suite above the office is available for a few days. It even has elevator access!" Dr. Julen not only became Katrina's caretaker, he became our landlord. We negotiated a price, something on the order of first-class floor space in Tokyo's Ginza district, but we had a home.

We spent the rest of the evening luxuriating in indoor plumbing, cooking facilities, and actual furniture. Over the next few days as we waited for Katrina's follow-up appointment with Dr. Julen, e-mails started to pour in from friends offering us free accommodation from Stockholm to London during Katrina's convalescence. We demurred, preferring to take things one day at a time.

Along with everyone else on the planet, we had been counting down the number of days to the new Harry Potter book. The day arrived as we were contemplating how a broken leg was going to impact us in the coming weeks.

> *John's Journal, July 17*
> *. . . we then spent the day pushing Katrina around town in her wheelchair, looking for a place to read a chapter. After Katrina and Jordan had gone to bed, I tore the apartment apart looking for the book, but I couldn't find it anywhere. Only the next morning did I find that Katrina was hiding it under her*

*pillow. She and Jordan had been co-conspirators, having laid out
their diabolical plan months in advance to keep me from reading ahead.*

We simply could not afford to live indoors in Zermatt; it became time
for us to move on. Dr. Julen wrote up a letter in both German and
English explaining Katrina's diagnosis and advised us, "She should
have her leg x-rayed again in about four weeks. It is possible that she
could get a knee-length cast at that time. Don't expect her to be ready to
have the cast completely off until at least six weeks from now. Possibly
eight. After that, it will be at least two weeks before she can walk without crutches. Good luck."

Before we had arrived in Zermatt we'd hit our stride and gotten into
a rhythm of homework-cycle-sleep-repeat, and for the first time since
we left London, cycling to Istanbul had seemed within our grasp. For
years I had been anticipating the thrilling descent from Zermatt to Visp
on my bicycle. We had also been talking up the hike to "our" apple tree.
This was all impossible now.

www.360degreeslongitude.com/concept3d/360degreeslongitude.kmz

"Hey, Mom! Why is that American family with those big bikes changing their clothes in our parking lot?" Use Google Earth and the *360
Degrees Longitude* layer to find out.

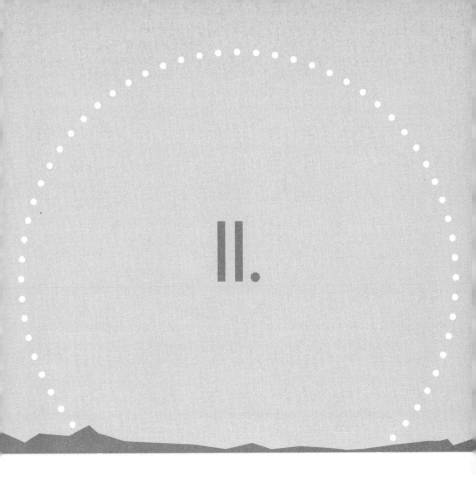

II.

SHATTERED BONES, SHATTERED PLANS

5.

Gargling with Razor Blades

July 21–August 1
Czech Republic/Poland

Children do not have an adult's apprehension about landing in a new city, late at night, hungry, not knowing the local language, not having any local currency, nor knowing where to stay. To them, it's all part of a grand adventure.

The broken leg changed everything. A week after Katrina's fall we found ourselves standing on the train platform in Cesky Krumlov, late at night, hungry, not knowing the local language, not having any local currency, nor knowing where to stay. Traveling by bicycle brought changes in our surroundings slowly. Arriving in the Czech Republic by train, our entire environment had changed in the course of a few hours.

We had left our tandems in storage at Zermatt's train station. Still unable to use her crutches due to her sprained wrist, and now with no wheelchair, Katrina was perched on my shoulders just like when she was three years old. We watched the train slowly depart, leaving us in this strange new place. September announced that she was going to look for information about accommodations, then disappeared.

My gaze turned from our massive pile of bicycle panniers scattered about my feet to Jordan. I said, "Well. Now what happens?"

Jordan looked up at me with a complete lack of comprehension. "You're silly, Dad."

I lifted Katrina off my shoulders, sat her down on a bench, then turned to Jordan and said, "I'm not silly. I'm tired and could use an ice cream cone." I pointed to a small convenience store. "Go over there and get me an ice cream cone, and when you're done with that, see if there's a tourist office and find us a hostel."

"Dad. I never know when to take you seriously."

With some relief I spotted an ATM in the distance. One problem solved.

We were refugees from the high prices of Western Europe. We had briefly considered the offers to stay at friends' homes during Katrina's convalescence but decided to head for Eastern Europe where we believed living indoors would be affordable. Camping in our current state was simply out of the question.

While I was negotiating with Jordan for an ice cream cone, September was perusing the bulletin board at the train station. She returned with a small piece of paper she'd found posted there. "This was the only thing I could read," she explained, handing me the flyer. "Hostel Skippy offers free pickup from the train station."

"I like the name. Sounds like a winner." After our ice cream issue was resolved, September pulled out the cell phone that had been faithfully serving us since London and dialed the number printed on the flyer.

"It reminds me of the Burrow," Jordan commented as we approached the hostel.

I was having the same thought. Hostel Skippy was on the banks of the Vltava River and appeared to be held together by paranormal means; one good exorcism and the entire structure would dissolve. Of course you knew that the Burrow is Ron Weasley's house. If you didn't, ask a kid to explain.

Skippy, the Rastafarian half-Cuban, half-Czech matron of the hostel, greeted us at the door. She was a walking, talking TMI telling anyone waaaay more about herself than polite conversation would dictate. We stepped into the entry when suddenly, with no provocation, she proceeded to tell us her life story and how she came to be matron of the hostel that bears her name.

"I bought this place for 800 U.S. dollars ten years ago when it was in shambles," she explained. "I did all the repairs myself."

I glanced at the rope holding up the front door frame and made a mental note that building inspectors are underappreciated.

In the microcosm of our nuclear family, Katrina and Jordan are . . . well "nuclear" is a good adjective. But to the casual observer they are reserved, perhaps even shy children. Katrina began to attract adults who wanted to hear how her leg came to be encased in plaster, and she had to confront her injury without pretending it away. For Katrina, this was more difficult than the broken leg. In a matter of just a few weeks this matured her from a little girl who avoided eye contact into a young lady who could look adults in the eye when speaking to them. Skippy was simply the first person to help Katrina through that transition.

"What happened to you!?" Skippy asked when she saw me carrying Katrina.

Katrina pretended to be invisible.

"She was rock climbing and the rope snapped," I said after an awkward silence. "Not only did she break her leg, but her wrist is sprained."

"You are lucky you just broke your leg!" Skippy exclaimed. "Did you bite your tongue, too? I bit my tongue once. Fell off a ladder and needed stitches, then couldn't talk for a week. Do you want to see the scar?" Skippy stuck her tongue out and simultaneously tried to give more details about her injury.

Katrina started giggling. I couldn't imagine Skippy not being able to talk. I needed to change the subject before she started showing us any more scars. "I was hoping," I interjected, "that you could help us find a wheelchair we could use while we're here."

"A wheelchair will not be of much use in Cesky Krumlov," Skippy explained. "The town is a maze of cobblestone streets built on hills with long flights of stone steps."

We discovered there was a lot more to Skippy than her scar and that she essentially built her hostel herself, albeit with the help she received from the spirits that lived with her right there in the hostel. She was a capable and resourceful woman, but I still went to bed each night praying I wouldn't wake up in the Vltava River.

• • •

Just as it had taken time to develop a routine when we were cycling, it was going to take time to adjust our routine to Katrina's limited mobility. This meant a hundred little things and one big thing: I started participating more when school was in session.

I had big hopes for school results over the year. In public school, both Katrina and Jordan had approached mathematics with the same enthusiasm they would have for cleaning hair out of a floor drain. I *loved* math and science as a kid. When teaching my children, my infectious enthusiasm was going to bubble over in class and before long they would be receiving grants from the National Academy of Sciences and having sweet dreams of partial differential equations.

I hit our little school like a gigantic belly flop.

The following Saturday while I was talking on the phone with my mother a half a world away, I complained about the children's lack of academic focus. "This shouldn't surprise you. You used to have a bite of dinner and then run around the kitchen table before you sat down for another bite." I thought I heard the faint hint of a snicker on the other end of the phone.

"My point is you couldn't sit still either," she continued. "Remember what your junior high English teacher told you."

That was really hitting below the belt. I have a selective memory for a reason; it is much more convenient than electroshock therapy. I may have done well in math and science, but I once had an English teacher who told me, "The only reason I'm giving you as high as a D minus is so that I will never have you in class again."

I was keener to teach Katrina than Jordan. Not only could Jordan not sit still, he was plowing through blatant memorization of the times tables. Katrina, on the other hand, was learning algebra, a "real" subject that applied to everything from cake recipes to Newton's Third Law of Motion.

"You know, there's a reason you're a rocket scientist and not an elementary school teacher," September said, pulling me aside after a particularly dismal morning of school. "You lost Katrina with that rock example."

"The relationship of kinetic and potential energy is a straightforward application of algebra. What's wrong with that?"

"Listen," replied September, "a lot of Katrina's friends still play with Barbies. If you want a real-world application of algebra that she can relate to, you need to stick with, say, how many cans of cat food you need for a litter of ten kittens."

With my help, Katrina liked math even less than when we'd left California, if such a thing was possible. "You help Jordan with his times tables," September told me one day, "and I will help Katrina with the Pythagorean theorem."

It wasn't long before I was banned from teaching Jordan as well, after a class we held in a small park.

"All I said was that seven times eight is the same as eight times seven." I stood my ground—as the teacher, I didn't want to get expelled from school. "And then he started throwing things at me."

"It isn't what you said, it's what you where doing when you said it. I understand that Jordan wants to swing from a branch, but you shouldn't. You're setting a bad example. You can't imitate a monkey and hope to get anywhere." September was folding her arms across her chest and looking at me sternly.

I don't think the kids dreamed of partial differential equations once.

· · ·

We had started taking P-Days in England roughly once a week so we could get caught up on various mundane tasks, such as laundry, but also to take a break from sightseeing and to recharge our batteries. Our first full day in Cesky Krumlov turned out to be a P-Day and we didn't get very far past Hostel Skippy's; on day two it was time to see what this new place was all about.

Cesky Krumlov is a UNESCO World Heritage site and rich with lots of sights to see. The castle, situated high on a hill, was built in the thirteenth century overlooking the Vltava River. The walled center of the city is full of quaint stone buildings that time has preserved from the 15th and 16th centuries. Walking down the narrow cobblestone paths with Katrina perched high on my shoulders made me feel as if I were indeed living in a long-ago century . . . except that there was an Internet café on every street corner. And due to its location in a former Eastern Bloc country, everything was incredibly cheap. But—true to the Eastern Bloc stereotype—by the looks on people's faces walking down the street, everyone looked miserable, as if they'd all recently had root canals and expected another one wasn't far off.

We climbed up a long hill to visit the castle in town. The castle had hundreds of stairs and the ceiling was low enough that I couldn't carry Katrina on my shoulders inside. Defeated, we milled about the castle courtyard looking as though *we* recently had root canals.

This was a low point. We were barred from doing the things we love and had come to do: cycling, hiking, swimming. We were even barred from the things that we merely tolerated: sightseeing at an old castle. Later, back at the hostel, we sat on the rear porch overlooking the Vltava River and watched people in canoes attempt to go over the locks. At least half the attempts resulted in the canoe capsizing. It lifted my spirits somewhat to watch people get thrown into the chilly water.

"Let's do that!" September was speaking, but I was wondering if one of the spirits that possessed the hostel had found a new host.

"You're joking, right? Katrina can't get her cast wet. Have you observed the capsize rate going over the locks?"

"Well, yes I have, but you're just noticing the canoes. Watch the rubber rafts. Not one has tipped over."

There were probably ten canoes for every raft, but she had a point.

"All we have to do is get a big garbage bag and wrap her cast in it. Worst case, she gets her cast wet and we get a new one."

Next thing I knew we were at a rafting outfitter in town. I was anticipating a release form of some kind that I would have to sign—you
know, the standard legalese mumbo jumbo stating that if I die, my
descendants waive the rights to sue or haunt the outfitter from beyond
the grave. Instead, the nice person who was helping me smiled and
handed me a bottle.

"What's this?" I asked. The man who was helping me spoke exactly three
words of English: "Hi" and "Monica Lewinsky." Actually, "Lewinsky" is
Polish, so make that two words of English, but he knew more English
than I knew Czech. Context is everything, so asking "What's this?" while
holding up the bottle was sufficient to frame the question.

"Grog," he grunted.

I didn't think I needed "grog" to captain the raft, so I tried to give it
back. The man looked affronted, so I slipped it into my pocket.

He led us to the water where we would shove off, but I wanted life
jackets, if not for all of us, at least for Katrina, who couldn't swim with
her cast. I made the universal sign-language symbol of a person drown-
ing and then pantomimed someone putting on a jacket. The man looked
perplexed. Had no one ever requested a life vest before? After a few earnest pantomiming motions he disappeared from view. ● Since about
the time we'd met the Harley-riding Frenchmen, I had been taking a
mental inventory of differences we found in people and cultures. I wondered if the U.S. Coast Guard had ever considered The Grog Approach
to boating preparedness.

> *Jordan's Journal, July 23*
>   *Today we went river rafting. Katrina wore a plastic garbage
> bag over her cast. We went down a small waterfall and rap-
> ids. We got soaked. On one canoe there was a person who was
> standing up and singing "I drank too much and now I'm drunk
> and I sound like an idiot." He sang it in Czech, so we just had to
> guess what he was saying.*

There were so many people plying the waters of the river—for the afternoon or even for the week—it was clearly the thing to do in the area.

The four of us were the only sober people on the river. Everyone else was stinking drunk and clearly enjoying themselves way more than they should have been. It was an interesting glimpse behind all those root-canal grimaces that greeted us around town. A little grog and the next thing you knew folks were trying to dance in a canoe. People must have been confused as to why we were sober because *many* made friendly gestures to give us as much booze as we wanted.

. . .

We had no agenda, no itinerary; in six weeks we planned to have Katrina's cast removed, return to Zermatt, pick up our tandems, and resume cycling. In the interim, we packed up and caught a bus to Prague, city of a thousand spires and perpetual graffiti.

Our first priority in Prague was to find a wheelchair. Katrina was now able to use her crutches for short distances but still needed help to cover more ground than that around our new hostel.

"Where are my crutches?!" Katrina demanded after breakfast one morning. "I *obviously* used them to come and sit down at the table, but they aren't here now!"

Of course we all knew where they were; the crutches were a cool toy. Jordan was constantly taking the crutches out for a spin.

Looking for a wheelchair to rent isn't a standard tourist activity, but for the next several weeks it became the first thing we did once we got settled in a city. Anyone who feels like they need an extra challenge in their lives is invited to travel to an unfamiliar place where you don't speak the language, and then make finding a wheelchair to rent a top priority.

Being illiterate really had its disadvantages. We just couldn't fake the language in Eastern Europe. In France and Switzerland, we could see the English words hiding, disguised as French or German, whether on the street signs or on a bottle of aspirin. For example, any fool can see that the German word *schweinefleisch* means "ham," yet in Prague you could think you were buying a box of sugar only to get it home and find out it was foot powder. This could be a big surprise if you had already sprinkled it on your cornflakes.

In Western Europe we were *danka*-ing and *merci*-ing with every other multilingual wannabe the day we arrived. I think you need to gargle with razor blades before you can acquire a Slavic dialect. And the letters no longer are faithful to the sounds that a boy from California would expect, having some other variant invented for the entertainment of the locals. Despite the language barrier, we found we could communicate most of our needs; all it took was a smile while pointing with one hand and holding up a credit card in the other. Of course this didn't work so well over the phone.

We obtained a wheelchair from an obscure social services agency and went to discover Prague. We found a lot of beautiful architecture—every building, every bridge, every corner has received a lot of detailed attention by some ancient craftsman. Luckily, it all survived World War II. But the reality is that unless one enjoys looking at a statue of a nobleman made anonymous by centuries of grime and soot, the overall impression is that the entire city needs a good scrubbing.

We ventured on a few short side trips from Prague, such as Kutná Hora. Kutná Hora rose to fame in the 13th century as one of the richest towns of medieval Bohemia, thanks to a nearby silver mine. Today it is probably most (in)famous for the Sedlec Ossuary, commonly known as "The Church of Bones," final resting spot of 40,000 souls whose bones are arranged into works of art.

The ossuary is a functioning church, holding services every Sunday; it also does a steady business in tourists. We paid our entrance fee and walked down a flight of stairs into a macabre chamber in which the bones were used to construct ordinary objects. I wondered how the dearly departed would take the news that their bones were being used as chandeliers and tables.

The bones started piling up in 1278 when King Ottokar II of Bohemia sent Henry, a bishop from Kutná Hora, to Jerusalem. Henry returned with a little bit of soil from Golgotha, the hill on which Jesus was crucified. For centuries the local townsfolk wanted to be buried on the land because of the holy dirt, and it eventually became the resting place to an estimated 40,000 souls. In the mid-1700s a church was placed on the site and bones from the cemetery were stockpiled in an ossuary. What does one do with an ossuary full of bones? Decorate, of course! A century after the church was built an artist was commissioned to do just that. Not exactly what I would have done with thousands of centuries-old skeletal remains, but I clearly do not have the imagination it takes to build a world-class chandelier made entirely of human femurs or a garland made of skulls. ● We spent time examining the teeth on various skulls. Dental work sure has come a long way over the centuries.

While returning to Prague, the four of us were sitting on a train facing each other. "That was cool," Jordan remarked. "Better than any of the other churches we've seen."

"I thought it was creepy," September disagreed. "Who would want to go to Sunday school with a bunch of skulls staring at you?"

"What's creepy about it?" Katrina asked. "It's not like they're going to spring to life and start chasing you."

"Although that'd be cool, too," Jordan quipped.

I stared at Jordan and imagined his *real* reaction if bones sprang back to life and started chasing him. "All talk," I said. "You'll be having nightmares tonight."

"The flying monkeys kind of nightmares?" Jordan responded. He was referring to my prediction of the impression that *The Wizard of Oz* would have on him when he was five. He thought the flying monkeys were cool, too, and never did have nightmares.

"The flying monkeys still creep me out," I said, recalling how I was terrified of them when I was five.

September and I had been discussing visiting another place that could give someone nightmares, but we'd been warned about taking the kids there. Turning to September, I whispered, "I think if they didn't freak out in the ossuary they can handle Auschwitz. It's something we shouldn't shy away from."

"Shy away from what?" Jordan demanded.

"What don't you think we can handle?" Katrina asked excitedly.

"Can't your mother and I have a simple conversation without you both interrupting?" I said, exasperated.

"We are discussing the fact that we should get tickets to Krakow, so that we can visit Aushwitz." September explained calmly.

The journey from Prague to Krakow, Poland, was an all-day affair in one of those trains built before air-conditioning was invented. We once again found ourselves on a train platform, watching the train depart, with a mass of bicycle panniers at our feet.

"The panniers worked out great when they were attached to the tandems," September said, "but they're a terrible choice as general luggage. Maybe we could attach wheels to them."

"We'll look for a luggage cart along with a wheelchair," I replied. "For now, let's just grab a taxi to our hostel." Taxis aren't exactly the budget traveler's transportation of choice, but after a long day with so much luggage to schlep and a daughter who needed to be carried, we splurged. As I tumbled into the back of the cab, my ears were affronted.

"Wasn't 'Stayin' Alive' banned by the United Nations or something?" I asked on the way to our hostel. "Isn't it like 30 years old?"

"Yes, dear. And so is *Dark Side of the Moon*."

The door-to-door service was pleasant, despite the disco. And the fare was so low I couldn't see how the driver could cover the cost of fuel. Taxis in Poland became a habit, even though, much to my chagrin, disco was the genre of choice for four out of five cab drivers surveyed.

We came to Krakow for the sole purpose of visiting Auschwitz, but stayed longer than planned because we really liked it. Krakow was everything Prague was not. It was clean, it was a manageable size, and you could buy a train ticket without having to stand in the information line, followed by the reservation line, and then the purchasing line. Krakow was also teeming with just the kind of history that we wanted the kids to see.

. . .

"It's bloody hot," I complained. Europe was in the grip of a heat wave, and we were preparing to go out. "I'm going to have to hand wash this shirt before we go. It'll feel nice to put it on damp, though."

"What happened to your other short-sleeved shirt?" September responded.

"It's in Zermatt with the tandems. I figured if we weren't cycling I wouldn't need it, so I left it with the other camping and cycling gear."

September gave me the same look of feigned patience she gave Jordan when she was trying to teach him the multiplication tables. "Well, we'll have to get you another one then. We need to divide and conquer. I'll look into getting a wheelchair with the kids." She gave me a stern look. "You go buy yourself a short-sleeved shirt. Get a pair of shorts as well."

"Can't I get you to pick me up a shirt and a pair of shorts?" I asked. "Most wives prefer to pick out their husband's wardrobes."

"Be brave. You can do this."

"What if I just ordered some stuff from Lands' End and had it sent with our next box of books?"

"We haven't received our first box of books yet."

I was defeated. "We will meet you back here in a couple of hours," September said, as she and the kids disappeared out the door of our hostel.

I proceeded down the street and walked into the first department-looking store I saw. On one of the upper levels I found some men's clothes on clearance. I picked out a shirt and a pair of shorts, tried them on, and purchased them. Victorious, I went back to the hostel, donned my new stylish threads, and waited for September and the kids.

An hour or so later I could hear them coming. They were still across the street, but the traffic was not enough to drown Jordan's voice in his excited state.

"Do you think Dad's back? Can I tell him? He'll be so surprised!" The door to our hostel room burst open. Two simultaneous conversations started up immediately.

Jordan was saying, "Guess what we saw? You'll never guess!"

September wasn't actually saying anything, at least not yet. She just stared at me, slack jawed, for several moments. Then, ignoring the fact that Jordan was playing twenty questions with me, she said, "You bought that just to get back at me."

I was confused. "What?"

Jordan said, "I want you to guess!"

September said, "That shirt. It is the ugliest shirt on the planet. You bought it to get back at me for not shopping for you."

I replied, "I wouldn't do that. Okay, maybe I would, but I didn't. It was on sale and it looked decent enough. What's wrong with it?"

"Dad! You aren't guessing!"

September explained, "It looks like . . . well, it looks like you work for some drive-up hamburger joint in the Midwest. It looks like a uniform for Bill's Burger Barn. Where's your name tag?"

Jordan was on the verge of hyperventilating. "Dad! You're not guessing!"

I decided that September was not a professional fashion critic. The shirt was a huge step up from a simple T-shirt. It was tan with navy blue sleeves and had buttons and even a collar. But I needed to focus on Jordan before he passed out. "Jordan," I asked, "what did you see?"

"We found a go-kart track and Mom said we could go!"

Go-karts weren't exactly what we came to experience in Krakow, but I agreed with Jordan; the brochure he had with him looked fun. It also provided a cultural counter to where we were headed the following day.

As part of the kids' education we had been studying World War II ever since we arrived in Europe, as it arguably had the biggest influence on world affairs for the last fifty years and likely will continue for the next fifty years. We tried to present a balanced view of the war by having the kids read accounts written from the perspective of both the Allies and the Axis powers. We talked about both viewpoints, that people on both sides did some really horrible things, and as in any war, it is the civilians who suffer. September and I both believe that most people the world over are innately good, but we aren't so naïve as to believe evil doesn't exist. We wanted to show the kids what can happen if evil goes unanswered. So, in our World War II discussions there was no denying or sugarcoating the atrocities of the Nazis. We were going to see those atrocities firsthand. I *wanted* the kids to be horrified. 🐚

The day after we went to Jordan's go-kart track, the Auschwitz tour company we'd arranged for came to pick us up at our hostel. It was a hot August morning. When the van arrived we stuffed Katrina's wheelchair, which we had rented from a hospital, into the back and settled in for the ninety-minute drive.

"Auschwitz" is the German pronunciation of the Polish town of Oświęcim, about 40 miles west of Krakow. The extermination camp was established by the Nazis in 1940 in what was then Nazi-occupied Poland. The exact number of people murdered there, mostly Jews, is not known, but most experts agree the number is between 1.1 and 1.5 million people.

Arriving at the site of the former camp, our van maneuvered into the parking lot. We set Katrina in her wheelchair and made our way through the infamous gates that read ARBEIT MACHT FREI which translates to "Work makes one free." The morning sun was scorching and we waited for our tour to begin along with the other tourists.

Our group of fifty was eventually led through the camp by a guide. We scurried from display to display. As there was no handicapped access and plenty of stairs, we eventually abandoned Katrina's wheelchair, but even with me carrying her it was difficult for us to keep up with our group. The rooms throughout Auschwitz were so crowded there was little chance to see the displays or to hear what was being said, even though our tour guide did her best to accommodate the large crowd.

Much of the extermination camp of Auschwitz is still intact, from the gas chambers used for the mass murders to the ovens used to cremate the remains. Some of the most grisly reminders of what occurred at Auschwitz are the things the Nazis kept in storage and historians preserved. As all entered the gas chambers shaven, the resulting hair was baled and over two tons of it is prominently on display in sacks that are splayed open. Room after room of personal effects are also displayed. There is the shoe room and the handbag room and the eyeglasses room. These items were taken from the prisoners after their arrival. Decades later they are on display behind glass, an echoing reminder that their owners never saw them again.

After visiting the various rooms of personal effects we walked across the compound to the ovens that were used for cremation. "I want to sit in my wheelchair in the shade," Katrina said. Similarly, Jordan had grown weary of being herded along and was on the verge of a meltdown—and not from the heat.

"I'm sorry, guys," I said. "This is a tremendously important part of history. Think of the millions who died here, what it was like for them to be herded through like cattle to slaughter. Remember, we will go home; we have a safe place to sleep tonight."

Nearby two teenage girls were in total hysterics, sobbing uncontrollably as they imagined the horrors of the site. As for us, I wanted *my* kids to be horrified, but the heat and the crowds dampened that effect. Our emotional meltdown was to come six months later at the Killing Fields near Phnom Penh, Cambodia.

Later that evening, in the comfort of our hostel, we talked to the kids about our experience at Auschwitz.

"I can't believe the people that did all those horrible things are the same ones that we see around town," Katrina said. "Everyone in Poland has been so nice."

We explained that the Germans occupied Poland at the time, and most people in the area probably had no idea what was happening at the camp, and most Germans probably didn't know, either.

"How can that be?" Katrina asked.

"There was a big war on," September replied. "It was a scary time. I think most people didn't want to know. But, remember, many people were heroes, like in the book you're reading." As part of her reading curriculum, Katrina was in the middle of *The Diary of Anne Frank.*

There is much more to Krakow than go-karts and Auschwitz. We visited the local salt mine and learned how it thrust Krakow into power in medieval times. In the historic Jewish Ghetto is Oskar Schindler's factory where visitors can learn his story that inspired the book and movie that bears his name. More important, we were reminded that there were good people in the midst of the ugliness of the Nazi era.

. . .

"Before we move on tomorrow," September said one afternoon, "we really need to do something about our panniers."

"Yup. We should probably hit a mall and see if we can find a luggage cart." Our eight panniers had metal hooks on the back for attaching to the tandems. The hooks had a nasty way of catching on things you didn't want them to, say, like flesh. Transferring them and a daughter on crutches from platform 1 to platform 9 during a three-minute dash was more than we'd bargained for.

The mall in Krakow was my first visit to such a place in roughly a decade, my shopping habits being nominal at best. The whole establishment seemed like it would blend in nicely in any suburb in the United States, right down to the cineplex playing the latest Hollywood blockbuster. We shopped valiantly, carrying a pencil and notepad wherever we went, but clerks laughed at our artwork. "Luggage cart" just didn't translate, no matter how hard we tried.

"Maybe they don't make luggage carts anymore," I suggested to September at a Samsonite luggage retailer, "since essentially all luggage these days comes pre-equipped with wheels."

"Then we need to improvise," September said. "I saw a sporting goods store. We could buy some rollerblades and strap them on."

"I think a skateboard is more like it."

Before we could execute on the skateboard idea, September took a 90-degree turn as she passed the hardware store at the mall. She emerged ten minutes later, with a full-fledged moving dolly. Now we could strap our panniers to the dolly and off we could go. And if we decided to move a refrigerator along the way, we could do that, too.

www.360degreeslongitude.com/concept3d/360degreeslongitude.kmz

"I've been Pragued!" There's nothing like a good Praguing to make one convert a noun into a verb. Use Google Earth and the *360 Degrees Longitude* layer to get Pragued.

6.

Have You Hugged Your Lawyer Today?

August 2–August 19
Poland/Sweden

Dad. How does it feel to be half of 90?" Katrina asked, as we clambered onto the train. "I think I see a new gray hair."

"It is only because of you, dear."

My birthday meant an extra helping of good-natured grief from my family. September was next. "I ordered a cheeseburger, no mayo," she quipped.

"Oh yeah, thanks for sewing on my button." My "Bill's Burger Barn" shirt had already lost more than one button. "You must love me."

"I do. I'll love you more if you let me burn that shirt."

When we found our compartment someone was already in it. We made our presence known by bursting in and shattering the solitude. Jordan spread out paper and pencils for his newfound love—making his own comic books. Katrina propped her cast up on the bench across from her and started reading. It's remarkable how much noise two kids can generate when pursuing "quiet" activities.

Five people in a compartment meant for four was a tight squeeze. Our neighbor sat quietly for a while, but I soon noticed him sniffing the air and looking puzzled, and then he got up and left. I didn't feel too bad. We had the compartment reserved, but for all I knew, so did he.

"Katrina, you really should put a sock on that foot," September said. "You know why that person just left, don't you?"

Wounded, Katrina replied, "Well, I can't actually wash under my cast, can I?"

"No, you can't," I said, "but you can save the rest of us a lot of grief if you would just seal up the offending fume factory by putting a sock on it."

After three months on the road, we thought we were a well traveled, "been there and done that" family, but nothing could prepare us for the Hostel Baltic Ocean in the Polish port city of Gdansk.

After we clambered off the train we phoned every single hostel in our guidebook and many, many more, only to find that every bed was taken. The whole of Europe, which had more or less been following us around since we'd arrived in Paris, was in Gdansk for a festival. The *Hostel Baltyk*, as it is formally known, was not listed in our guidebook, but when we found that it had four beds available we made reservations, sight unseen.

We had pushed the budget travel envelope a little too far.

Hostels can come in a wide variety of flavors. Of course, a hostel is not a hotel, where you obtain a room in exchange for cash. At a hostel, you get a bed in a room and a bathroom down the hall. A good hostel will also have cooking facilities, and a great hostel will have a coin-operated laundry.

Most hostels are well aware that people do not really like to share a room with others they do not know. Gone are the days when a hostel was two large dorm-style rooms—one for the men and one for the women. Hostels nowadays are a collection of smaller rooms where families or friends traveling together can all have a room to themselves. We never had to share our room.

That is, until we stayed at the Hostel Baltic Ocean. My first impression of the hostel was that the insides hadn't seen a broom since the Russians liberated Gdansk from the fleeing Nazis. My second impression was of the *Blues Brothers* scene were Elwood brings Jake home to his apartment above the train station, and Jake asks "How often does the train go by?" to which Elwood answers, "So often, you don't even notice."

As the staff was showing us our room, I noted seven beds. The woman helping us must have read my mind. "You probably will not have to share your room." The word "probably" rattled around in my head as I trundled off to the shower.

"I have a surprise for you," September said when I returned 20 minutes later. "What Ms. Hostel-Person failed to mention when she showed us our room was what was behind Door Numbers One and Two." September pointed to two innocent-looking doors in our room. I was drying myself off just as she was ready divulge her secret, when in bounced a sweet young thing through Door Number One. "Surprise!" September said, "behind these doors are more rooms. And the only path to those rooms is through *our* room."

I smiled thoughtfully at the young lady as she sped through our room, diverting her eyes and trying not to giggle.

The following night we were able to upgrade so we were no longer in the corridor room; we were in the room behind Door Number One.

Our old room—the corridor room—was now inhabited by seven very large and very hairy Polish men with booming laughs, affectionately known to us as the Bathroom Joke Septuplet. Not that we could tell what jokes they were really telling, but the hand gestures for bathroom jokes appear universal.

We now had the pleasure of bursting in on the Bathroom Joke Septuplet every time we left or returned to our room. These were clearly fun-loving guys who were very friendly, totally unrefined, and all the happier for it. They did not seem to be fazed in the least by the fact that the rest of the guests used their room as a hallway. Every time we passed through they were all sprawled across their beds in various stages of undress and joke-telling. During every transition through the room we would be reminded of just how hairy and large they were.

And that they wore blue boxer shorts. With red stripes. Not all of them, of course. Others preferred polka dots.

Quietly opening the door to the corridor room the following morning, I found the Bathroom Joke Septuplet had completely vanished! Not a single trace of them was left, save for a single pair of blue-and-white polka-dotted briefs on the floor, and the blue striped boxer shorts hanging from the curtains. Gratefully, there are some questions in life we will never know the answers to.

We made up a song to commemorate our encounter, to the tune of "Hotel California":

We're living it up at the Hostel Baltic Ocean
What a big disgrace
Such a scary face . . .

www.360degreeslongitude.com/concept3d/360degreeslongitude.kmz

Naked aggression encased in 4,000 pounds of steel. And you thought Boston had bad drivers.

Sweden was not on our radar screen when we left Zermatt; our intention had been to stay in Eastern Europe until we could resume cycling and camping. Yet around the time I was putting foot powder on my cornflakes, September simply announced that we were going to Sweden. "It'll be easier to find an English-speaking doctor for Katrina's follow-up exam," she noted. I couldn't argue that, as we had already speculated that everyone in Scandinavia speaks excellent English. Lutefisk had to be better than cornflakes mixed with Dr. Scholl's, so it was arranged.

www.360degreeslongitude.com/concept3d/360degreeslongitude.kmz

Got cabin? September has this way of always getting what she wants. She missed a career opportunity in politics, sales or as a con artist. Use Google Earth and the *360 Degrees Longitude* layer to find at least one reason I would marry my wife all over again.

We took a ferry from Gdansk to Gotland Island, Sweden, situated in the Baltic Sea 110 miles south of Stockholm. Gotland, literally "God's Land," was a Viking stronghold for centuries and the main city of Visby is now considered one of the best-preserved medieval cities in Scandinavia. Visby was hosting a medieval festival and on the Internet, September had found a cabin for us. The cabin gave us something we hadn't had since we left Silicon Valley—a mailing address.

When we arrived we found the cabin was surrounded by forest, situated on a cliff overlooking the bay that surrounds the town of Visby. When we first walked inside we took a look at the dining room table and found a large package waiting for us—our August shipment of books! It cost about three times the value of the contents of the package to have it FedEx-ed from the United States to Sweden, but it arrived on time. Our July shipment of books was still at the mercy of the U.S. Post Office.

Not only was our package of books waiting for us, but also friends had sent Katrina and Jordan a care package. It was better than Christmas. "COOL!" Jordan shouted, climbing the furniture and jumping from the kitchen table to the couch, his way of coping with the flood of emotions that came with the new *Essential Fantastic Four* comic book he received.

After Jordan's Fantastic Fill, we ventured inside the old city walls to the medieval festival. Entrepreneurs had set up booths to sell their wares and the townsfolk and tourists alike were dressed in period clothes.

"Omigoshlookatallthecoolknivesandweapons!" Jordan started talking so fast and excitedly that all the words ran together. The focal point for all this enthusiasm was stall after stall of shiny weaponry: bows, arrows, spears, knives, battle-axes, maces. You know, the run-of-the-mill stuff that any knight in shining armor or Freddy Krueger wannabe would need. All available for sale, all available for any hyperactive eight-year-old to handle and impale himself with in a spasmodic frenzy of activity.

Jordan picked up one particularly massive-looking sword and started to wield it in a fashion that should not be allowed in public. I rushed over to avoid a reproduction of the Black Knight scene from *Monty Python and the Holy Grail.* "Wow," he exclaimed as I helped him put the sword back in the scabbard, "they would never let you do that in America."

"Right you are, my boy. And for good reason."

Mixed in with all the weaponry was Ye Olde Tie-Dye Shoppe and Ye Olde Internet Café. At the grocery store we observed battle-axe-wielding Vikings helping their fair maidens peruse produce.

"There's a jousting tournament tonight," September commented after reading a brochure. "Could be interesting."

"What's that?" Jordan asked.

"It's a demonstration of how to use all these weapons," I replied.

"Cool!"

The "cool" tag should have been a warning. The men and women who participate in these tournaments are certifiable.

Later that night Katrina's wheelchair scored us front-row seats at the tournament. Brandishing a 15-foot-long lance, two "knights" would charge at each other on horseback at full gallop. The sole safety measure in place was that instead of an armor-piercing point, the lance had a spherical cushion about the size of a volleyball. There was a convincing thud on impact, throwing the loser off his horse. The time lag between the person hitting the ground and when he actually started moving again was a signal that these tournaments are not faked.

It didn't take long for us to understand that the Swedes take jousting seriously. "That hurt," I said. "He's not moving."

"How do you know it's a he?" Katrina asked. "They're in full armor."

"Women aren't that stupid," September replied.

When the archers came out and started shooting real arrows in a show of their marksmanship, September was not amused. "All it would take is a tiny slip and those arrows would come straight at us!" It was one of the few times that I wasn't grateful for front-row seats.

"You can hear the arrow slice through the air!" Jordan exclaimed. When the real arrows gave way to flaming arrows, we gave up our premium seats and opted for five rows of human shields for the remainder of the tournament.

. . .

The day of Katrina's four-week checkup arrived. Visby Tourist Information helped us to make an appointment at the local hospital.

"Dr. Julen told me that I might be able to get a cast after four weeks where I could bend my knee," Katrina said as we made our way to her appointment. "I would really like that."

Dr. Julen had given us the original X-ray before we left Zermatt. We found that our Swedish doctor was a semi-retired Dane working in Visby for the duration of the summer tourist season. The hospital was new and sparkling clean and our doctor probably spoke better English than I did. It was impossible to tell if we were in Sweden or California.

The doctor took the original X-ray and put it side by side with the one he had just taken. "Katrina's leg is healing nicely," he said, "but it is still much too early to replace this cast with one that would allow her to bend her knee."

I looked at the two X-rays, and to my untrained eyes, they looked no different from each other.

The doctor continued, "We cannot disturb the healing process by replacing the cast with a shorter one. There is still a visible five-millimeter gap at the break point."

We were all disappointed. Katrina tried her best not to show it; we dealt with the setback by not discussing it. We shuffled to the payment desk and paid our bill. It suddenly became clear we weren't in California.

"We just got an X-ray and consultation for 50 dollars," I commented to September as we walked away. "At that price, we should get two."

"One's enough," September said. "Let's go home." By now it was natural to refer to the place where our stuff was as "home."

When we arrived we found a note: Our friends' friends in Paris had received the package of books that had been mailed more than two months prior. Excited, we arranged to have it FedEx-ed to us in Visby. Within the space of a week we had gone from being marooned in a virtual book desert to being able to compete with the local library.

• • •

One of the things that gives Gotland Island its character is the Viking Village, a working museum that keeps the old traditions alive. But old traditions aren't always worth keeping alive. Two days after we had flaming arrows shot at us during the jousting tournament, we found ourselves once again running for cover at the Viking Village, where anyone who wanted could go to the axe-throwing booth, pick up an axe, and give it a toss. Or the archery booth, the mace booth, and so on.

We stood in line to test our own axe-throwing powers. When it was my turn, I reached for an axe; if I hurled it hard enough it would either stick into a pile of logs or bounce off them, ricocheting back to test my reflexes.

"One at a time," a young man said in perfect English. He then motioned to a little boy, about three years old, to take his turn. I had noticed the little boy, but assumed he was with an adult, never dreaming he was actually waiting for a turn.

"You can't be serious," September said. "He can barely lift the axe! Where are his parents?"

The little boy hurled the axe and it landed about three inches past his toes. September was upset that the Viking Village would let a toddler throw an axe and she let the young man next to the booth know it.

"I don't work here, ma'am. My friends and I like to hang out here, that's all."

"You know," I said, walking away, "this morning I was reading a news article that was headlined, 'Sweden bans import of irradiated food.' It's one of the EU stumbling blocks."

"So, what you're saying," September said with a mixture of frustration and utter befuddlement, "is my health is protected from the onslaught of irradiated tomatoes, but . . . "

" . . . one ill-timed stumble could cause you and your radiation-free cucumbers to be chopped by a battle-axe, yes." I finished her thought to the logical conclusion.

There are those who believe that we should take responsibility for our own actions; I even like to think I am one of them. But obviously

I am a mama's boy by European standards. "I've been noting a severe shortage of lawyers in this part of the world. Ever since a ... "

" ... certain rope broke?" September asked.

"Well, that too," I said. I had also been thinking about how we were given grog when we went rafting, but had to demand life jackets, and how we had arrows whiz past our heads at the jousting tournament. And there were other, more subtle differences we had observed. "I've been taking a mental inventory about how everywhere we go people are a little bit different. It's taken a couple of months before I could start to appreciate how *we* are different."

"What do you mean?" Katrina asked.

"The Swiss are always on time, and they love their rules. But just to the south, the Italians are always late and as far as rules go, don't mind looking the other way. The French enjoy their leisure, which is why stores are always closed. The list goes on."

"And what are Americans like?" Katrina asked.

"I'm not so sure I want to know. But I suspect that among other things, Europeans must think we have an over developed sense of liability. But I beg to differ on that."

John's Journal, August 18

Frank Zappa once wrote a song called "Stink Foot." I wonder if he had a daughter with a cast. I never appreciated the fact that after five weeks one small cast could pack the wallop of a laundry truck filled with old gym socks. Wherever we go, people suddenly start looking about and begin testing the air as if some industrial accident just occurred upwind.

We are constantly second-guessing when the cast might come off and changing our plans, such as they are, to satisfy that event in the undefined future.

Stockholm is a city surrounded by water. We arrived in August at the peak of Europe's travel season and had just visited the *Vasa*, a ship built in the early 17th century. It was to be the grandest vessel on the water, and it was for about 40 seconds, until it sank on its maiden voyage. There it sat on the bottom of Stockholm Bay, until it was found and raised in 1961 and restored with a museum built around it. We were now on a pedal boat in the waterways where Lake Mälaren meets the Baltic Sea. The kids were entertaining themselves by blowing long strings of soap bubbles as September and I pedaled along.

"Science Moment!" I declared. I had introduced Science Moments as a way to stay in the classroom, even though I had been unofficially expelled. Anytime I saw something cool, I would explain *why* it was cool. Nevertheless, I heard a collective groan from my captive audience.

"Dad's in a good mood because he is pedaling in the sunshine," September said. "Humor him with his Science Moment."

"I was just thinking about that ship, the *Vasa*," I began. "It floated for 40 seconds and then flipped upside-down and sank. What makes a boat float? What makes it sink? What made that boat flip upside-down? Why doesn't the boat that we're on right now flip upside-down?"

The kids desperately avoided making eye contact.

"Don't everyone raise your hands at once."

Jordan held up his bottle of bubble soap. "These bubbles have special powers in them. 🌑 Every third Thursday they generate a force field around children that Science Moments can't penetrate!"

I let it go. True, I was only pedaling a paddle boat and not my beloved tandem, but in August the Stockholm days are long and the skies clear and it's a great place for anyone who likes the color blue. We weren't progressing toward Istanbul, but pedaling in the sunshine made me think that perhaps it didn't really matter.

7.

Chocolate Vomit *Is* a Medical Emergency!

August 20–September 8
Denmark/Germany

 e began to slowly make our way back to Zermatt to pick up our tandems. On Katrina's six-week anniversary we planned to stop wherever we happened to be and have her cast removed. A week or so later we would arrive in Zermatt, ready to ride.

That was the plan. Step one was to take the train from Stockholm to Copenhagen, Denmark. There is nothing like "real life" to screw up a good plan.

> *Jordan's Journal, August 19*
>   *Today we went on a train. I ate two candy bars then I barfed. Some of the barf went into Katrina's cast. Then we went on two more trains and then we went to our campground. We are in Copenhagen, Denmark now.*

The smell emanating from the cast had been bad enough, but now it was horrid beyond words. Unless we had a wheelchair, I carried Katrina on my shoulders when we had to walk anywhere significant, so I had a front-row seat to the offending fume factory, as the top of her thigh-high cast was only inches from my nose.

It had been nearly six weeks since Katrina's accident and it was time once again for a follow-up visit to a doctor. With the cast in its current shape it simply needed to come off, even if it meant another would replace it. We arrived at a campground near Copenhagen eager to find a doctor, but the lone attendant at the campground was occupied with a couple ahead of us.

The couple's thick accent was clearly Italian, the camp manager's Dutch, yet they were speaking in English. I had been impatient, but the paradox soon got the best of me and I listened. The Italian couple was making friendly comments about Tivoli Gardens, a famous landmark of the city. The Italians spoke loudly and with their hands. The Dutch camp manager kept backing away, as if threatened, yet the couple advanced, unaware they were slowly backing their prey into a corner.

A few moments later the Italian couple left and the manager seemed relieved as he turned his attention to us. "Italians," he said. "They come every August and are so loud. I'm sorry that there is a group of them near your cabin."

"That's not why we're here," September explained. "I need to speak to a doctor."

"You will not be able to find a doctor this late on a Friday," replied the manager. Writing on a slip of paper, he continued, "Here is the phone number for the emergency room at the hospital. This is the only doctor that will answer a phone until Monday morning."

September got the on-call physician on our cell phone and explained the situation.

"I'm sorry," said the unsympathetic doctor on the other end, "but office hours for the week are over throughout the entire country. If you have an emergency, you can bring the patient to the emergency room at the hospital where someone is always on call."

"This *is* an emergency!" September pleaded desperately into the phone. "We can't get into the same room with that cast smelling the way it does!"

"I should have been more exact," explained the physician. "A *life threatening* emergency. I'll tell you what, though. Bring your daughter to my office first thing Monday morning and we'll do what we can."

"Whoever heard of an entire medical system shutting down for the weekend?" September protested, placing the cell phone down on the table.

It was time I took matters into my own hands. I contemplated our options and then . . .

"What are you looking for?" September asked.

"That blasted wilderness survival saw that I couldn't get you to part with."

Suddenly September's countenance brightened. "You mean the one you tried to throw out, but I rescued? The one that you thought was a total waste of space? You want it now? You *need* it?"

"Yes," I said through gritted teeth.

"What do you need it for? Does this have anything to do with the fact that Katrina can't see the doctor until Monday morning?"

"Well, yes, it does." I shared my plan with September. "The contaminated part of the cast is over her thigh. Doctor Julen told us we might be able to get a shortened cast at four weeks that only comes to her knee. The doctor in Sweden didn't want to do that because he didn't want to disturb the leg by removing the cast. I'm going to cut off the top six inches so that her cast will come to the knee. That will get rid of the contaminated section *without* disturbing her leg."

"We could just remove the entire cast and be done with it," September suggested. "The six-week point is only a few days away."

We had been discussing Katrina's leg so much in recent days and second-guessing doctors' diagnoses that it was difficult to separate fact from wishful thinking. We had gone so far as to practically force-feed Katrina yogurt and ice cream, thinking the extra calcium was going to perform some miracle, even though my Internet research showed this was of dubious merit. I pulled out Katrina's two X-rays, taken four weeks apart, to re-establish fact.

"The two X-rays look so similar," I said, scratching my chin. "Didn't Dr. Julen tell us she would have to wear the cast for six to eight weeks? We've been counting on six, but . . . "

I had this "vision" in my head. I would remove the cast, Katrina would take one step and then collapse onto the ground. "We can't just cut it off if there is any risk of reinjuring her leg," I contemplated. "But it should be okay to remove the top six inches."

The "saw" was nothing more than a wire with teeth. I took Katrina outside and propped up her leg on a picnic table; she grasped the edge of the bench with rapid shallow breathing and white knuckles. Yet I don't know who panicked more, September or Katrina.

"Don't you think scissors would be safer?" exclaimed September, maneuvering herself between me and her daughter.

"No, I don't. Trust me."

Katrina's fear of the saw was overcome by the yearning to get rid of her cast, if only the top few inches, so she could bend her leg.

It took much longer than anticipated, in no small part due to Katrina squealing in terror at the slightest hint of pressure on her leg. But eventually the top six inches was removed, along with zero bits of flesh.

"Try bending your knee, Little One," I said. After weeks of immobility, she could bend it only slightly. "Monday morning we'll go see the doctor, tell her it's been six weeks, and hopefully be done with it."

• • •

We celebrated the last weekend of Katrina's cast by going to Tivoli Gardens and also to the planetarium. Tycho Brahe, the astronomer who was instrumental along with Johann Kepler in formulating the planetary laws of motion that I had studied in graduate school, was a Copenhagen native. To go to Copenhagen and not visit the planetarium that bears his name would be a disgrace. In the following months Jordan would inform us repeatedly that the Tycho Brahe Planetarium was the only "museum" he liked. I think that's because it came with an IMAX movie.

Sunday night came and with it big plans for the following day. It had been a long, waterless summer for two kids who love to swim. To celebrate, we planned to visit Copenhagen's biggest water park as soon as we were rid of the cast. The following morning came with a brilliant sun and a beautiful blue sky that seemed to be full of hope. "It's over a mile to the train station," September said as Katrina and I made our way out the door. "Are you sure you'll be able to carry her?"

"Been there, done that," I replied. We had outgrown our tradition of looking for a wheelchair immediately upon our arrival in a new city; Katrina and I had both gotten a lot stronger. I would carry her for a few blocks, and then she would use her crutches for a few blocks; in that fashion we could cover a lot of ground. "Once we get out of the doctor's office," I said, "I'll call the cell phone and we can rendezvous at the water park."

At the examining room I gave the doctor a rundown of our plight: We were cycling from London to Istanbul when Katrina broke her leg in Switzerland. We hoped to return to cycling before the summer was over, yada, yada, yada. It was Denial 101. I had told myself so many times that we were going to return to Zermatt and cycle off to Istanbul that I created a scenario in my mind in which, if the doctor felt sorry for us, she would give Katrina the desired diagnosis.

The physician was a competent pediatric orthopedic specialist and listened sympathetically. Of course, our plight didn't change the facts.

Examining a fresh X-ray she said, "There is a five-millimeter gap in the bone at the fracture point." She looked at me with pity. "With this kind of a break, it can take months for the bone to heal."

Katrina started sobbing right there in the examining room.

"It is very important to keep the cast in place until the calcification process is complete and a callous has formed over the entire fracture," she continued. "You *must* have the leg x-rayed to verify this before the cast is removed." Maintaining eye contact, she spoke slowly and clearly while enunciating each syllable with the proper inflection to emphasize her point. As if she could read my thoughts, she continued, "Do not expect any significant change for at least two to three weeks, and probably much longer."

By the time I crossed through the doorway, the doctor was making me feel grateful she didn't replace the cast I had shortened with one the original length.

On our way out, I stopped at the receptionist's desk to settle the bill. "Can I have your E.U. card?" the woman behind the desk asked.

I had been asked this question in Sweden, so I gave the same response. "I don't have one. I'm a U.S. citizen traveling in Europe for an extended period. I'll just pay cash and my insurance company will reimburse me directly." This worked in Sweden where they were happy to take my cash. Not so in Denmark.

"Cash?" She gave me a look as though she had never heard of the stuff before. After much hand-wringing she concluded that she really didn't know what amount to charge me, nor how to accept the filthy lucre if she did. Finally the receptionist handed me a yellow Post-it note and said, "Just write down your name and your address in the United States. We will send you a bill in a few days."

They never did. Danish travelers we later met were aghast that the hospital would even consider sending a bill, reacting the way an American might react to, say, the concept of censorship of the press.

John's Journal, August 22

In the past six weeks Katrina has occasionally seemed on the verge of depression, but 90% of the time she has been a real trouper. Now all pretense of keeping a stiff upper lip is gone. It is doubtful we will be able to continue cycling to Istanbul.

I don't want to write about it anymore.

The following two weeks were spent in the company of Mrs. Happy. She was the disembodied too-chirpy-for-her-own-good voice of our German rental car's GPS device. We flew to Munich from Copenhagen knowing we needed to return to the tandems in Zermatt, but unsure when and under what circumstances. Our budget had been calibrated for camping and cycling throughout Europe. Now we were driving through Germany from hostel to hostel; every time I opened my wallet it was to the accompaniment of a giant sucking sound.

Mrs. Happy led us all over Germany, from the Black Forest to the Neuschwanstein castle, rarely leading us astray. Occasionally she became confused, such as when she demanded we drive straight into the Danube's flooded banks; even then it was impossible to get angry with Mrs. Happy, who became the family's arbitrator whenever deciding which exit to take and when. We concluded every married couple should have two sinks in the master bath and an in-dash GPS device.

Eventually there was no denying our cycling trip was over and we needed to return to Switzerland to ship the tandems home. We arrived in Friedrichshafen on the German side of Lake Constance as we were making those preparations.

www.360degreeslongitude.com/concept3d/360degreeslongitude.kmz

Mrs. Happy led us to Mr. Helpful. Use Google Earth and the *360 Degrees Longitude* layer to see why "helpful" isn't always such a *super* idea.

If it hadn't been for *cyclus interruptus,* we would have passed through Friedrichshafen about two months earlier. The broken leg had all the drama of an eight-week-long root canal; being on the shores of Lake Constance with warm sunshine put the fine point on our forced change in plans. I busied myself looking out over the water and counting people cycling the path along the shore. I then heard a voice. "It's been two weeks. We should get Katrina's leg x-rayed again." It was September speaking.

"Why?" I said. "One definition of 'crazy' is doing something more than once and expecting a different outcome. The doctor in Copenhagen said *at least* two or three weeks, but it was pretty clear to me she was trying to sugarcoat the real prognosis of two or three *months.*"

"Well, that's completely different from what Dr. Julen told us way back in Zermatt. More data can't hurt."

Ah, it was the familiar "more data" debate. "Have I ever told you—" But I was cut off.

"Yes, I've heard your 'analysis paralysis' stories a thousand times. This is different. We aren't about to launch a rocket."

We went back and forth for a while, but I was really arguing for the intellectual stimulation; it lifted my spirits. September understands this about me.

Once again, we took Katrina to see a doctor and have her leg x-rayed, explaining to the doctor how we came to be in his office. He looked at the X-rays of her leg that we had in our possession. "The cast *must* come off today!" he declared with authority. "I don't need an X-ray to tell me that!"

You could have knocked me over with a feather.

The doctor took an X-ray of her leg anyway and the 5-mm gap in the bone was still clearly displayed, but he stood his ground. "The cast absolutely must come off today."

Not only was that contrary to the Danish doctor, but it was contrary to my gut instincts as an engineer. I exclaimed, "But doctor, there is no bone there. No structure to support the weight! Won't she just refracture her leg?!"

"It's a risk," he said, reaching for his electric saw, "but the bone will heal much faster if it is out of the cast. I'm surprised that the bone has healed so little in the past eight weeks. If we leave it in the cast it will be *months* before it heals completely. In cases like this, the bone needs some stimulation as a catalyst for the healing process."

I couldn't help myself. "Why didn't they tell us that in Denmark?"

"There are many kinds of fractures." The good doctor smiled and pointed to several framed photos on the wall of skiers schussing down impossibly steep inclines. "Denmark is a flat country."

I stood there with a stupid expression, trying to take in this meaning, but his saw was already cutting the plaster. "Her leg is still broken," the doctor said, removing the cast. "It will be several weeks before Katrina will be able to walk without crutches. Absolutely no running, cycling, or other contact sports for several weeks. Katrina will know when she is ready." As we were making our way from the doctor's office, he remarked in an offhanded way, "Just don't trip or stumble!"

Thanks for the confidence boost, Doc.

• • •

We packaged up our bicycle panniers and shipped them home. Then we purchased bona fide suitcases at Wal-Mart and abandoned at the train station the moving dolly we had purchased in Krakow. We then said our good-byes to Mrs. Happy and boarded the 5:30 p.m. ferry across Lake Constance to Romanshorn, Switzerland.

www.360degreeslongitude.com/concept3d/360degreeslongitude.kmz

Intellectual Man Strikes Again! Jordan loved making his own comic books, but scoffed at my suggestion of a superhero named Intellectual Man. Use Google Earth and the *360 Degrees Longitude layer* to see what happens next.

8.

Touch It, Wimp!

September 6–September 17
Switzerland . . . again

"You've gotta be joking."

Katrina gave me a hurt puppy dog look and asked, "Why not?"

Jordan and I had left September and Katrina 13 hours earlier to retrieve our tandems from Zermatt. After zipping across Switzerland by train, whiling away the time reading or watching sitcoms on my e.brain, Jordan and I were now rendezvousing with September and Katrina in the small mountain valley of Lauterbrunnen according to plan. September and Katrina had found us a place to stay and were waiting at the train station. Katrina wanted to ride the tandem. Now.

"Little one," I said, "your leg is still broken. You're not supposed to put any pressure on it whatsoever."

"It's about a 45-minute walk back to our cabin," Katrina said. "My arms are so tired from walking here on my crutches to meet you and Jordan. I hope I don't get too tired on the walk back and slip and fall."

I couldn't believe I was being talked into this. That I was on the *opposing* side of the debate. A thousand arguments ran through my mind in the span of a few seconds.

"It's downhill all the way from here," September added. "She wouldn't even have to pedal. And it isn't like we're loaded down; we're light with no panniers."

"But she can't even bend her knee far enough to follow the pedal around in its arc. We don't want to . . . " I stopped midsentence, then reached for my tool bag. A moment later I was holding Katrina's left pedal in my hand. "There," I said. "No pedaling required."

With Katrina's crutches strapped to the rear rack, we rode for the first time in eight weeks. Oh, what a joyous feeling! To be in this beautiful valley and feel the cool mountain air and the wind ruffling my hair, there just isn't anything like it to lift one's spirits. Well, maybe one thing . . .

Lauterbrunnen literally translates to "loud springs." The "springs" are actually waterfalls, 72 in total, circling this high mountain valley, but they are anything but loud. The effect is actually quite peaceful. We were returning here to visit our apple tree, the one we'd planted in a precise location three years prior. How we were going to accomplish this with a daughter on crutches we still didn't know.

We were also in Lauterbrunnen to send the tandems home. I made a silent commitment to not even think about sending for the bikes again until I saw Katrina run just for the fun of running. Watching her hobble around on crutches, I knew that was still many weeks away.

While we waited for our tandem cases to be sent from David and Carolyn's in England, we spent the next few days taking short bike rides along the valley floor, Katrina's crutches strapped to the back, her left foot dangling unused.

. . .

"I wouldn't touch that if I were you." We had been out for the day and were picnicking in a place known to us as "Nutella Nirvana." Jordan's hand had been transformed into a fighter jet, and it was just about to come in for a landing.

Jordan looked up and said, "Why not?"

"It's an electric fence," I explained. "It'll attack you like it's a rattlesnake."

"Dad. I never know when to take you seriously."

"I am being serious now."

Jordan eyed me with suspicion. He asked, "How can a fence attack you?" and while he was saying it, he brought the fighter jet in for a landing on the wire. For a very brief moment he wore a smug expression on his face, but then he leapt a tall building in a single bound, a primal yell punctuating the feat. Upon landing he started to karate chop the air near the fence.

He looked at me with a mixture of anger and awe and said, "How did you do that?"

"I did nothing." I was trying my best to stifle a laugh. "It's an electric fence. Farmers use them to keep their animals inside." I then taught him how to distinguish an electric fence from a normal fence. "See the wires embedded into the weave of this fabric? That's only the first clue. The thing you really want to look for are these babies," I said, pointing to the ceramic insulators.

Nutella Nirvana is known to the world as Gimmelwald, population no more than four or five families. In the summertime a traveler can stay in Nutella Nirvana at the hostel, or in the local "sleep-in-straw." Farmers all over Switzerland let out their barns during the summer months while their cows are out to pasture. It is a very inexpensive night's accommodation in a country that isn't known for anything inexpensive. The barns are far, far cleaner than some places we would stay in months later.

We came to Nutella Nirvana for the locally made chocolate. "Here, try this," I said, passing Jordan a rather large piece of confection.

Jordan eyed me with suspicion. "I never know when to take you seriously."

"It's good. You've had them before, you just don't remember."

"It looks like . . ." Jordan paused. He didn't want to say what it looked like.

Meet Doña Lupe from chapter 23. She has the power to make you instantly both respect and like her. This photo was taken shortly after Ciprián repaired the Unimog with a peanut. Doña Lupe opened her doors in the middle of the night and is preparing our last box of macaroni and cheese for Jordan. Never mind that she had never seen macaroni and cheese before, and perhaps had never seen an actual box. *Photo credit: John Higham*

Could someone call AAA? That's Patrick from chapter 22 smiling nervously from the passenger-side window. If you look closely, you'll see a plastic sandwich bag covering the gas tank's spigot. There was a message there, but unfortunately, we didn't pick up on it until about the time this picture was taken. *Photo credit: John Higham*

The Higham ancestral home. This photo was taken when getting into the rhythm of riding in jolly ol' England. Would we have been smiling if we'd known what the next fifty-two weeks had in store for us? We can laugh about it now, but somehow I think if we had known, we would have chickened out and just gone home. *Photo credit: David McHale. (used with permission)*

We started our days with a formal math lesson six mornings a week, the only exception being if we had to catch an early plane, bus or train. When the kids returned to the local public school system they reintegrated with their peers without skipping a beat. This picture was taken at the breakfast table aboard the famous Navimag of chapter 24 and also shows me using my e.brain to keep the journal that would eventually morph into this book. *Photo credit: September Higham*

A picture is worth a thousand words, isn't it? After receiving a fresh supply of books from Antonili (chapter 9) Katrina and Jordan simply sat on the floor in St. Peter's Basilica and read. Note that they are both at the beginning of their books. *Photo credit: John Higham*

Part of the kids' education during our year was to have them read something about the places we were to visit. Hopefully this would make an impression on them that would last a lifetime. This picture was taken at the American Cemetery in Normandy, France. *Photo credit: John Higham*

I know that look on Katrina's face. It is the look of denial. In this photo, Katrina is denying that she is in excruciating pain because her tibia has been shattered. Our cycling trip from London to Istanbul has just been terminated, but I don't know it yet. *Photo credit: John Higham*

When Katrina broke her leg, she also sprained her wrist. It was weeks before she could use her crutches for any significant distance. Hence, I carried Katrina in this fashion throughout Europe, and yes, we got stares from everyone as this photo records. This picture was taken in Cesky Krumlov, Czech Republic. *Photo credit: John Higham*

We were very concerned about Jordan's lethargy while hiking the Inca Trail. In extreme cases altitude sickness can be fatal, and Jordan simply wouldn't eat. This picture was taken a few moments after we stopped for lunch. It broke my heart that I had to wake him up and force him to eat, then get moving again. I was prepared to carry Jordan but he wouldn't have anything to do with that. *Photo credit: John Higham*

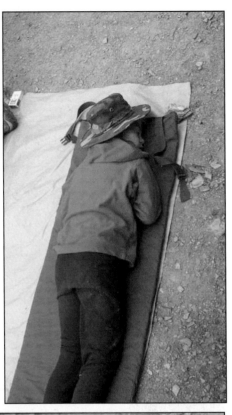

BELOW: More than anyone I've ever met, Ishmael from chapter 12 embodies the Good Samaritan; I should be half as charitable as he is. Katrina and Jordan were fascinated by the chameleons and how they would change color. Ishmael would catch one and by the time he gave it to one of the kids to hold, it would be a chocolate brown. *Photo credit: September Higham*

It is six-thirty a.m., so why are these people smiling? Our first couple of weeks on the road weren't the smoothest but catching the ferry in Poole, England that would take us to France was a major mental milestone. The sun was bright and we would soon be able to cycle on the right-hand side of the road. If that isn't worth a smile, I don't know what is. *Photo credit: John Higham*

We tried to go to church wherever we were so we wouldn't get our thou shalts confused with our thou shalt nots. Note the full laundry bag and the tent acting as a makeshift clothesline. When traveling on a shoestring budget, laundry is a constant chore. *Photo credit: John Higham*

Gotland Island, Sweden. Gotland literally translates to God's Land. In the summer months the frequent cruise ships (above Katrina's head) reinforce that the Vikings occasionally do name a place appropriately, unlike Iceland and Greenland. *Photo credit: John Higham*

Proof that Switzerland is the most beautiful place on the planet. *Photo credit: John Higham*

This picture was taken above Lushoto in the Usambara Mountains (chapter 12). These girls wanted to walk with us, just to hold Katrina's hand while we walked. They talked to us in Swahili and we responded in English, but it was enough. Chameleons are considered bad luck but we didn't know that and Katrina had one under her hat. Moments after this photo was taken these three girls saw Katrina's chameleon and ran away in terror. *Photo credit: John Higham*

This picture was taken the day before we came home. The look on September's face is only achievable after successfully circumnavigating the globe in fifty-two weeks. The 'do on Jordan's head is a science experiment in maximum entropy. It is achievable only after living through four weeks of repeated applications of pool water and ocean water, with none of that shampoo stuff mucking it up (chapter 27). *Photo credit: John Higham*

Katrina is coaxing The Cute One with a bouquet of flowers and weeds. This method of befriending an elephant is recommended (chapter 18). *Photo credit: Marie Blanchard (used with permission)*

Rene was fond of calling me John-Rambo (chapter 25). I'm certain it is because of my striking likeness to the movie character. *Photo credit: John Higham*

Meet Plastico, the pasta-eating alligator of the Amazon (chapter 25). Somehow, Plastico lost his threatening menace with spaghetti dangling from his incisors. *Photo credit: Dale Blanchard (used with permission)*

The end of the Inca Trail and proof that Jordan made it. Moments before this picture was taken, Jordan was puking right where we are standing. It was captured on (digital) film, but he wouldn't let me publish it. *Photo credit: September Higham*

For most of its length, the Great Wall of China is in disrepair, victim of centuries of weather and raiding Mongols. The parts that are most frequently visited have benefited from large-scale renovation. *Photo credit: John Higham*

BELOW: Lunch stop along the Great Wall. The Water Bottle Lady (chapter 14) is lurking just around the corner. She had never eaten a sandwich until we offered her one of ours. *Photo credit: John Higham*

The sea of sand near the border of Oman and the United Arab Emirates seems to stretch forever. Note the stuffed toy animal in Jordan's pocket. "Tiger" was a powerful connection Katrina and Jordan had to home and each other. *Photo credit: John Higham*

The legendary Serengeti more than lives up to its reputation, as it is bursting with activity. *Photo credit: John Higham*

Typically the Maasai will not tolerate having their photos taken, but for $50 the chief of this small commune let us take all the photos we wanted. Still, this little guy was a reluctant subject. The women of the village make the huts from cow dung. *Photo credit: September Higham*

We learned that the "brave" Maasai children are allowed to become warriors and the not-so-brave are sent to school in the towns. A few days after this photo was taken I sat next to a Maasai Warrior at an Internet cafe in Arusha; I didn't have the guts to ask him what he did that made him not-so-brave. Off to school for me! *Photo credit: John Higham*

Happiness is a Roman Candle taller than you are (chapter 13). The best thing about Mauritius: giant fireworks at the grocery store. *Photo credit: John Higham*

This friendly fellow just wanted to groom someone (chapter 17). It just happened to be Katrina. Note the expression on Katrina's face. She started shaving her legs after this incident. *Photo credit: John Higham*

According to my highly unscientific "Sphincter Factor" method, Phnom Penh has the dubious honor of the most dangerous place to go out in traffic. There are five human beings on that moped and the traffic in Phnom Penh makes Istanbul seem sedate. This is a common sight around Phnom Penh. *Photo credit: John Higham*

Shock and Awe. The images depicting life under the Khmer Rouge are horrific. We wanted the kids to be horrified, and got our wish. This picture was taken at Aki Ra's Landmine Museum near Angkor Wat in Cambodia. *Photo credit: John Higham*

Tonle Sap near Seim Reap, Cambodia, is home to a floating village, one of many such villages in this part of the world. The lake rises ten meters in three months during the wet season so the village floats to accommodate. The friendly children of these villages like to paddle out to greet tourists. *Photo credit: John Higham*

This young woman is taking refuge from the sun in her "house." Little children are frequently seen naked in Cambodia. They simply grow too fast to be outfitted with something that they neither need nor will be able to use a few months hence. *Photo credit: John Higham*

"Horse poop?" I said, finishing his sentence. "These are actually called 'Horse Shit Balls' and . . . "

"*Dad!*" Katrina protested. "I can't believe you said that!"

"Hey! It's what they're called! People here speak German so they probably don't know that it's a bad word." Which of course is not true—the people responsible for the name knew exactly what they were doing. "They're made to look this way and are yummy. Try one."

"See?" I said. "They're good, aren't they? You can't always judge something by the way it looks. Sometimes a fence can attack you. Other times something that appears disgusting can be fantastic. You just need to try it first."

As we returned to our campground, Jordan searched for electric fences. When he found one he looked at me with glee and issued a dare, "Touch it, wimp!"

"Okay," I said, reaching out and grabbing the fence, holding on to it for dramatic effect.

Jordan ogled me with awe. Over the next several days, whenever Jordan saw an electric fence he would issue the same dare. On occasion I would casually reply to his dares, "I have touched every fence you dared me to, it's your turn to do it." This would always end with a yelp, a leap, and him karate chopping the air.

What Jordan didn't understand is that I grew up around electric fences and could guess with about 90 percent accuracy the conditions under which a farmer would actually turn the fence on. So, Jordan didn't stand a chance. I'll tell him. Eventually.

• • •

During our stay in Lauterbrunnen we had become good friends with a Swiss-American family that owned and operated the local campground. September was celebrating her birthday and over cake, I mentioned to one of the young men of the family that he was lucky to live in such a beautiful place.

"This place drives me crazy," he said. "I want to move to Las Vegas."

"Trust me; you do not want to move to Las Vegas," I replied.

"Why not?"

A million responses flooded my mind. I looked up toward the end of the valley where the Eiger, Jungfrau, and Mönch stood as sentinels, the sun glistening off their white peaks. September and I had been discussing Lauterbrunnen as an escape from the buzz of our fast-paced lives; it was on a short list of places never to return from. On either side of me waterfalls cascaded over the cliffs onto the lush valley floor. If there was an antithesis of Lauterbrunnen, it would be Vegas. "Las Vegas is dry, brown, plastered with neon signs, and buzzing with people," I replied, as if that settled the matter.

"Exactly," he said enthusiastically. "Nothing ever happens here."

I thought about human nature and the tendency to want what we can't have.

"I've been wondering if we can ride our tandems down from the top of Männlichen," I said, changing the subject. "We have a spot we visited three years ago that we want to return to, but it's a bit problematic with Katrina's leg. I remember a service road that goes to the top. Do you think we could put our tandems on the gondola and ride down?"

"Sure. I see bicyclists on that service road all the time."

The plan to return to the apple tree was set. On the appointed day, we put our bicycles on the cog-wheel train to Wengen. Wengen is situated on the edge of a cliff about eight hundred feet above the Lauterbrunnen Valley, but it is also situated at the base of Männlichen, the peak of World Ski Cup fame. Männlichen is essentially a cliff towering above Wengen; the ski slope is on the far side of the mountain. We would take the tandems to the top via the gondola and ride the service road down the far side into the town of Grindelwald.

"I'd like four one-way tickets for us and two for bicycles, please," I said, reaching for my wallet.

"Bicycles are not allowed on the gondola," the woman behind the ticket counter informed me.

"But I've taken them on gondolas before!"

"Not on this one you haven't."

"We were told we could ride down the service road into Grindelwald."

"You can. But in order to ride down, you must first ride up. It is the rule."

It was the rule thing again. The Swiss and the Germans can't function without their rules. "But my daughter has a broken leg!"

Mrs. Ticket-Lady sneered, "Then she shouldn't be riding a bike."

I pleaded, but to no avail. I left the ticket booth and summed up the situation to September and the kids. "We are screwed. They will not allow the tandems on the gondola, and it's too far for me to carry Katrina."

"We could get a wheelchair and try again another day," September offered.

"We could," I said. "But the forecast is for rain. If we try to outlast the weather, we may not see much of Italy or Turkey before we have to catch our flight out of Istanbul."

"I'll hike it!" Katrina said, weighing in on the conversation. "I'll hike the entire trail by myself on crutches if I have to. I *want* to see the apple tree!"

Determined. Or stubborn. Or both. I had been carrying Katrina around Europe for the last eight weeks only to find now that sufficiently motivated, she could hike three hours down a mountain.

We took the gondola to the top of the mountain and Katrina doggedly hobbled down the long, curvy road until we reached the place where we'd had our picnic three years ago. And in the exact location where the kids had planted their apple seeds was . . . a tree! It was about twelve inches high, and, well, it sort of looked apple-ish. 🍎 So, it's an apple tree. That's my story and I'm sticking with it.

Of course now the kids want to visit it again in a few years to watch it grow. And they want to bring their kids to it and eat its apples, once it starts bearing fruit. Sounds like a great plan! I don't have the heart to tell the kids this is a world famous ski course and as soon as this tree gets very large it will be firewood for Heidi's great-great-grandkids.

When we returned to our campground in Lauterbrunnen, there was a package waiting for us. "I see UPS came while we were gone," September said.

All I could manage to get out was a feeble "Yeah" in response. David had sent the tandems' cases from England. I looked from the tandems back to their shipping cases. It wasn't as though the cases had arrived unexpectedly, but seeing them made what was about to happen real.

Feeling the tension in the silence as I gazed at the cases, Katrina asked, "What's wrong?"

"I'm grateful that all that happened when you fell was a broken leg," I said. "If that rope had snapped when you were higher, the result could have been much worse." There was a long pause, then I continued, "In a few weeks the broken leg will just be a memory, but the tandems need to go home. To resume cycling fully loaded, Mom needs your full pedal power, not just with one leg. That's still weeks away. There could be snow on the ground by that time."

Katrina gave me a hurt look. I knew what she was thinking. It was the same thing I was thinking, the same thing we had *all* been thinking for the last eight weeks; that accomplishing our goal of cycling across Europe had been stolen from us by a rope that had been sitting in the sun too long. But the pain of it was too fresh to vocalize. No one dared speak those words.

September broke the silence. "We have had an eventful summer. But we knew before we left there would be setbacks. Things rarely work out as we plan, but they often work out for the best. They key is to be flexible."

"Right!" I agreed. "Highams, one: fate, zero."

• • •

Autumn was firmly entrenched in the Swiss Alps. The air was crisp in the mornings and the mist from our breath sparkled in the sunshine. Coming back to this place had been very therapeutic in helping me, if not the rest of the family, put the broken leg behind us.

The locals say that when it is raining, God is merely washing the mountains. The morning we made our way to the Lauterbrunnen train station the sunshine had gone away and the mountains were being washed thoroughly. The tandems were already on their way back to California, and we were on our way to Italy.

www.360degreeslongitude.com/concept3d/360degreeslongitude.kmz

Wengen has the dubious honor of being the location where I did the second stupidest thing I have ever done. Use Google Earth and the *360 Degrees Longitude* layer to see how we fared.

9.

The Incredible Disappearing Force Field

September 17–September 24
Italy

Jordan eyed me with suspicion.

"I am being totally serious. If you don't believe me, ask Mom."

So he did. "Dad says that we have force fields around us and they get smaller the further south we go."

"Well, in this case, he's correct," September replied casually. "In Sweden your force field was about three feet, and people couldn't get closer to you than that. Your force field shrinks as we travel south and by the time we cross the border to Italy it will only be about six inches. Remember our campground in Denmark? The manager there complained about the 'loud Italians' and when he talked to them he was always backing away? That's because the Italians were always bumping into his force field."

Jordan narrowed his eyes to slits and clenched his jaw tightly shut as if a stranger had the nerve to actually talk to him, or perhaps ask him a question, such as, "Where did you get those beautiful blue eyes?" We thought it important to prep him as we ventured south.

The morning we left Switzerland's green, idyllic Lauterbrunnen Valley, Katrina decided that she was ready to try to walk using only one crutch. 🌑 "Katrina, there's no reason to rush things. You don't want to put too much weight on your leg too soon because then . . . "

She cut me off: "Da-ad!" When my name gets extended to two syllables I'm in trouble. "You've told me a hundred times! I am *not* trying to rush it" (adding weakly) "very much. I just *hate* these crutches and I can tell that my leg is going to be okay. I can just tell."

I thought of her series of X-rays continuing to show a 5-mm gap in the bone. The last X-ray hadn't been that long ago.

"The doctor said I would know when it was time."

I let out a long, slow breath.

And so it was that Katrina started to walk with only one crutch. The funny thing was Jordan was now gleefully on the other crutch. The two of them really looked pathetic dragging their suitcases in one hand, and limping along with a crutch in the other.

"People are going to talk," I said to September, motioning to Katrina and Jordan limping along the train platform, each with one crutch. "Have you noticed people's gazes darting from Katrina, to Jordan, and then to us?"

"Yeah. Maybe we could get Katrina and Jordan some tin cups."

Jordan couldn't cover ground as quickly with a crutch as Katrina. As a result, he would fall behind. Suddenly, when he decided the gap between them had grown too large, he would realize that he didn't *need* a crutch, and would run to catch up with his big sister.

We were off to Milan—we picked Milan merely based on the train arrival time, figuring that was about as far as we wanted to travel in one day. After our first connection on the Italian side of the border we saw a family with three children traveling together. September said, "Hmm . . . those people look American."

"How do people *look* American?" I asked. Ever since I'd decided that Europeans have an underdeveloped sense of liability, I had spent a lot of time thinking about how the world perceives Americans. The

United States is such a melting pot I had never considered it possible that someone could "look" American. When we lived in Japan, there was no question that we stood out. Conversely as we traveled through Europe I felt we blended in. But September was right—the people she was referring to *did* 'look' American somehow.

"Oh, I don't know," September replied. "Gregarious. Kinda swagger when they walk, thunder when they talk, slouch in their seats and put their feet up. In general act like they own the place."

"Like us?"

"Yeah. Their kids should be in school."

"*Our* kids should be in school."

"That's my point. I'm going to check it out."

I said, "Don't . . ." but it was too late. September was on her way down the aisle.

Katrina looked up from her book. "Where's Mom going?"

"She is going to go get those people's life story. I'll give her twenty minutes and if she hasn't returned, we'll need to send out a rescue party."

Twenty minutes later I made my way down the aisle. September was chatting with a pleasant woman as if they had been friends for years. "I'm here to rescue you from my wife," I said to the woman, although it was clear she didn't want to be rescued.

"This is Anne from the D.C. area," September said with an I-told-you-they-were-Americans sort of wink. "They are in Italy for six weeks as part of their homeschooling."

I smiled at the two American ladies as they traded embarrassing anecdotes about their spouses and in general acted like they owned the place.

 . . .

It was ironic how we had spent weeks agonizing over bicycle panniers, purchasing the highest-quality panniers money could buy. Yet, when it came to buying luggage, without a thought we had asked Mrs. Happy to take us to the nearest Wal-Mart in Friedrichshafen.

The rain was coming down in biblical proportions in Milan and by the time we reached our campsite it was clear that our new luggage was not as waterproof as the panniers had been.

The next morning we were awakened by the sound of farm animals and loud noises. "What is that banging?" September croaked, trying to get her head off of the pillow.

"Someone's building an ark." I had already gotten up and was sneaking a look out, but saw nothing. We gathered ourselves together and looked out into the pouring rain. "What is it you want to do in Milan?" September asked.

"Catch a train to Venice," I answered. I knew there were wonderful museums in Milan, but Jordan was getting museum weary; we were budgeting our museum time for the Vatican.

It was a 15-minute walk from the campground to the metro station in the pouring rain, and our umbrellas were no match for the deluge. Yet Katrina and Jordan failed to notice because they were so engrossed in hobbling along with their one crutch each and chatting about the plot of the latest comic book Jordan was creating. After nearly four months of being on the road, nothing seemed to faze them. This is a really annoying quality; you want to be miserable, but those around you refuse to yield their sunny dispositions.

Staying in Venice proper would have approached $200 per night, and that was if we could find accommodations. For about $40, we could pitch our tent in Fusina, a short five-minute walk from the ferry terminal, then another 20 minutes on the ferry to Venice. We had just recently retrieved our tent from Zermatt. In the weeks we had been without it, when we stayed at campgrounds we got a cabin. Now that Katrina was out of her cast, the idea was to get back on budget, which meant sleeping in the tent. Yet, while I was standing in line at the reservations counter in Fusina, I hoped with every fiber of my soul that they had a trailer or cabin available. I tried to approach this subject delicately. "I sure am glad it stopped raining."

"Yes, but it still looks like it'll be unsettled for a few days," September replied.

She was playing right into my hands. "Yeah." I let out a long breath. Then I said, "The ground sure looks soggy. I guess it was raining as hard here as it was in Milan."

The subtlety cracked. September had been holding our tent but at that moment she thrust it into my arms and with a wicked smile exclaimed, "Sleep in it, wimp!"

www.360degreeslongitude.com/concept3d/360degreeslongitude.kmz

There are only two things you need to know to be a civil engineer. First, you can't push a rope. Go to the *360 Degrees Longitude* Google Earth layer to discover the second one. Then, try to not think about how many times a toilet flushes somewhere in Venice on your visit to San Marco Basilica at high tide.

The weather gave us a reprieve as we strolled the narrow walkways of Venice. September and I were in awe of the city's history, the Venetian architecture, and the romance of the gondolas, even though we were too cheap to actually ride in one.

I looked at the gondolas and remembered the advice my friend Al had once given me about his time in Venice. He had cautioned, "The gondolas are expensive, but cheaper than the alternative." He explained that when he and his wife, Rania, were in Venice he balked at the cost of a gondola. But after years of feeling guilty for denying her the experience, he ultimately took her to the Venetian Hotel in Las Vegas to make it up.

After being solicited about a dozen times by men in ridiculous black-and-white striped outfits, I turned to September. "It is our only chance. What do you say—should we spend the hundred and fifty euros?"

She choked back a laugh. "Are you kidding? We can take the water bus down the Grande Canal for about a fiftieth of that!"

That's my girl! But I didn't want to suffer Al's fate, so I pressed, "But we don't get the guy singing to us."

She rolled her eyes. "I would pay extra *not* to be serenaded."

Which is exactly how I felt. You need to be careful who you marry, because you'll end up just like them.

To a kid, however, the highlights of Venice are the pigeons and the gelato. Just not at the same time. As I sat on a bridge, looking up something in our guidebook, Jordan read over my shoulder, as a serenading gondola operator passed underneath the bridge. Jordan's face brightened and, grabbing the book from my hands, he ran to his sister, shouting, "Hey, Katrina! It says here that Venice has the seventh-best gelato in all of Italy!"

Suddenly there was purpose in Katrina and Jordan's existence. Being in Venice means being lost, as the "streets" are impossibly narrow and all look alike. Looking for Italy's seventh-best gelato was apparently a common tourist activity, because all we had to do was show a local resident our guidebook, open it up to the page with the sidebar, and they would smile and point us in the right direction.

Italy's seventh-best gelato was pure heaven on earth. I could only imagine what the first through sixth must be like, but that would have to wait for another trip.

We would have traded all the pigeons in San Marco Basilica for more time in Venice, but our pace needed to quicken. By the time we arrived in Rome, we had made the decision to hit the highlights as quickly as possible and then do the same for Pompeii and get ourselves to Turkey. Italy was turning out to be more expensive than we had estimated, as was the whole of Europe, which was in no small part due to the change of plans after Katrina's broken leg. Turkey, we expected, would be easier on our budget.

We had arranged to have a package of books sent to Antonili, a friend of a friend in Rome. As we got ready to go into the city to meet her, September asked, "What are you doing with that?"

"It is called a backpack," I said. "You put stuff into it. I thought we'd need an empty one for the books."

"Not the backpack, the shirt. You aren't going to wear that, are you? You haven't worn it for ages and now when we're about to meet someone for the first time you pick that out of your suitcase? She's going to introduce herself and then order a cheeseburger."

"It's hot today. I haven't worn it because it was too cold in Switzerland and then it was raining so much. Now it's sunny and hot, and there's nothing wrong with this shirt." I started to smooth out my shirt to demonstrate how stylish it was. "I can't believe it! There's a hole in this already."

"Just to show you what a good wife I am," September said, reaching for her needle and thread, "I'll mend your shirt so you can wear it." September had learned long ago that I am a danger to myself with sharp objects.

After we met Antonili, our mobile library made a beeline for Vatican City, arguably one of the most influential seats of power in the last two millennia. But who needs history after a shipment of new books? Katrina had just received book two in a long, involved trilogy and Jordan a thick new comic book. They simply sat on the floor in St. Peter's Basilica and read, although we did make them look up in the Sistine Chapel. Then it was time for the museum.

I had been talking up the Vatican museum for a couple of years. "Maps of course haven't always looked like this," I'd said, pointing to our giant wall map that we used for planning before we left. "In the Vatican, there are maps and globes that date back to Christopher Columbus." Now we could study how our perception of the world has evolved over the last 500 years.

I knew much less about other parts of the Vatican museum. For instance, many, many statues on display were missing an important body part. A nose, or a finger, or a hand, or even a head. More often than not, they were also missing a penis. That raised the question as to why all the statues were male and nude in the first place. And those statues that had all their important bits looked as though they could benefit from the medication that I find advertised in my e-mail spam folder. I thought it might be some Freudian commentary on celibate priests, but I kept those thoughts to myself. Jordan did wince and hold his crotch every time we walked past a eunuch statue.

"Easy there, Little Dude," I said. "You're safe as long as you're with me."

"Shush!" Jordan exclaimed, while hitting me in the arm.

"I don't get art," I said to Jordan, pointing to a pedestal. "You'd think the missing body parts were simply damage, but that doesn't explain this one."

There were some toes on a pedestal that was clearly set up to display a full-sized statue, but, the only thing on it were some toes. Not even an entire foot. At least humor me with a statue.

"It seems to be missing its body," Jordan noted.

We spent the rest of the day trying to one-up each other's art jokes.

• • •

History is a fickle friend. And foe. The people of Pompeii—how many died? Maybe 20,000, or even 50,000? All those people got up one morning worrying about their jobs, or their kids' health, or the neighbor's dog who barked all night, and by the end of the day they were all dead.

Pompeii was a must-see ever since September and I read Richard Harris's *Pompeii*. The city of Pompeii was a huge, bustling port city buried by Mount Vesuvius, located across the Bay of Naples, when the mountain erupted on August 24, A.D. 79.

On top of my agenda was to swing by the brothel, but it was closed. By this I mean the brothel ruins in Pompeii, which hasn't been opened for business in two millennia. I wanted to visit the archaeological site, but it was roped off.

In Pompeii it's possible to see many aspects of Roman life on display in suspended animation. "Times have changed," I said, looking at a bas-relief in the House of the Vetti. Compared to the statues and paintings of naked men in the Vatican, the statues and paintings of naked men in Pompeii looked like they all OD'd on the medication that I find in my e-mail spam folder. "We've been noticing differences in people as we've traveled from place to place, but here we can see differences in people over time."

"Time has changed nothing!" September exclaimed, looking at the same bas-relief. "Men are still enamored with their private parts."

There are many places within the city where we came across plaster casts of people where they died, with expressions of agony clearly visible on their faces. One such place is known as the Garden of the Fugitives; we studied a cast of a man as he lay on the ground with his arm over a woman and child, as if he was trying to protect them.

"I wonder if history would have turned out any differently if Pompeii hadn't been destroyed," said September. "If all those people had been allowed to lead normal lives and pass their DNA to the next generation, what would be different today?"

"Hard to imagine," I said. "Would the Roman Empire have played out in largely the same manner, with Constantine converting to Christianity? The world as we know it would be vastly different otherwise."

"Maybe. It's interesting to think about," September said. "I remember reading in Jordan's *Horrible History* books that toward the end of World War I a grenade exploded in a foxhole with seven German soldiers in it, six of whom died. The seventh was Adolf Hitler and he barely had a scratch. How different history would have been if that had ended differently."

To see the entire city of Pompeii would take days, but it is possible to take in the highlights in a few hours. Jordan's attention span for this sort of activity was about 30 minutes, so we put him up to the task of moving a specific pinecone from one end of the city to the next without using his hands.

Jordan's Journal, September 24

I played the Pompeii Pinecone Challenge. I kicked a pinecone, like a soccer ball, all the way through Pompeii. I had to make sure it didn't go over any fences, and I had to figure out a way to get it up the stairs. The scariest part of the challenge was when a stray dog wanted to play "fetch" with the pinecone. When I would kick it, the dog would fetch it, and then he would chew on it. Finally, we gave the dog some bread so he would forget about the pinecone.

When we got back from Pompeii to Sorrento, where we were staying, we found it had been transformed in the hours while we were in Pompeii. Merchants had their wares out on tables to the edge of the street. Pedestrians were out in huge numbers, engaged in vigorous hand-to-hand conversation.

I nudged Katrina. "Watch people as they talk to each other." We had been people watching throughout Italy, but the warm summer night and the sea breeze coming off the Mediterranean seemed to make the scene more Italian, with people practically bumping noses as they talked.

"So do force fields get smaller than six inches?" Jordan asked.

"Nah. Six inches is as small as they come," I replied with vacant authority.

We had started our twelve-month around-the-world trip in Europe for a reason: to get into the rhythm of traveling in a place where it was easy to find a rhythm. You can expect things to work. Things like the rail system, or the phones. You can eat a salad at a restaurant or drink the water coming out of the tap and expect not to get sick. Stuff that, as Americans, we simply took for granted. That night before we left Sorrento, I fretted sleeplessly just as I had before we left California.

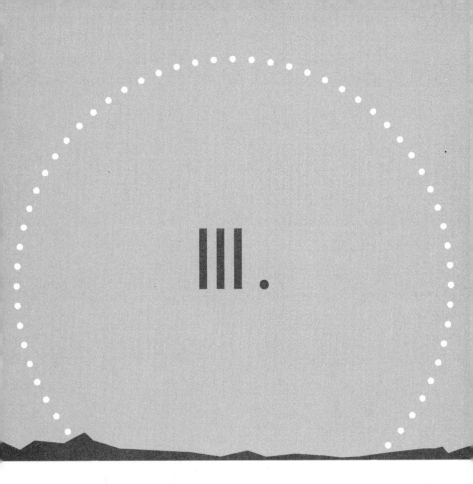

III.

OUT OF OUR
COMFORT ZONE

10.

Exploding Postal Scales

September 25–October 13
The Planet of Turkey, with a Dash of Greece

Thirty-six hours after leaving Pompeii, we found ourselves sitting in the main cabin of an all-night island-hopping ferry leaving Athens, Greece. An elderly woman about 200 pounds overweight went up and down the aisles singing at the top of her very capable lungs. No one paid her any attention, because she seemed the most sane person in the crowd. This was our first experience with Greeks in large numbers. I was reminded of a scene from the movie *My Big Fat Greek Wedding* in which a lamb is being roasted in the front yard, except we were missing the guy with the bottle of Windex.

Pulling out of port we had to leave behind any notion that we could ever blend in again. Our Northern European skin and hair betrayed the fact that we were not members of the surrounding clan; two little girls, about ages four and five, stood staring at me through wide and unblinking eyes, mouths so agape that I could scrutinize their dental work.

Although we could no longer *blend* in, *fitting* in seemed within reach—at least in the midst of a ship full of Greeks. Surveying the scene before me, I could not help but sit back and fully relax for the first time in ages, realizing that my noisy children and our tendency to spread our belongings out for all to trample would not raise an eyebrow. Throughout Europe I had felt like we were water buffalo stampeding through a delicately constructed society.

But no worries here; people were setting up little fiefdoms throughout the cabin, with blankets on the floor, sleeping bags, pillows, boomboxes, and all manner of stuff. Each fiefdom had its own crowd and they all seemed to be making political ties with the neighboring tribes.

This wasn't some college student's coming-of-age drinking party, either. With each tribe having its share of kidlets, aunts, uncles, and cousins, this was an affair the entire family could enjoy. While nobody was roasting a lamb on board, it looked like all the maternal types had brought a potluck dish to share.

"I thought we'd try and find a quiet corner of the deck and try to sleep," I said. "But I don't think this deck comes with a quiet corner."

September gave me a mischievous look. "Well, then . . . when in Rome, do as the Romans. When on a party boat, party. Did you bring the Bundt cake?"

* * *

We were dumped unceremoniously on a Greek island I had never heard of at 3:30 in the morning. The Greek party boat sailed onward into the night toward its final destination. Rumor had it that at dawn we could catch another boat to Çesme on the mainland of Turkey, 30 or so minutes away.

Ordering a round of hot chocolates gave us, I assumed, the privilege of sitting at a table in an outside café overlooking the pier; we waited to see what might happen when the sun rose. I thought for sure that the kids would fold their arms on the table, put their heads down, and collapse, but they both put their books in front of them and nursed their hot drinks.

Thus composed, I spent a few hours contemplating what it meant to leave easy, predictable Europe. Ahead of us were a few weeks in Turkey, then the Arabian Peninsula, Africa, East Asia, and eastward. In Europe it was possible to blend in with the local population; going forward, this was simply not possible. With disconcerting news stories filling up my e-mail inbox from well-meaning friends, I was not feeling completely confident about setting foot in this new land. It was beyond dispute that folks in most of the Middle East were not too keen on Americans at the moment. There was the wretched war going on in neighboring Iraq, and as hard as I tried to wish it away, every morning when I woke it was still there. Whispers of doubt echoed in my mind: "You are all walking targets." What was I getting my family into?

Yet, we were on this trip to get past the stereotypes and prejudices in order to "know" and "experience." But talking the talk is one thing; it was now time to walk the walk. I looked at my children lost in their books in the predawn hours. I was envious. They didn't feel my anxiety, because they weren't encumbered by the stereotypes of my generation. I simply had to appear completely confident, even though I wasn't.

While I was lost in my thoughts, another ferry arrived and with it, a young Turkish woman named Dilara. She asked if she could sit at our table, explaining that it was, of course, rather dangerous for her to sit alone outside in the dark, in "the West."

"Of course!" September answered, as she pulled a chair up to our table. "Can I offer you something to drink?"

September excels at extracting life stories from the unsuspecting. Maybe it was because being lost in their books, Katrina and Jordan never entered or otherwise aborted the conversation. Or, maybe it was just because I was too tired to take one of my normal "wireless walks" where I wander off looking for an unsecure Wi-Fi network. Whatever the reason, I was able to quietly observe an artist practice her craft and I would grunt approval or disapproval when prompted by the Lean, Mean, Talking Machine.

Dilara was returning home to Turkey with only hours to spare before her student visa expired. "Some of my family disapproves of my study-ing in Europe," she explained. "But I want a career in which I can meet lots of different people and do something important." She explained that she loved studying in Europe, even though she bristled at the idea of the upcoming "ascension" talks for Turkey to be admitted into the E.U. "As if Turkey needs to 'ascend' to Europe!" Then she added, as if an afterthought, "I simply *must* make it to Turkey today; otherwise my student visa will be lost. Do you know when the Çesme ferry leaves?"

"No idea," September replied. "The good folks on our ferry gave us a gentle shove down the plank when we asked them that question. We've looked, but there's no obvious ferry service, no postings, nothing. The waiter is pretty sure we can find 'something' in the morning, though."

Dilara informed us that she keeps abreast of world events by watching CNN. "I watch it in English to help learn the language better." Over a period of an hour Dilara gradually approached the subject of life in the United States. It felt like she was tap dancing around something; finally, it came out. "Life in America must be . . . difficult with so many guns and all those gangs."

That comment caught me off guard, but I let September do the talking for the two of us. I gave her a one eyebrow raised, one eyebrow furrowed look, to signal her to probe deeper.

"You've been watching too much CNN," September replied conversationally; then she shot me a meaningful glance. "A lot of us are guilty of that."

Dilara was proud of her liberal cosmopolitan attitude. She told us that in spite of all the "obvious" dangers, she even planned to visit the United States someday. "I'm certain that some parts of the U.S. are safe," she explained. "By the way, could you please tell me which parts those might be?"

My reaction was to blurt out, "It's safe everywhere!" But I knew that wasn't true, nor was Dilara's view that nowhere was safe. The truth was somewhere along the continuum between "nowhere" and "everywhere" and it was impossible to portray that concisely with economy of words. After being together for so long, September and I are able read each other with just a glance; I could tell she was thinking of the best way to respond. After a pause she said, "You'll find most people in the

United States are friendly wherever you want to go. Just go, and trust your instincts; you'll be fine."

That is, after all, what we were doing now. I saw in Dilara a reflection of my apprehension of traveling to an unknown country. Thus continued the process of discovering how alike we humans all are, no matter which passport we hold.

• • •

Several hours later we found ourselves on Turkish soil. We hadn't yet been through customs when a machine gun-wielding official at passport control decided that Jordan's blond hair looked too flat and tousled it. Trying to keep the encounter positive, I said, "Wow, Jordan. A guy with a machine gun touched your hair. Can I touch your hair, too?"

"Dad," Jordan protested, pushing my hand away, "when we left Italy you said personal force fields didn't get any smaller than six inches."

"I wouldn't worry about it," I said. "Guys carrying machine guns feel like they can get away with anything. It probably won't happen again."

The pier and passport control in Çesme is a long walk from anywhere. We started to slowly make our way toward town. Katrina was hobbling along with her one crutch, pulling her suitcase with the other hand. Jordan was still using the other crutch, occasionally for its intended purpose, occasionally to pole vault himself over some imagined obstacle.

Suddenly, ten weeks of frustration came out. "*I hate this crutch!*" Katrina exclaimed, tossing it aside. "I'm going to try to walk without it."

September and I froze. "Katrina, you don't want to rush it," September advised. "Remember your last X-ray wasn't that long ago and . . . " But September couldn't finish the thought.

"You've already told me, but the doctor said I would know when I was ready, and I'm ready *now*." Katrina had come out of the womb with her will forged in iron. Nothing we could say would change her mind. I just stood there with a look of horror on my face as she took her first steps, preparing myself to pick up my daughter from the sidewalk after her leg folded under the weight.

Her stride was slow and each step deliberate, but she left her crutch there on the sidewalk and never looked back. Picking up this newly discarded treasure, Jordan exclaimed, "Cool. Can I have it?"

Fresh off the boat, we hadn't yet acquired any local currency. It was time to feed ourselves and I had a hunch the corner shop by the dock would accept my euros, but had no idea what the exchange rate was. Selecting a few food items, I handed the cashier a 20-euro note and acted as though this was a perfectly normal transaction. To my relief, he simply handed me a bunch of Turkish lira as though this were a perfectly normal transaction.

When I got out of the store, I looked at what the clerk had handed me, eager to familiarize myself with the exchange rate. To my extreme befuddlement I found myself holding three five-lira notes, three one-lira coins, and a one-MILLION-lira note. Being an engineer, I can only work with two, sometimes three, significant digits. Looking at the one-million-lira note I wondered why I cared about the fives and the ones.

"Check this out," I said, handing Jordan the one-million-lira bill. "They gave me a million dollars." We had been using the word "dollars" to denote the local currency, whatever it happened to be, because through Europe it seemed we changed currency types every other day and couldn't keep track of what they were called.

Jordan's eyes bulged to the size of saucers. "COOL! Can I have it?"

What we later found was that Turkey had recently devalued their currency by a factor of one million (!) and that there are both new and old flavors of lira in circulation. The one-million-lira bill and the one-lira coin were equivalent.

The difference between the "new" and the "old" money, however, was lost on Jordan. Over the next few days whenever I got another one- (or five-) million-lira bill, Jordan would hoard it, thinking that the store clerks kept making mistakes. By the time we left Turkey he almost had enough to buy himself a Happy Meal, but to hear him talk about it, you'd have thought that Donald Trump had better watch out.

. . .

Çesme is a beach town; in late September Çesme skies were a brilliant blue and the sun seemed to be brighter than normal. After a quiet day of recovering from disembarking at 3:30 a.m., we were ready to head to the beach. It was pleasantly warm and the lightest piece of clothing I owned was my Bill's Burger Barn shirt.

"Cheap communist construction!" I said, pulling the shirt on. "It's little wonder that this shirt was on the clearance rack."

"Mmmm?" September looked up from what she was doing.

"Oh, it's just this cheap shirt. Now the seam across the shoulder is unraveling. That's the last time I buy a shirt from the clearance rack in a former Eastern Bloc country. I'm throwing it away."

"You don't have to. I can fix it," September said, reaching for her needle and thread. "It'll only take a minute."

"I thought you hated this shirt."

"I do. But I'll fix it if you want."

"That's okay," I said, wadding up the shirt and tossing it into the circular file. I put on my old T-shirt.

We strolled along the shops on the way to the beach when a man approached us. "Hello my friend!" he said. "Where are you from?"

"California."

"Really? Me too!"

I eyed my new "friend" with suspicion. Then he continued, "We have all types of beautiful handwoven carpets that will complement your home in California."

"No thanks," I said, without breaking stride. "I don't need a carpet."

We continued to make our way toward the beach, but it wasn't long before we were approached by another carpet salesman, then another.

After we had disappointed a few carpet salesmen, Katrina gave me a devilish smile and said, "You need to replace your Bill's shirt with one that says, 'No Thanks, I Don't Need a Carpet!'"

"Yes, I suppose I should," I said, but something at the beach took my mind off shirts. "Wow! Check out the bikinis!"

"No thanks. Doesn't do much for me," September replied.

"No, that's not what I meant. Well, perhaps a bit. But I never would have guessed I'd see women in bikinis in a Muslim country."

"I guess there are Muslim countries, and then there are Muslim countries."

"Yeah, if it weren't for the five-times-daily call to prayer blasted over loudspeakers from every street corner, I'd have thought we were in Mexico."

Of course, I didn't have a clue what the *muezzin*, aka Mr. Singy-Person, was saying during the call to prayer. In fact, he doesn't *say* anything. The call to prayer is a *song*, sung in a bluesy, country-western twang. I speculated that it is really a song about how Mr. Singy-Person lost his job, lost his dog, and his mother-in-law is moving in. But I didn't have the nerve to ask the locals if this was the case.

Turkey is a huge country, but with much less transportation infrastructure than Europe. There are few trains that crisscross the country, nor are there villages around every bend. Distances between towns and regions can be vast and the terrain desolate. Our options for getting around were limited to renting a car, taking the bus, or flying. When it was time to move on, we opted for the clean, efficient, and ridiculously inexpensive bus network.

As we made preparations to leave Çesme, I glanced around our hostel room to be sure we hadn't forgotten anything. Katrina had already left the room but her crutches were leaning against the wall near the door. As I went to retrieve them, September shot me a glance; the glance was all I needed to tell me that it was time to leave them behind.

Katrina hadn't used the crutches since setting them aside after first arriving in Çesme, though her stride was slow and deliberate and would be for weeks to come. Jordan wanted to keep the crutches as they were a cool toy, but September and I hoped they would find use by someone who needed them. We quietly slipped away.

Initially the broken leg was a bitter blow, but it changed us, *improved* us, somehow. In the first weeks of our trip we had struggled with the issue of too much time together. When Katrina had her accident, for a brief moment packing up and going home seemed the logical thing to do. I struggled with emotions from rage at the person who had hung the rope to despair that we couldn't engage in the activities we had come for. In the weeks that followed somehow the fact that we couldn't "do" as much seemed less important and our ability to enjoy simply being together gradually increased. Without warning, our original problem of "too much together time" simply evaporated. Now what once threatened to beat us was quietly left behind without fanfare. We would be challenged again before coming home, but we faced these challenges differently from the outset—with the experience of knowing that if we banded together, we could overcome almost anything.

• • •

We boarded a bus to Selçuk, the modern city near ancient Ephesus. September and Katrina plopped down onto a bench seat and Jordan and I took the bench directly behind them. Jordan and I busied ourselves with watching a sitcom I had downloaded onto my e.brain an hour earlier. We spent half an hour glued to the tiny two-by-three-inch screen when I noticed September and Katrina giggling and shooting me the occasional glance, telling me that whatever they were laughing at, I was the butt of the joke.

"What's so funny?" I asked.

"Tell him, Mom!" Katrina begged.

"Yeah, tell him," I said.

"Your shirt wasn't cheap Commie construction," September said, trying to keep her composure. "It was *robust* Commie construction."

I had no idea what September was talking about. Katrina and September looked as though they had just won the lottery. Relying on one of the wittiest retorts in my arsenal I said, "Huh?"

"It was virtually indestructible," September replied. "Tightly woven poly-blend fabric, triple-stitched seams—the works. It wouldn't have come unraveled without a little sabotage." I should have suspected such from the woman who once sewed the flies of my underwear together to remind me to either sit or put down the seat.

"I'm sorry," she continued, "but I just couldn't bear to be seen in public with you wearing that shirt."

My mouth was moving but nothing came out. Finally, I was able to form the words, "And so you waited to tell me until we were well out of the city so I couldn't retrieve it from the landfill."

"Something like that."

Jordan, in particular, was scandalized to learn that his own mother was capable of such seditious behavior. "Well, Jordan," I explained, "I should have known better. Your mother once donated my California Superbike School T-shirt to a homeless shelter. But she *promised* that she would never throw away any of my shirts again."

"And I kept my promise. *You* threw it away."

Katrina, not being able to hold back any longer, burst into giggles. This called for more than just soap squished together. Jordan and I started scheming over how to get even with Team Estrogen.

* * *

We pulled into Selçuk and checked into a hostel near the bustling town center. One of the hostel workers decided to make it his mission to get Jordan to smile. He knelt down so he was at Jordan's eye level and, tousling Jordan's hair, said, "Such blue eyes!"

"Smile, Jordan," I said.

He ignored me. He was rapidly learning to avoid every adult he saw; our intention of giving the kids an appreciation of other cultures was backfiring in Turkey. Jordan's blond hair and blue eyes were something of a novelty, and he was getting way more attention from well-meaning strangers than he wanted. Initially, we were having some success getting him to smile as strangers rumpled his hair and told him how cute he was. But by the time we hit Selçuk, we were judging these encounters as successful if Jordan didn't grimace and clench his fists.

"You're getting attention only because they love children here," September explained.

"I don't like being treated like a little kid!"

We didn't want Jordan to have ill feelings for those who were trying to be friendly, but a kid from the United States is used to having strangers keep themselves at arm's length. Katrina, being a middle-sized girl in a Muslim society, was largely immune to the pats, pokes, and prods, and so every time we transitioned through the hostel, she became a human shield to protect her little brother from "Mr. Patty-Head."

Selçuk is adjacent to Ephesus, one of the greatest cities of the ancient Mediterranean world. Ephesus was first occupied by the Greeks, then the Romans, and was abandoned in the sixth century when the harbor silted up. Ancient Ephesus was best known for the Temple of Artemis, one of the Seven Wonders of the Ancient World. 🐚 When *we* went to see the Temple of Artemis it was just a stone column sticking up out of the ground, pieces of it having been carted off to the British Museum some decades earlier. Of course when we were at the British Museum the previous June, we naïvely assumed that this Wonder of the Ancient World would still be on location and not relocated to downtown London.

Luckily for us, the amphitheater where Paul the Apostle preached had *not* been relocated to downtown London. Interestingly, the audio guide we rented didn't tell the story of Paul the Apostle. It told the story of local artisans, whose livelihoods depended on making figurines of the many-breasted Artemis, Goddess of Fertility.

As the story unfolded, we heard about a new-fangled religion being preached by someone named Paul, claiming to be an apostle. Paul started gaining converts and preached that the worship of Artemis was wrong. The local artisans whose livelihoods depended on the Artemis figurines saw Paul as a threat to their livelihood, as the Temple of Artemis was famous and drew crowds from far away. The artisans incited the crowd at the amphitheater to jeer at Paul by chanting "Great is Artemis of the Ephesians!" A riot ensued and Paul was obliged to leave.

If only those artisans could have seen 2,000 years into the future, they would have known they could still make a living crafting crosses and crèches for the hundreds of pilgrims who now file in daily.

Jordan's Journal, October 1

Today we went to the ancient city of Ephesus. It has a marble street. It is really slippery when it rains. We played hide-and-seek. I got "gum" flavored ice cream, except I think it was actually like the tree-sap kind of gum. It was really bitter. We hid it in a napkin and threw it away. All of the patting on the head and tickling and poking is getting even worse. I hope the next town we go to isn't as bad. I want a hat with metal spikes on it.

The following morning September was doing laundry by hand and I was doing homework with Katrina and Jordan in our room. "I'm going to make breakfast," I announced. "Finish what you're working on and come down in 15 minutes."

As the kitchen was located adjacent to the lobby, Jordan's eyes narrowed to slits and he clenched his teeth. Omar—Mr. Patty-Head—was usually found busying himself in the lobby.

Fifteen minutes later, I heard Katrina and Jordan talking as they approached me in the kitchen. Then I heard the heavily accented voice of Omar. "What's wrong, don't you like me? I just want to be friends."

I thought about intervening, but I also knew that if Omar was successful in coercing a smile from Jordan, he would let the kids pass. Then I heard Katrina say, "My brother doesn't like that." I knew something was up; Katrina wouldn't stand up to an adult, especially a stranger, unless something was wrong.

I hurriedly finished what I was doing only to hear her repeat the same words, louder, "My brother doesn't like that." I peered around the corner in time to see Jordan on Omar's lap, struggling for freedom. There was nothing nefarious happening. I believe Omar simply wanted to make a friend and took Jordan's reluctance personally; he was reaching out in his way.

As I was about to make my presence known, Katrina took hold of Jordan's hand and said pointedly, "Jordan has to come with me," and she pulled him free and then walked into the kitchen where I was.

I knew confrontation was difficult for Katrina. "You're a good big sister," I said.

Katrina turned a chair toward the wall. I heard a sniffle and saw her hand dab at her eyes.

"Jordan," I said, "Omar wouldn't pester you if you simply gave him a smile."

Jordan looked up. With ferocity in his eyes, he growled, "Sometimes it's no fun being a kid."

Later, when September and I talked about this incident, we agreed that Omar's motivation was innocent and he was merely trying to be friendly. We had observed that open gestures such as this were part of the culture. But at home, picking up a child of an acquaintance and placing him on your lap might land you in jail. Nevertheless, the situation had become so uncomfortable for us that we couldn't stay, and we made arrangements to leave earlier than planned.

A few hours later we were on a fourteen-hour overnight bus ride to the interior of the country. We stepped off the bus at four in the morning in the tiny town of Göreme. The gray sandstone towers gave the landscape an alien feel.

"Ramadan starts soon," I commented.

"Your point being . . . what?" September replied.

"Back home, the terror alert is being raised to orange because unrest is expected." I paused. "My mom thinks we're nuts being here during Ramadan."

"Funny," September replied. "*My* mom doesn't think that at all."

"What's Ramadan?" Katrina asked.

"Ramadan is the ninth month of the Islamic calendar. To Muslims, it's a holy month marked by fasting."

Katrina looked surprised. "Wow. I don't think I could fast a whole month."

"When the sun goes down at night people can eat all they want, and when the sun comes up in the morning, the fasting starts. This goes on every day for a full lunar cycle."

Katrina looked confused. "I don't get it. You mean people at home are nervous about a bunch of hungry Muslims?"

"It's human nature to be afraid of things you don't understand," September said. "Remember Dilara, who we met on that island before we came to Turkey? She was afraid to visit the United States because she saw news clips about gang violence, but we think of the United States as safe. It's the same kind of thing."

"I still don't get it," Katrina said.

"Some believe that during Ramadan Muslims become more devout, and therefore, terrorists act more extreme," I said.

"But not all Muslims are terrorists!" Katrina protested emphatically. "Nor are all terrorists Muslim! Everyone we've met here has been so nice!"

"You're forgetting about all the Mr. Patty-Heads," Jordan said, scandalized. "They are *not* nice!"

Isn't it interesting, I thought to myself, how we can share the same experiences, and reach such different conclusions.

• • •

Göreme is in the heart of the vast Cappadocia region of Turkey. Large towers of rock adorn the landscape. The canyons are riddled with tunnels, caves, and spires of stone. The stone is actually volcanic ash, solidified into soft sandstone that has eroded over eons leaving behind tall, chimney-shaped rock formations. Many homes and dwellings are dug out of the rock, as was our hostel.

Just a few steps from the front door of our cave hostel a gentleman named Karim tended his shop, where he sold fruits and vegetables. Karim could frequently be spotted sitting outside his shop making small talk with passersby; even when he wasn't, it was impossible to walk by unnoticed. He wanted to know all about our trip, where we had been and where we were going, and how we liked his country. Karim always had a piece of hard candy for each of the kids, and always had a pat on the head or a pinch on the cheek for Jordan.

Karim explained that the popular thing to do in Göreme is to go hiking in and through the weird rock formations. As Katrina was still walking stiffly, he suggested an easy walk from our hostel into Göreme National Park and into "Love Valley."

That afternoon as we started out our hostel door toward Love Valley, Jordan protested. "I don't want to go outside the hostel."

"Just put on your baseball hat and sunglasses," I said, "and come along. Remember to smile if Karim talks to you."

"I already smiled once today!" Jordan protested, but he dutifully grabbed his hat and sunglasses as we headed out the door.

Love Valley is so named because of the three-story-high phalluses that nature has made out of the sandstone. Surveying the arid landscape from the road above the valley, it looked as though nothing could grow here. As we descended into the little valleys between the rock outcroppings we were surprised to find an abundance of wild grapes along the valley floor, despite no evidence of water.

We stopped for lunch. "Don't you just love this place?" September asked, grabbing a handful of deep purple grapes.

"Yes!" Katrina responded. "Turkey has the friendliest animals. Jordan and I love to feed all the stray cats."

"I meant right here in this place—Love Valley," September said. "It feels like a whole different world. I love the feeling of being lost, wandering around these stone towers. We should come back here in a few years and spend more time exploring—"

"We should plant these apple seeds!" exclaimed Katrina, cutting September off, holding an apple from our picnic lunch.

"I think one long-distance apple tree is enough for one family," September said.

As we left Love Valley we walked past homes that appeared the same as they would have a thousand years ago—conical towers of stone excavated to make a living space, then sealed with a simple handcrafted wooden door and window.

I was studying one of these homes when a woman opened the door and smiled at us, then beckoned us in. While from the outside the house may have looked the same as it would have a millennium ago, inside the floor was covered with wall-to-wall Turkish rugs, and the home's one room sported a big-screen satellite TV.

Jordan's eyes bulged. "Wow, Dad! Can we get a cool TV like that?"

Our host then announced, "I wove all these carpets myself. Where are you from?"

I groaned. We had been asked that question at least once an hour since arriving in Turkey and I had long since begun making up home countries at random. It seemed that no matter how we answered, the would-be salesperson had either lived there or had a cousin there. "Namibia," I answered.

"Oh, I've never heard of that place, where is it?" the woman replied.

I was suddenly embarrassed for being so flippant. I also wasn't entirely sure where Namibia was. Luckily, September came to my rescue. "On the west coast of Africa, bordering South Africa. Your carpets are beautiful, but I'm afraid we have no way to carry them with us."

We all came out with several Nazar Boncuk stones to ward off the evil eye. The "stone" is actually a blue glass bead set with a white "iris," and a black "pupil" in the center. Our host was aghast when she realized we weren't wearing them.

"You must wear one so it is visible at all times!" She exclaimed. "It is our tradition."

As we were returning from our walk, Karim surprised us by sneaking up behind and pinching Jordan. *"Argh!"* Jordan screamed.

Karim held out two pieces of hard candy, one for Jordan and one for Katrina. Jordan scowled, but took the candy anyway. As we walked away Jordan removed the Nazar Boncuk from his belt loop. Handing me the stone, he scowled. "This doesn't work."

• • •

"Make it stop!" I groaned. For all practical purposes it was the middle of the night, the silence shattered by the now-familiar call to prayer.

"Why so early today?" September asked. "Mr. Singy-Person wasn't up so early yesterday."

You would think that the room in our hostel, carved into solid sandstone, would be impervious to Mr. Singy-Person. You would be wrong. "Today's the first day of Ramadan," I croaked. "It's time for the feast before the fast. Go back to sleep."

Mr. Singy-Person does the call to prayer and the call to begin the Ramadan fast based on *local* sunrise and sunset. I couldn't help but wonder if the less devout ever moved north of the Arctic Circle during the summer, when the sun doesn't set for weeks. I would make a lousy Muslim.

We enjoyed several days exploring the sites of Cappadocia, such as the underground cities and second-century churches, using Göreme as a base, and learned to love the friendly people, inexpensive food, and other-worldly towering stone landscapes. Eventually it was time to move on and we took the opportunity to comb through our belongings, culling items no longer needed and packing them to be shipped home.

I took a fairly large package to the fairly tiny Göreme post office. The lone postal clerk looked up from his crossword puzzle. I made the internationally recognized hand signal of mailing a package surface mail to the United States, which consists of pointing to the address on the label and then using an imaginary pencil to draw a boat.

We went through the motions of mailing a package. As the clerk made to weigh the package, I noted that the scale was a modern-looking digital unit, and that it needed to be plugged in. After plugging in the scale, the clerk placed my package on it, noted the weight, and proceeded to fill out a bunch of paperwork, leaving the package sitting on the scale.

I watched the clerk for a few moments while he filled in the forms. Suddenly the sound of a gunshot ripped through the silence. The clerk gave me a look of abject horror and put his hands up as if he were surrendering. My ears were ringing from the blast. The sound clearly came from the direction of the scale . . . or from the package sitting on top of the scale? A few seconds passed that seemed to stretch in an unnatural fashion. The clerk gradually began to realize that the Göreme, Turkey, post office was not under siege by a lone American. Ever so slowly, he put his hands down.

He gave a quick nod toward the package sitting on the scale and with a quizzical look, it was clear that he wanted to know just what in the hell I was mailing. My mind raced as I tried to think of what item in the package could have exploded like that, but I just couldn't fathom how our REI Four-Man Half Dome tent could spontaneously combust. Plus, the package looked perfectly tranquil sitting atop the scale.

I shrugged, a gesture I hoped was universally understood as "beats the heck out of me."

It wasn't long before we understood it was the scale that had exploded. To the casual observer the scale looked perfectly innocent, but it had weighed its last package.

My time in Göreme convinced me that for an American family, Turkey was at or near the end of the safety continuum. We found most Turks friendlier and easier to talk to than Europeans, but, curiously, they were cautious about talking freely about the United States. It seemed they did not wish to offend us by discussing the current state of affairs back home or the war in Iraq. My experience with the shaken postal clerk reinforced the notion we had gotten from Dilara: that we Americans were viewed as approachable, but also as quite possibly hazardous.

With our package in the mail, we were ready to make our way to Istanbul. It had taken fourteen hours to get to Göreme on the bus. It would take another fourteen to get back out. At the appointed time, we left our hostel in our familiar formation: Dad, Katrina, Jordan, and Mom, walking with our suitcases in tow to the bus station. Seemingly out of nowhere someone streaked in, swooped down, and hoisted Jordan into the air.

"You are mine now!" came the familiar voice.

It was Karim.

"I have three lovely daughters at home, but no sons." Karim put Jordan back on the ground but held him by the shoulders. Karim turned to me. "I will trade you your son for all three daughters!"

I knew Karim wasn't serious, but Jordan didn't; he was fighting back tears and not doing very well at it. The situation was very awkward, as I thought of Karim as a friend. He had been very kind, reaching out to us in his way, but it just didn't bridge the gap in the cultural divide, especially not to an eight-year-old boy who was still trying to find his place in the world.

I told Karim I was tempted, but I would keep Jordan with us. And with that, I took Jordan in my arms and carried him the rest of the way to the bus station.

* * *

Perhaps the most historic place in all of Istanbul is the site of the Blue Mosque and the Hagia Sophia. The Blue Mosque, which isn't blue, and the Hagia Sophia face each other across a large public park.

The Hagia Sophia was built and destroyed a few times before the current structure was dedicated by the Byzantines in the year 537 A.D. It remained the largest cathedral in the world for roughly a thousand years, despite suffering from the occasional earthquake. After the fall of Constantinople to the Ottomans in 1453, the cathedral was converted to a mosque. Across the street from the Hagia Sophia is the Blue Mosque, which was completed in 1616. In 1935 Turkish president Kemal Atatürk concluded that the good people of Istanbul didn't need two massive mosques across the street from each other and the Hagia Sophia was secularized and turned into a museum. Both structures are impressive and historically important to Christians and, more recently, to Muslims. Shortly after we visited, the Pope visited the Hagia Sophia. All the buzz on the news was about what would happen if the Pope decided to genuflect while at the Hagia Sophia.

Since the Blue Mosque is a place of worship it has specific dress codes, especially for women and for girls over eleven, who must cover their heads. We weren't in the Blue Mosque very long when Jordan grabbed my arm. "That lady over there isn't wearing her head scarf!" Soon we saw another woman sans scarf. Jordan's little body quivered with excitement at the thought of someone openly disobeying the rules. Soon, he was clutching his notebook while darting in and out of the crowds, creating a tally of all women without head scarves: forty-two in about thirty minutes.

The entire area surrounding the Blue Mosque had been transformed while Jordan busied himself with his Naughty Tally. It was approaching dusk when we exited and families had put down picnic blankets covered with towering plates of food. On their faces people wore eager expressions and were poised to pounce on their dinners. Folks kept glancing at their watches and as soon Mr. Singy-Person shattered the silence, there was a great blur of elbows as the picnickers broke their daily fast.

John's Journal, October 13

In a few hours we will leave Turkey for someplace altogether new and different. Although Jordan may disagree, Turkey has been a high point of our trip so far. Not just because of the friendly people and the stunning sights, but also because of what we have learned about ourselves. I'm embarrassed that I was nervous to travel here. There were no mobs trying to find us because September wore shorts, and Mr. Singy-Person aside, Ramadan at the Blue Mosque has been more like a carnival than a terrorist recruiting ground. My preconceived notions were completely off mark and I've never been so pleased to be wrong.

Upon leaving Turkey, I felt much lighter, leaving behind prejudices I had brought with me. As travelers, we were starting to walk the walk.

www.360degreeslongitude.com/concept3d/360degreeslongitude.kmz

Sunset at the Blue Mosque was livelier than a tailgate party at the Superbowl, only more family oriented. The carnival like atmosphere of Ramadan was enhanced by the mosque's minarets, which were lit up like, well, like Christmas, for the occasion.

11.

A Dangerous Place to Be a Chicken

October 13–October 18
Dubai, United Arab Emirates

"Breakfast is until four? That's nice, we can sleep in and still eat." We reached our hostel near the Dubai airport just before 2:00 a.m., and the price included breakfast. The receptionist was in the process of explaining breakfast hours, but the gravity of what he was saying didn't make it past the throbbing temples that result from sitting on a plane for several hours.

"Oh no, sir," the receptionist replied. "Breakfast begins in just a few minutes, and continues for only two hours until 4:00 a.m. If you want to sleep in, I suggest you get your breakfast . . ."

I stood rooted to the spot, swaying slightly, trying to process this information. Ah, yes. Humor. He was making a joke. That's okay, I can do humor, even with a 20-pound headache.

" . . . now. Breakfast hours have been moved up to accommodate the Ramadan fast. You *are* aware that Muslims fast from sunrise to sunset during the holy month of Ramadan?"

He wasn't joking. We were given our meal tickets and were escorted to the cafeteria, where, at 2:00 a.m., we found many people dressed in white robes, reading newspapers and eating their breakfasts.

Not surprisingly, none of us felt much like eating. We collected our breakfast and took it to our room so we could enjoy it cold and stale after we woke up.

• • •

"Trust me."

Those were the words uttered by a well-traveled friend in California when he was trying to convince us to stay a few days in Dubai instead of just making a plane connection on our way to Africa. "If you don't believe me," he continued, "just type 'Dubai water park' into the Google search box and then click 'I'm Feeling Lucky.'"

Our ersatz travel agent had been trying to convince us that Dubai had the world's best water park, and that we should pay it a visit, but a layover there made me nervous. "Don't they paint a bull's-eye on the forehead of every American as part of clearing customs?" I asked.

"It's not like that at all. Trust me."

So, we did.

The promise of the world's best water park brought us to Dubai, yet nothing was more important to the survival of our little troupe's emotional health than going to Chili's. Yes. That Chili's.

You must understand that the "molten chocolate cake" from Chili's is a necessary dietary component. We knew at the outset it would be one of the things we missed most during our travels. A few days before we stepped on the plane to Iceland we were having what we thought would be our last molten chocolate cake for an entire year.

"I have a bit of news," September announced. "I did some research on Chili's locations worldwide and compared the list to our itinerary."

Spoons stopped in midair. Everyone held their breath.

"There's a Chili's in Dubai. In fact, there are two."

Of course we hadn't thought of Ramadan. In Turkey we knew that the devout were fasting but businesses still conformed to normal hours and practices. In Dubai, Ramadan ruled our existence.

Having our priorities in order, on our first day in Dubai we arose, passed on the stale breakfast from the previous night, did the homework ritual, and then took a bus straight to Chili's at the Deira City Center mall. The bus was mercifully air-conditioned, but September was compelled to sit in the front, where she and the rest of the adult women were walled off from view. Since September couldn't see me and the kids, I just hoped we would all get off at the same bus stop.

Luckily, the mall was massive and there was no mistaking the stop. Stepping off the bus, Jordan remarked, "There's nothing wrong with chocolate cake for breakfast. It's loaded with milk, eggs, and flour—just like scrambled eggs and toast, only different."

A large portion of the population in Dubai are immigrants, imported to fuel the explosive growth in the area. As in much of the world, English is the second language widely used. Luckily for us, this meant most signs were posted in both Arabic and English.

Even without the aid of being posted in our native tongue, there was no mistaking the familiar Chili's logo on the map by the mall's entrance. Jordan and I ran ahead while September and Katrina did a bit of window shopping en route. A few moments later we were looking at the darkened interior of Chili's.

"There will be no chocolate cake for breakfast today," I announced to September and Katrina when they finally caught up. "The sign says it is closed for Ramadan. It will open later after sunset."

"Then what are we going to do for breakfast?" Katrina asked.

"It's actually almost lunchtime. I saw a food court on the mall's map," September said

We followed September a while and consulted a sign or two along the way. Eventually we made it to the food court. It seemed that every major fast food chain on the planet was represented, but the food court was dark and virtually deserted. We wound our way past Cinnabon, Baskin-Robbins, Starbucks, McDonald's, KFC. By their dress, it was apparent that half the people wandering around in the mall were European or Hindi who were surely hungry at lunchtime. But everything was shuttered for Ramadan.

"I'm hungry," Jordan stated. None of us had eaten since the flight from Istanbul.

"We knew sooner or later we would have to go hungry," I responded. "We may have to tough it out until tonight."

"I think I hear something," September said.

Faint voices were coming from the rear of the massive food court. Katrina and Jordan went toward the voices, then called back, "There's a Subway open!"

As we stood in line we found it was open *only* for take-out. The tables in the center of the food court were all roped off and there was a guard posted to be sure they stayed that way.

I perused the menu. "Hey!" I said, "the ham and bacon are missing!" Nor was there any sign of a roast beef sandwich or a BLT. In their stead were roast chicken sandwiches, teriyaki chicken sandwiches, chicken salad sandwiches . . .

"In a place where the Muslim locals don't eat pigs and the imported Hindus don't eat cows," September noted, "Dubai is clearly a *very* dangerous place to be a chicken!"

We ordered our take-out food and then tried to find a place we could eat without being busted by mall security. "We could eat in the restroom stalls," I suggested.

"I'm not going to do that," September said. "Let's keep going toward the back of the food court." It turned out that behind the darkened food court was a darkened video arcade, also off-limits during Ramadan. Venturing to the back of the arcade we heard voices again. At the very rear of the arcade was an area that looked like a dark box canyon. Anyone in the box canyon could see someone coming so that if they were doing anything forbidden, say, like eating their take-out Subway sandwiches, they could quickly hide the evidence.

This is where we found a group of British teenagers eating their chicken subs in the dark, sitting on the horsies of a tiny merry-go-round.

Feeling somewhat like junkies getting our fixes, we took our seats next to the motorcycle racer game.

Just as I was about to take a bite, September gently prodded me in the ribs and gave her head a quick nod in the direction of the almost pitch-black cockpits of the fighter jet arcade games. Sitting in the cockpits quietly eating *their* Subway takeouts were two grown Arab men.

I made the same subtle motion to Katrina and Jordan that September had made to me. "I can't believe they're doing that!" Katrina said in a tone that was both whispered and insistent. "I mean, they are not *supposed* to be eating!"

Simultaneously, Jordan was in awe. "Cool!" he intoned.

• • •

The afternoon was devoted to trying to see the city of Dubai, which at the moment was imitating the inside of an oven. At 6:00 p.m. we returned to Chili's at the mall to get our molten chocolate cake. No longer shuttered, the restaurant had completely transformed. It was packed with men in robes and women in head scarves sitting in front of untouched plates of food, anxiously checking their watches. Suddenly, Mr. Singy-Person crackled to life over the mall PA system, and there was a whoosh and blur of bending elbows as great quantities of chicken were enthusiastically consumed. I made a mental note that if I am ever reincarnated as a chicken in Dubai, I will immediately emigrate to Oregon, where I hear people exclusively eat granola.

John's Journal, October 14

In mid-October the sun is relentless. Parking lots are all covered by tents. One of the weirdest things I can't figure out is that at our hostel there is one kind of water in the faucet: hot. When we asked how to get cold water, they looked at us like we were from an alien planet. Why would anyone want cold water? Even the water flowing into the toilet bowl is hot, giving new meaning to the term "steamed buns."

> *The cross section of people at the mall was hugely varied;*
> *about one-third of the people were Arabs, with the remain-*
> *der being transplants from India, Africa, the Philippines, and*
> *Europe.*

Dubai has been described as Las Vegas, minus the casinos, set on the Arabian Peninsula. This is accurate. There are endless ways to keep yourself entertained, one being Wild Wadi, touted by our well-traveled friend as the best water park on the planet.

Wild Wadi justifies a trip halfway around the world. 🌐 The park has spared no expense in presenting its theme: an Arabian desert adventure with high canyon walls that mercifully block the afternoon sun. If you ever wondered what the sensation of being shot out of a water canon would be, Wild Wadi is your place. The lifeguards, twentysomething kids mostly from Northern Africa, seemed to be placed in the water solely to torment Jordan by patting him on the head.

For more sophisticated entertainment there is Dubailand. Dubailand is, or will be, the *ne plus ultra* of theme parks. When completed, Dubailand will be over twice the size of Orlando's Walt Disney World, currently the largest theme park in the world, but comparing it to Mickey leads to the wrong conclusion. When we were in Dubai the only part of Dubailand that had been completed was the autodome where you could rent a Ferrari and take it for a spin on the 3.4-mile FIA-sanctioned track. It was one of those things where if you had to ask, you couldn't afford it. Coming soon to Dubailand is everything from indoor skiing to the Mother of All Water Parks, promising to dwarf Wild Wadi.

• • •

The concept of a desert safari is simple enough: You are driven out to the middle of the desert and abandoned to spend the night hoping that in the morning your driver remembers where he left you.

I tried to make a case for not going. "Americans aren't exactly on the Arabs' 'Most Admired' list."

"What do you think they'll do?" September asked. "Take us out in the middle of the desert and leave us to rot?"

"Well, the thought crossed my mind. Worse things have happened to the naïvely trusting. Look what happened to Terry Waite."

"Who?"

"The British hostage negotiator. The second he shed his bodyguards he was taken hostage himself."

"Wasn't that like 20 years ago? Whatever happened to him? Did he get released?"

"I don't remember, but I don't want to meet him the hard way."

"I already paid the travel agency."

I wondered how many wives had used that line to get their husbands to accompany them on the *Titanic*.

We were picked up at our hostel by a nice young man in a turban and flowing white robes, driving a shiny new Toyota Land Cruiser. We headed out of Dubai toward the country of Oman, making small talk, gliding down an ultra-modern freeway, passing the occasional camel and miles and miles of endless sand.

While we were driving I desperately wanted to ask our driver and guide, "So, how about those Israelis and Palestinians?" But I was chicken. Since we had concluded being a chicken in Dubai is a dangerous thing, I kept my mouth shut.

The city skyline was quickly swallowed by the vast dunes. The desert was everything I thought it would be. Sand stretched as far as the eye could see. I imagined I was on the ocean, the rolling dunes disappearing on the horizon as if they were waves. After many miles, our driver pulled off the smooth blacktop highway, into and over the rolling sand dunes.

"Crossing the dunes is a lot like riding a roller-coaster!" I exclaimed. The young driver was clearly enjoying ferrying folks over the sand in his shiny, company-provided Land Cruiser.

"Yes," September replied. "Just like a roller-coaster, but without the assurance that comes with being on a steel track."

Later, as we cleaned up the vomit that Jordan had deposited all over the back seat, I asked our guide about the various vehicle parts strewn across the desert. "Over yonder looks like a fender from a Land Cruiser," I said. "And isn't that a bumper off a Hummer?"

"This part of the desert is set aside for dune bashing," our guide replied. "There used to be a lot of accidents here, but in the interest of tourist safety, all guides are now required to pass a rigorous off-road test and to be knowledgeable in emergency first aid."

"I feel so much better knowing that. What about the drivers that aren't guides? Do they have to pass any special training?"

"No, but most people who come here are very good drivers. You do have to be careful, though, when you see one of the off-road Lamborghinis. They are driven by the very rich and very crazy."

Our driver neared the drop-off place for our overnight stay. I looked about and noted the sun setting in the west, but apart from that everything looked the same from horizon to horizon. Our guide unloaded the back of the Land Cruiser with efficiency and then he was gone. He had left us with some water, a picnic basket full of chicken, and some blankets.

"How does he know where to pick us up?" Katrina asked.

"Good question." My eyes were scanning the horizon for any off-road Lamborghinis. I turned to September and asked, "Did you notice a GPS device?"

"No," she replied.

Jordan, having recovered from motion sickness caused by "dune bashing," was running about wildly, delighting in the freedom of the open space and being utterly alone. "Cool! Is this where we're staying tonight?!" he asked.

The vast sea of sand all looked the same. "Have you ever noticed," I said, "that if you put enough miles between you and a place, that place just seems to evaporate?"

"What do you mean?" asked Katrina.

"It's hard to remember the carpet salesmen of Turkey," September replied, "when the streets are lined with glistening chrome buildings and the banners hanging from the streetlights advertise the Real Estate Channel. It's fun to be in a new place, but it's sad that it's so hard to remember the place we just left."

"Dubai seems so different," Katrina commented.

"It is different, isn't it?" I said. "Mom couldn't sit with us on the bus today because men and women aren't allowed to mix in public. At the mall we saw men with three and four wives, and they were completely veiled."

"The writing we see looks like someone tried to pull the paper away," Jordan offered.

"But has anyone noticed how much *the same* things are?" September asked.

"What do you mean?" Katrina asked.

"The grown men at the mall eating their Subway takeout," September continued. "Classic human behavior, trying to be anonymous when being sneaky. At the end of the day, we aren't all so different from one another."

Everywhere we had visited it was possible to see what was different about it and the people. Yet I was beginning to see how much things—and people—were *alike*. Was it like that in Europe, and I was too distracted to notice?

The desert was very dark at night. And the stars brilliant. And we all felt very, very small.

www.360degreeslongitude.com/concept3d/360degreeslongitude.kmz

Not lost in a sea of sand. I'd just like to express my gratitude to the young man in the turban for paying attention in Boy Scouts.

12.

Stranded by Our Stupidity

October 18–November 2
Tanzania

The nice man with the machine gun at passport control wanted two hundred dollars for four visas. Cash.

We knew visas were fifty dollars each, payable in good ol' Yankee currency, before we stepped on the plane in Dubai, but I didn't want to withdraw a bunch of dirhams only to discover that I couldn't exchange them in Tanzania. Our strategy was to hope we would find an ATM in Tanzania before we reached passport control. We didn't.

As I explained our predicament to Mr. Machine Gun, he replied, "No problem. There are ATMs outside of the airport near the taxi stand. Just be sure to come back."

I left September, Katrina, and Jordan as collateral to ensure my return and proceeded past passport control and out of the airport. As promised, outside of the airport two ATMs, on different networks, awaited. But there was also a pride of cab drivers waiting for a fare and a legion of beggars waiting for relief. All eyes were upon me. Due to low transaction limitations, to get enough cash I had to make eight separate transactions, four on each network. I pretended to be invisible as I stuffed an inch-thick wad of Tanzanian shillings into my pocket. I shuffled off to exchange them back into dollars for our visas.

Access to cash was our biggest problem in Tanzania. It would also be the catalyst for our appreciation of the people of a tiny village in the Usambara Mountains.

• • •

The power was out citywide in Dar es Salaam, the largest Tanzanian city, and it was expected to remain out for two weeks due to lack of replacement parts for a key generator. That every third or so shop owner was ready with a portable generator told me that power outages were not uncommon. This was my first experience in a large African city. Gone were the shiny chrome buildings of Dubai. In their place was dense, chaotic traffic and street peddlers lined up elbow to elbow, each more desperate than the last. The effect of fumes from generators mixing with trash rotting on the sidewalks and in the gutters was choking.

This was the kids' first experience in a third world city. "Why is there so much trash in the streets?" Katrina asked as she leaped across a pothole.

"No garbage cans," Jordan responded matter-of-factly.

"Well, why don't they just get some?"

"Most likely no collection service," yelled September as we passed a particularly noisy generator.

The garbage-in-the-street question was the first of many that the kids started asking. *Why won't they accept Tanzanian shillings for visas? Why are there so many people trying sell the exact same things?*

We were spared any generator noise and fumes at our hostel; this also meant we were spared electricity. What could we expect for five dollars a night? Going without power was actually very nice. We spent a pleasant evening in the courtyard of the hostel talking with some of the other guests as Jordan zapped flies and mosquitoes with the hand-held, battery-powered zapper he'd acquired from a street peddler.

Beth, a middle-aged woman from Philadelphia who worked with the Peace Corps, was vocalizing some of her frustrations. She was in Dar, as it is known locally, for a few days before returning to the village where she was trying to raise AIDS awareness.

"The ugly truth," Beth said, "is that 'safe sex' has taken on a sinister twist in the bush areas." With a cautious glance at Katrina she continued. "'Safe sex' is taken to mean sex with younger and younger girls who are not yet infected."

We had brought the kids on the World-the-Round Trip to experience the good *and* the bad of humanity. Just over 24 hours after arriving in Tanzania, Katrina and Jordan were already asking hard questions about why this place was so different from others we had visited. I had been wondering that myself, and had yet to find a very satisfying answer.

With no power in the city it was very dark in Dar es Salaam and the Milky Way was stunning in the African night. Even though Katrina wasn't meant to be part of our conversation with Beth, as we had learned in our first weeks on the road there were no private conversations in our foursome. As soon as the syllables " . . . younger girls" had left Beth's lips, Katrina spun around and looked at us and said, "What? What are you guys talking about?"

It was a segue into a discussion I really didn't want to have. Beth quietly slipped away and we spent the next hour or so discussing everything from AIDS to the meaning of life, corruption in governments, garbage collection services, and the vastness of space with Katrina *and* Jordan.

I had naïvely thought that these philosophical discussions would occur almost daily on our trip. Not that I liked talking about AIDS with my kids, but the vastness of space is right up there on my top ten list. I had presumed our year together as a family would be spent learning about each other on a new level, debating politics, and discussing the wonders of science. What we found was that the days were filled with the trivialities of existence, just like at home. So, to be able to have a long meandering conversation with my kids under the starlight on an African night was worth the entire trip.

. . .

We stayed in Dar just long enough to purchase bus tickets to Arusha, the center of Tanzania's safari circuit. We were careful to use the bus company recommended by our guidebook as "least likely to break down." I grabbed a local paper in English for the ten-hour ride.

Local papers are always an interesting read. Prominently highlighted on the cover was a story about a little boy who was mauled to death by a leopard while on safari near Arusha. This was, of course, exactly where we were headed and our activity of choice once we arrived— the viewing, not the mauling. I decided to keep this information to myself and turned to local politics. Tanzanian elections were coming up. One of the presidential hopefuls claimed to know a famous scientist in America, and the candidate's platform was built on the promise of using this connection to cure AIDS in the next eight months. But he would do it *only* if elected. It would have been funny instead of sad if the guy had been considered the lunatic fringe by the electorate, but he was a serious contender.

A few hours on the bus and we had left the confines of the city, but the trash of the city still followed us. The major culprit was the lowly plastic bag, similar to what you might get at the local supermarket, but black and much thinner. There wasn't a square foot along the side of the road that wasn't carpeted with black plastic bags for at least the first two or three hours out of the city. Plastic simply doesn't biodegrade, and the concept of landfills and what they are supposed to be filled with simply hasn't entered the public consciousness. It is a problem continentwide.

Once we were well out of the "no turning back" range of Dar, the bus's engine started to emit a noise that sounded like my '68 Schwinn Sting-Ray when I clothes-pinned a playing card in the spokes to get the "motorcycle engine" effect. The bus driver pulled over, opened the hood (accessible from inside the bus), and after a few whacks with a hammer, we were happily motoring again. But not for long.

"There's that sound again," September said. The driver once again pulled over and removed the cowling that covered the engine. But this time he gave the hammer to a gentleman in the front seat. For the next several hours as we made our way to Arusha, whenever the sound returned, the gentleman in the front seat administered a few random whacks while the driver continued to motor happily down the road.

Dubai, with its 24-hour cable TV real estate channel and the wan-nabe Team Ferrari racetrack for rent seemed a lifetime ago. The United States seemed as though it was a previous existence. I certainly would never have seen a passenger whacking a bus engine with a hammer in the United States, or anywhere else in the Western World for that matter. I recalled a trip to New Zealand several years prior; the bus we'd been on developed a noise and the driver pulled over and we were stuck on a remote mountain for hours until help arrived. Things may be done differently here, but who's to say which is better?

When we stepped off the bus in Arusha a mob scene ensued. "We have the best safari in town!" one man shouted as he tried to grab my hand. Another man, walking off with my luggage, pointed to the first man and proclaimed, "He is a thief! You do not want to do business with that man!" Bodies were pressing up against us, tearing at all of us, trying to pull the four of us and our luggage in different directions. Each was desperate to tell us that they had the best safari and hostel in town.

Tempers in the crowd were starting to flare and for a moment it seemed a fight was going to break out over who got our business. Even though we were outnumbered, simply raising my voice dispersed the mob efficiently. We pulled out our guidebook and went to a hostel that it recommended, leaving behind many very disappointed people.

Once settled into the hostel I remarked to Jordan, "Kinda makes the carpet salesmen in Istanbul seem like kinder, gentler entrepreneurs."

Either I was making more out of the scene than I should have or the kids were becoming road hardened, because Jordan ignored the comment and asked, "I wonder if they have that same kind of cherry soda like they had in Turkey."

. . .

Arusha is the gateway to the Serengeti and we started to research our options to experience this natural wonder. Our guidebook warned us to choose a safari operator with care. Some operators try to cut costs a little too aggressively, which could leave you stranded in the Serengeti without an operating vehicle, food, or communications. Worse, the odd criminal has been known to try to pass himself off as a guide.

We chose a four-day budget camping safari run by a company recommended by our guidebook. We eyed the VISA ACCEPTED sign in the window as a good omen.

"We charge a ten percent fee for credit cards," the owner of the safari company said as I pulled out my Visa card. That seemed a bit steep, but due to small transaction limits on the ATM networks, it would take a few days to accumulate enough cash.

"Ten percent is okay," I said.

"Actually, the person who handles our credit card transactions is out sick."

"That's all right. We can wait until tomorrow."

"Well, uh . . . she is going to be out for a long time. We don't know when she will be back."

"I see." We eventually learned it is a rare business in Tanzania that accepts credit cards, even if a sign advertises such. It takes capital to run a business the way Westerners like us would expect. However, essentially all African businesses run on near zero capital and they have learned to adapt. The safari company simply needed our cash up front to pay for items like food, gas, and park entrance fees.

We settled into Arusha for a few days until we could withdraw enough cash to pay for our safari, but we soon found that withdrawing cash from an African ATM involves much more than walking up to it, sticking in your card, and punching a few buttons. First, the things require power to operate, and you simply can't rely on the power company to supply the stuff. Second, the things need to be stuffed with cash before they can dispense any, but more importantly the maximum daily withdrawal from a Tanzanian ATM is really not very much.

It would take a few days to accumulate enough cash to pay for our safari if the ATMs worked as they should—longer if they didn't. Whatever. We weren't in a hurry.

John's Journal, October 21
This morning as I stepped out of the shower there was a sweet young thing standing there with her hand outstretched. I was a wee bit stunned. She wanted my dirty clothes so she could wash them for me. The maid in our hostel scrubs the floor twice a day. With a rag, on her hands and knees. There are a lot of very hardworking people here. Yet there is also mind-boggling idleness. Huge numbers of young men sit along the streets for hours doing nothing at all. People flock from the villages to the cities, but there are no jobs to support them.

Walking anywhere in the town of Arusha was like traversing an army-training obstacle course. As I made my daily rounds to the ATMs, I would leap over three-foot-wide open storm drains, squeeze past market stalls blocking the sidewalk, and weave through heavy traffic that showed no signs of following simple traffic laws like, say, stopping at stop signs. As I went about trying to coerce cash from the ATMs, street vendors would try to get me to buy some souvenir or food item, and beggars would simply ask for cash. To them, *I* was the ATM.

The various street merchants seemed hardworking, trying to make money to feed their families. It was clear that they were very, very poor and many were desperate. Still, it puts the traveler in an uncomfortable position, especially for people like us who weren't able to accumulate a lot of souvenirs.

Making daily rounds to the various ATMs in the city, it didn't take long for me to realize that people on the street knew we were accumulating cash. During our third night at the hostel someone entered our room at 3:00 a.m. I leaped out of bed screaming like a wild man, *"GET OUT!"* as the intruder quickly fled.

"How did he get in? Did you see who it was?" September was firing questions at me.

"I think he used a key. The door was locked, but now it isn't."

The hostel staff knew nothing, saw nothing. Suddenly we were in a hurry to acquire the rest of the money for our safari and go. The following morning the safari company arranged a cash advance on my Visa at a local bank, albeit with a massive transaction fee.

Our whole reason for being in Arusha came from years before, when our favorite family pastime was to gather in front of our giant world map with a stack of Post-it notes to discuss where our trip might take us. As plans firmed up, Katrina and Jordan were allotted one Post-it note each. Katrina decided that the Serengeti was the one place she wanted to see during the World-the-Round Trip. Jordan's choice, The Great Wall of China, was still a few months away.

The night prior to our safari departure was full of anticipation from both Katrina and Jordan. Tiger, a small stuffed animal, had accompanied them ever since we left California. As we lay in bed, Katrina and Jordan were whispering in hushed excitement as they made plans to "show" Tiger the Serengeti.

We met Bariki, our guide, and Tanfi, our cook, the following morning. The six of us would be constant companions over the next four days, covering great distances in a Land Rover, eating our meals together and camping under the stars. The first thing we did as we pulled out of town was to go grocery shopping. Tanfi bought all of the supplies, including two liters of bottled water per day for each of us.

The Land Rover pulled out of the grocery store parking lot and Bariki pointed it down the blacktop and toward the horizon. We had hours of blacktop before we arrived at our destination, and the Lean, Mean Talking Machine started to work her craft. September started with the basics, asking Bariki and Tanfi where they were from. When they found we were from California, they asked excitedly, "Do you know Arnold Schwarzenegger?" We were surprised. In Eastern Europe, Turkey, and Dubai, we were peppered with inquiries about Monica Lewinsky, despite the decade or so since her brush with infamy. Arnold was a refreshing change of subject.

"No, we've never met him," September responded. "Do you like some of his movies?"

"I have never seen a movie before," they replied simultaneously.

I was pretty astounded. Not just because a grown man had never seen a movie, but because they knew a famous movie star, even though they had never seen a movie. Nor had Bariki or Tanfi ever heard of a movie called *Star Wars*. We were a long way from Kansas.

• • •

Frankly, the idea of a safari didn't interest me. I arrived in Africa with a prejudice developed while September and I were cycling in Alaska, before Katrina and Jordan entered our lives. Although Denali National Park was famous for moose, bear, and other wildlife, after a week of cycling across the tundra we had seen very little evidence of them. I expected a similar experience in the Serengeti, but Katrina had romantic notions of seeing large prides of lions, herds of elephants, and a landscape teeming with big game.

Driving into the Serengeti, we were met by axle-breaking roads. So when we came upon a large truck with its rear wheels almost ninety degrees out of their preferred orientation, it was no surprise. The truck's driver was on the verge of tears. Bariki simply kept driving.

When we reached our camp on the Serengeti Plain, prominently displayed on a sign near the entrance was "Do not go beyond the camp as the wild animals may attact (sic) humans."

I stared at the sign, allowing the full gravity of its message to seep into my brain, all the while trying to reconcile the message with my expectations. Nevertheless, we pitched our tents in the center of the campsite, hoping to keep the other campers' tents as a buffer between us and the carnivores.

After dinner Bariki announced, "It is not advisable to leave your tent between midnight and 5:00 a.m."

I asked him what we should do if we needed a nighttime winkle. "Couldn't we just go outside of the tent, if we don't walk across camp to the latrine?"

"It is not recommended," Bariki replied solemnly. Shortly after we went to bed, I heard growling outside of our campground. I thought about the leopard story in the newspaper and wondered if camping was such a good idea.

Sure enough, at about 3:00 a.m. Jordan, who *never* needs to use the facilities in the middle of the night, informed me that he needed to use the toilet, and badly. What is a parent to do? Risk a bedwetting or risk allowing your child to become an early-morning breakfast?

I listened to the night for a good long time, poked my flashlight out of the tent, sniffed the breeze, and contemplated my next move. It is my strong desire that my finest moment in life, the moment I faced my biggest fear, will not end up being when I took Jordan out for a pee next to a tent. So I'll have to come up with something heroic in the coming years, because that is precisely what I did, and I was terrified.

Daylight broke over our camp and I felt a wave of relief at having survived the experience. I did, however, have regrets over my choice of using the laundry bag as a pillow for the night. I woke to find Jordan's dirty underwear pasted to the side of my face.

At breakfast Bariki told us that lions had in fact been poking around the campground during the night. So after breakfast, in the safety of our Land Rover, we went to look for them. Bariki soon located four fully grown females and four or five adolescents of both sexes.

He maneuvered the Land Rover about two car lengths away from them. Standing with my head and shoulders poking out of the viewing port in the roof, I locked eyes with one of the fully grown females, and for several seconds we considered each other, she with large, unblinking and inquisitive eyes.

How does one describe the cold stare of an animal that has only known being the top of the food chain? I couldn't help but wonder if she was thinking, "Mmmmm, plump and juicy!" I wanted to shout, "I'm on top of the food chain, too, you know!" Of course that's not saying much because with no natural predators, skunks are, too.

Awed by the scene, all I could manage to say was, "Well. This is nothing like Alaska."

"You're goofy, Dad," Katrina said with a giggle.

The safari was full of spectacular encounters with wildlife. Bariki kept us entertained with background information and anecdotes about the area and the animals. Some of his anecdotes seemed like the African version of an urban legend, like the German who wanted to photograph hippopotamuses up close, sneaking out of camp and wading up to his waist in a watering hole only to become dinner for same. But I wasn't about to wade into any watering holes to refute the authenticity, either.

Katrina's Journal, October 25

We got up early this morning. Tanfi already had our breakfast packed for us and we were off. We soon saw some giraffes. They were very close up, and we watched a mother eating lazily while its baby nursed. Farther down the road, we saw our next animal—a full grown male lion. I really like seeing lions, and am hoping to see all of "The Big Five," which are lions, elephants, leopards, rhinoceros, and cape buffalo. But I like the cats the best so I want to see cheetahs, too.

After seeing the male lion, we went somewhere nearby and saw a male and a female lion together. Counting these, I think we have seen seventeen lions.

Then we drove some more, seeing nothing besides gazelles and stuff, a few warthogs, and hyenas. But we did, after a while, see a crocodile. It wasn't very long, but I thought that it was pretty neat to see one. And after that, guess what? We saw a LEOPARD. It was kind of far away, but through the binoculars we could see that it was sitting in a tree, eating its kill. There were about ten cars surrounding the leopard, but wow. It isn't very common to see one.

After seeing the leopard, we headed back to camp and had lunch. After that, we got back in the car and began the long drive to a new camp at Ngorongoro, where we are now. On the way we saw two lionesses, one with her kill. And we also saw a cheetah. All three big cats in one day. The cheetah was very far away and even through the binoculars I couldn't see its spots, but I could tell by its shape that it was a cheetah.

Bariki's ability to spot wildlife was astounding. He had an uncanny ability to sight, say, a leopard that had dragged its kill up into a tree a kilometer away. Bariki would locate a *National Geographic* moment for us to gawk at, and then position our Land Rover as close to the action as he could. Then he would make himself busy while we took pictures and acted like tourists.

It took me a while to figure out what was occupying Bariki's attention while we were taking pictures; he had his cell phone out and was texting his girlfriend. I pulled my own cell phone from my pocket and noted I had five bars of coverage. Somehow, the coolness factor of being on safari in the Serengeti was diminished when I realized that my mother could call and check up on me to see if I had been eaten.

At the end of the dry season the Serengeti and Ngorongoro Crater are as dry as dust and just as brown. There is no replicating the sensation of slathering your skin with sunscreen and 'skeeter repellant only to have it act as a dust magnet. By the end of the day, we were nearly as brown as our guide. "I'd kill for a shower," I said.

"Not with rations of two liters of water per day, you won't," September replied.

"What do all the animals do for water?" Katrina asked.

"There are water holes around here but they must be getting mighty dry about now. It's food I wonder about," September answered. "The lions can fend for themselves, but there seems to be nothing for the zebras, wildebeests, and antelope to eat."

"The elephants are making runs to Costco when the sun goes down," I said. "It's the only way."

We divided our days between Lake Manyara, Serengeti, and Ngorongoro National Parks. Each of the parks we visited had its own personality, and in each it was simply not possible to go more than a few moments without seeing abundant wildlife including lions, elephants, hippos, baboons, giraffes, cheetahs, crocodiles, rhinos, leopards, and what seemed like a zebra, wildebeest, or gazelle for every brown blade of grass.

In short, our experience with Bariki was nothing like my experience in Alaska and it more than met Katrina's romantic notions of what an African safari should be.

. . .

Returning to Arusha, Bariki maneuvered the Land Rover into a shanty town for supplies. Bariki and Tanfi left us alone and a boy about ten years old approached the car.

"Bic? Bic?" Oddly enough an ink pen (known as a "Bic") is the preferred item that children beg for.

As I don't believe in supporting begging, I said, "I don't have a pen."

"One dollar!" he demanded.

"No."

"Give me your sunglasses?"

"No."

The young boy proceeded to recite a list of items he wanted.

Finally, he saw a bag of potato chips on the seat next to me and asked for those. I wondered if he was hungry. If he was, I don't think he would have asked for my sunglasses before he asked for the chips. Nevertheless, I didn't want the chips so I gave them to him. This turned out to be a mistake.

He quickly went over to his friends and held the bag of chips in the air like a trophy. I couldn't understand what he was saying, but it was clear he was taunting his friends that he had gotten the American to give him something. Soon, the Land Rover was mobbed by kids demanding everything from the hat on my head to the kids' clothes.

Clearly, a generation of well-off travelers before me had conditioned the kids in the area to expect handouts. This is understandable, as desperation is perhaps the only thing not in short supply in the area and well-meaning people *want* to relieve suffering. I *want* to relieve suffering. But as the scene unfolded before us, it was clear that handing out Bic pens to every kid who asks is not the answer. Within moments the scene started to devolve and we started to fear for our safety. Clearly the children from the area have learned to be brazen, and simply shooing them away wasn't going to work. Instinct told me that the primal yell I used to disperse a near-mob scene a few days earlier would have backfired. Reacting to the growing tension, Katrina and Jordan put down what they were reading and sat erect in uncomfortable silence. Fortunately, Bariki soon returned and drove us away.

We settled back into a hostel in Arusha that evening and opened our guidebook. We were looking for someplace off the standard tourist track and decided to visit Lushoto, a town in the Usambara Mountains. Lushoto is surrounded by rain forest, in the shadow of Mount Kilimanjaro.

The bus ride to Lushoto would take about seven hours and would start at 6:30 a.m. "We should get cash tonight before we leave in the morning," September said, "because the bus leaves before the ATM opens."

A trip to the ATM would have been a prudent move, but the thought of making a withdrawal at night was not on my must-accomplish list. On top of the incident with the intruder in our room the week prior, there had been the mob scene around our Land Rover and two unpleasant encounters with aggressive panhandling that very day.

"The guidebook says there is a bank in Lushoto—let's wait until we get there," I replied.

The next day our bus twisted and turned as it clung to the edge of a cliff, climbing out of the Great Rift Valley and up into the mountains. We passed small farms growing sugarcane and banana trees, and occasionally we would see monkeys climbing across the branches of an overhanging tree. We arrived in Lushoto just before 3:00 p.m. on a Friday afternoon. The bus pulled up into a town square of hard-packed, uneven dirt. The small square was surrounded by a number of wooden shacks selling anything from used car parts to packages of crackers.

The guidebook described Lushoto as a town of 100,000 people, with a bank. Glancing about the tiny town square, it was clear the guidebook was off by a couple of zeros.

Somehow I had acquired a card proudly advertising a hotel where we could "enjoy running hot water!"

"The bank is probably going to close soon," I said, handing September the hotel's card. "You take the kids and find this hotel, and I'll go to the bank."

The Lushoto Bank of Micro-Finance was just off the town's main square. I'm not even sure if the bank had electricity. I do know the teller was unimpressed by the fact that I had both an ATM card *and* a credit card. He simply laughed and dismissed me with a wave of his hand.

I found September and the kids at the hot water hotel. "We have a problem," I said.

September asked, "Did you find an ATM?"

"No," I responded. "And it gets worse. Here's our situation." Katrina and Jordan were listening most intently at this point, not interrupting every few syllables as they were prone to do. "We have one ten-thou-sand-shilling note (about US$9.50) and a handful of coins. We can't pay for even one night in this hotel, so we'll have to check out right now and hope they don't make us pay for the half hour we've been here. The closest bank with an ATM or Western Union is back in Arusha, and we only have enough money to cover one person's bus fare, one way."

"Arusha?" September exclaimed. "We just came from there! Are you proposing that just one of us take the bus 14 hours round-trip back to Arusha while three of us huddle in the forest, waiting, without food or shelter? Is that what I just heard you say?"

"Not exactly," I replied. "The buses only run in the mornings. So, even though it's fourteen hours of travel time, the person who goes can't leave for Arusha until tomorrow morning, then return the day after that."

September said "okay," with a faraway look in her eye. After a long pause, she said, "You would have to be the one to go to Arusha because I don't think it's wise for me to be traveling alone. And what would you do if you got to Arusha and found that the electricity was out? Or if you couldn't use the ATM for any other reason, like if your wallet was stolen? You would have no way to return to us here in Lushoto."

Everything she said was true. "Look, I can't leave until tomorrow morning anyway. First things first, we can't stay in the hotel, so we need to check out now. Then we can spend the rest of the day searching for a hotel and a restaurant that will accept a credit card. Maybe we'll get lucky."

Jordan spoke for the first time during this discussion. He calmly asked, "Does this mean I can't get a soda?"

Never before had we been in such a predicament. Our previous experience had taught us that to get money, you needed to go to the bank and the bank would take care of you. Now that this had failed us, we weren't sure what to do, and were quite anxious regarding how things might work out.

I went to the front desk to check out and September went into town to the Cultural Tourism Center to see if there was a place for us to camp in the surrounding forest. We had sent our tent back to the United States, but we still had our sleeping bags, as they were invaluable in hostels.

"I'm sorry, we can't stay here," I explained to the clerk behind the front desk. "We have no money to pay."

"It's okay," the woman helping me said as best she could, trying to overcome a language barrier. "You go to town and see owner Mr. Mkwati."

"Katrina and Jordan," I said, returning to the room, "wait here and tell Mom when she gets back I went to talk to the hotel's owner."

Exiting through the lobby a few moments later, I found a taxi waiting. The woman at the front desk had called it for me. "I have no money to pay for the taxi," I said. "I don't mind walking."

"But you will never find Mr. Mkwati. The taxi driver will help you find him. I will pay the taxi driver, you pay later."

I was speechless. This was so different from our experience in Arusha.

The taxi driver helped me locate Mr. Mkwati in town. I explained our predicament, telling him we needed to check out of his hotel and why.

"*Hakuna matata*, John. Do you know what that means?"

"Yeah, I've seen the movie."

Mr. Mkwati said, "What movie?"

I suddenly remembered I wasn't in Kansas anymore. "*The Lion King*," I replied. "Have you ever heard of it?"

"No."

I briefly explained that *The Lion King* was a children's movie, summed up the plot and then tied it up with how *hakuna matata*, which loosely translates to "no worries," was central to the plot. I felt pretty stupid, knowing full well what Mr. Mkwati was thinking—I was certifiable. I had brought my family to Lushoto from California without enough money to pay for a night in his hotel, and here I was talking about a lion cub who sang the "Hakuna Matata" song. But he was impressed that I knew a few Swahili words, such as *simba* for "lion." Which of course

I didn't, but since I mentioned the name Simba in connection with the lion cub who would someday be king, he presumed I was a Swahili master.

I learned something very important. *Hakuna matata* is more than a line out of a movie, and more than a casual greeting—it is a way of life. I didn't realize it then, but it would be a siren song for a new philosophy of life that we would need to make the difficult transition upon returning to Western civilization seven months later.

After listening to me talk about singing simbas named Simba, Mr. Mkwati started to fully grasp our predicament: that I couldn't feed my family, and that I stood a good chance of ending up stranded in a strange town the following day when I went to search for a working ATM.

He then did something most unexpected. He opened up his wallet, emptied it out, and gave me everything he had: thirty thousand Tanzanian shillings, or about $29. That wasn't a tremendous amount of money, but it *was* enough to feed my family, and also ensure that I would have a return ticket should my search for an ATM the following day be in vain.

I was not only deeply touched, but the experience left me pondering my own charity. Would I have done the same thing if the tables were turned? I'd like to think so, but twelve hours earlier I wanted nothing more than to get out of Tanzania altogether, motivated in no small part by the disturbing scenes around Arusha, which was, in no small part, why we ended up in Lushoto virtually broke.

"You'll never believe what just happened to me," I said upon returning to the hotel.

"Where have you been?" September said. "I was starting to think you had abandoned us in despair. I've been so anxious to talk to you. You'll never believe what just happened to *me*. I went to the Cultural Tourism Center and explained our situation. They lent me everything they had in their safe. Three hundred U.S. dollars. Cash."

I couldn't speak. This was roughly equivalent to the annual per capita income for Tanzania. No collateral, no paperwork, no specified repayment schedule, just a "here you are ma'am, and thank you for letting us serve you."

"Taking charity from the impoverished, it kind of puts the fine point on our predicament, doesn't it?" September said.

"It's more than that," I said. "The bank here let us down and the best plan we could come up with was to try a different bank. If everyone here thought like us, that *would* have been the best plan. What are the chances that if the three people who lent us money today showed up in Silicon Valley with no way to feed themselves, within hours they would have the equivalent of a year's worth of cash in their pocket?"

There was silence. It was a powerful, emotional lesson.

"I can't help but think of the kids yesterday who all wanted Bic pens," September said.

"I still don't think handouts are the right answer. But neither is watching from the sidelines. Poverty is a complicated problem, with no easy solutions."

• • •

The following day I was en route to find an ATM. September and the kids stayed in Lushoto and had a grand time hiking with Ishmael from the Cultural Tourism Center, so much so that they took me on the same hike when I returned.

Ishmael, our guide, took us through the rain forest, but he showed us much more than just the lush landscape and the green mamba snakes. He showed us that the people who live in the villages scattered throughout the hills were genuinely thrilled to see us. For the first time since entering Tanzania we felt welcomed for who we were, not because we might hand out Bic pens or buy a month-old newspaper. On a simple four-hour hike I lost count of how many families we found harvesting sugarcane by hand. Walking along we were frequently greeted with a "*hakuna matata!*" by women carrying into town bundles of cane balanced on their heads. Scattered among the sugarcane fields we occasionally found a group of children playing soccer with a ball made of rolled-up rags held together by string. They would run to us with their big, affable smiles shouting *Jambo!* (Swahili for hello) and then walk with us just for the simple novelty of holding our hands.

Ishmael was an orphan in his early twenties. He had a younger brother and sister to care for and was working hard to keep them in school. Tuition at US$100 per year was difficult to come by.

"Last year I was able to pay tuition for them but there are fewer tourists this year because of the drought. But I have my marriage cow. If I cannot save the money for their tuition, I can sell my cow."

September pressed for details and learned that the cow was a traditional bride price. Without it, his marriage prospects were bleak.

Ishmael had Rastafarian dreadlocks and wore a Bob Marley T-shirt. Had I met him in other circumstances, I might have judged him unfavorably, strictly based on his appearance.

We learned that the Usambara Mountains are filled with orphans. The day-to-day existence of the average African is full of hardships that the typical U.S. suburbanite can't fathom. For example, Ishmael lost his mother to a horrific bus accident. In two short weeks we had already seen the aftermath of two ugly accidents and had also witnessed how overcrowded trucks and buses become. Shortly after the accident took his mother, Ishmael lost his father to malaria. September remarked, "But malaria is so easy to treat!"

Ishmael replied, "Yes, but people are used to being sick here. We eat bad food and our stomachs hurt and we get chills. He didn't know he had malaria. My father finally went to the clinic, but it was too late."

Katrina's Journal, October 31

Normal morning. Today is our last day in Lushoto. Tomorrow we return to Dar and then we fly to Mauritius. Since it is Halloween, we went out looking for some candy in the little shops around the town square. There was none to be found. After asking at a couple of shops I started to feel like a spoiled kid who demanded sweets.

Living in the West, it is easy to be lulled into believing that wealth can be quantified by trailing zeros on a bank account or by possessions. In Zermatt there seemed to be a Rolex dealer or a specialty chocolate shop every other door along the main street. Although I may not be a Warren

Buffett or a Bill Gates, by world standards, I am still counted among the richest, and before I arrived in Lushoto, I would have described myself as a charitable person. But it was in Lushoto that I became the beggar, and the people of the town demonstrated a kind of charity that was frankly foreign to me. It took Lushoto to make me realize that what I lacked couldn't be purchased.

What I remember most about Lushoto is not looking over the Great Rift Valley nor the beauty of the forest nor the colony of African albinos we met. What I remember is receiving aid from those who had little to give with no thought of how they might be repaid.

www.360degreeslongitude.com/concept3d/360degreeslongitude.kmz

Who knew hanging with the guy sporting the dreadlocks would be so much fun? More than any other person, Ishmael saved the day when we showed up in Lushoto virtually broke.

13.

Eat First, Ask Questions Later

November 2–November 26
Mauritius/Japan

As we cleared the security checkpoint for our flight out of Tanzania, we came upon the customary large, clear plastic bin of items that had been confiscated over the months. I never understood what the purpose of this display is . . . is it a deterrent against bringing tweezers on board? By the time a passenger gets to this point, his or her luggage has already been checked. It is a little late to be reminding people how nefarious tweezers can be.

Jordan studied the objects inside the bin, fascinated by the different items that security felt obliged to confiscate. In a loud, boisterous voice Jordan commented on how stupid it would be to try to hijack a plane with, say, fingernail clippers. I was worried that he was drawing a bit too much attention to the subject.

Obviously some passengers just have different objectives in flying than simply going someplace new. It would seem that someone had been planning a picnic at thirty-three thousand feet, because nestled in with the Swiss Army knives, fingernail files, and hair picks were several ordinary table forks. What's up with that? I could understand how someone was caught off guard with a Swiss Army knife in his pocket, but a bunch of forks?

Less than an hour later, we were airborne and enjoying the in-flight dinner. I mean, *really* enjoying it. I realized that this was the best meal I had had in longer than I cared to remember. I was just thinking of how pathetic that was when Jordan stood up, held a metal fork above his head, and yelled from across the aisle of seats:

"Hey, Dad, look! The airline gave us metal forks with our dinner! If someone wanted to hijack a plane with a fork, they could just use this one!"

Right at that precise moment I took my metal fork and used it to skewer a green bean, and popped it into my mouth.

Only it wasn't a green bean, it was some kind of pepper. I pride myself on my tolerance for spicy foods, but the green bean that wasn't a green bean was in a category by itself.

As Jordan was shouting about hijacking a plane with a fork, I was gasping for air and holding my throat with one hand and waving a fork madly in the air with the other. I was desperately trying to form the word "water," but people in the vicinity were starting to react to the situation with alarm.

Why is it that airlines pass out all of the dinners and time it so just when you're finished eating, they come back around offering you something to drink? Most people I know enjoy their drink *with* their meal. It was some time before I could actually get water, first being obliged to demonstrate that I was to be pitied rather than feared.

"That's your father for you," September summarized. "Eat first, ask questions later."

We stepped off the plane in Mauritius without the accoutrements of handcuffs or leg shackles. It was the perfect temperature that's only possible in the tropics, where the air is warm, yet the breeze is pleasantly cool with a hint of salt spray. To top it off, we found that in Mauritius they sell fireworks in the grocery stores. Really big ones. How can you not love a place like that?

Mauritius is a tiny dot on the average globe, situated just above the Tropic of Capricorn and 530 miles east of Madagascar. The dodo bird, we discovered, is Mauritius's claim to fame. Our taxi driver from the airport was an Indian gentleman with a perfect French accent. I find it a bit unnerving when the person I am talking to doesn't have the accent that my stereotype has assigned him, for example, Africans in London with their perfect British accents, or Harley riders who talk like Inspector Clouseau.

"Ze French," said the taxi driver, "when zey first come to Mauritius, zey love to eat ze doo-doo. It ez delicious to them."

"How is that again?"

"Ze doo-doo, zey cannot fly and were eezee to catch. Ze French eat all ze doo-doo, so it eez extinct."

Mr. Taxi-Driver must have thought I was having spasms as I was forced to stifle snickers as visions of doo-doo eating French went through my mind. I had always thought it was the Dutch who drove the dodo to extinction, which is what research later confirmed. Even though inaccurate, I can't help but like Mr. Taxi-Driver's version of the dodo's demise better, as the French are so delightful to poke fun at.

September had found an apartment in Pereybere, a beach town on the northern coast of Mauritius, before we had left California. It was the only preplanned break in traveling that we had made, and we looked forward to a week basking in the tropical sun and recharging our batteries. Test-driving the fireworks on the beach was an unexpected perk. Even though we could buy fireworks at the grocery store, every time I lit a fuse I couldn't help but think that this much fun surely couldn't be legal.

"Jordan and I decided we're staying in Mauritius," I announced to September and Katrina one morning. "We're having some shirts made up patterned after the one you sabotaged in Turkey, and we're going to open up a hamburger joint."

September was doing homework with Katrina and Jordan. Jordan was in on the ruse, and got a big smile and started squirming in his seat. He'll never amount to much in a poker game. September didn't look up from what she was doing and merely said, "That's nice dear." Katrina started peppering September with questions. "They're not really serious, are they?"

"As far as you know I am," I responded. "Before we left Istanbul I found a place on the Web that can make us anything we want. Just send them a picture."

September started to look nervous. "Do we have a picture?"

"Oh, yes. You took one of me wearing it in Pompeii. It's a beaut. Having the shirts sent here made the most sense because we had an address. Little did I know then what a great place this was."

After a few nights we had graduated to fireworks that would not have been out of place in many civic Fourth of July celebrations. As window-rattling booms washed over the island and trails of flaming flowers of gunpowder lit up the night sky, I would look over my shoulder, expecting the police to storm the beach in riot gear and haul me away.

Katrina was mildly amused by the fireworks, but mostly she busied herself baking cakes. As our departure date neared I told Katrina, "We ordered you a shirt, too. We can serve burgers *and* cakes. We'll just hide the plane tickets from Mom until it's too late."

"Dad," Katrina responded, "Mom and I love it here, too, but *we* want to see the rest of the world."

When our departure date arrived, the custom Bill's Burger Barn shirts still hadn't arrived. Sadly, we made our way to the airport without them. We queued up at the Air Mauritius counter and handed the nice lady our tickets.

"I'm sorry," she said, "this flight departed yesterday. I'll see if I can't get you on the next flight, but we only fly this route three times a week."

What? Yesterday?! I grabbed my e.brain and looked at the date. For several seconds my gaze shifted from our tickets to the display on my PDA as if by looking at them hard enough the calendar would magically roll back. "I guess I lost track of time and forgot what day it was."

September looked at me in disbelief. "Did you make us late so we could get that package?"

"That's not something I'd do!" I protested. September looked at me like she wanted to believe me, but didn't know if she should. "Okay, maybe it is something I'd do, but I didn't. Really. I swear on the fish."

Swearing on the fish was code. Shortly after we married, September's parents had a great practical joke played on them that involved a wading pool and a catfish. The blame was laid at our feet, and although it was something we would have loved to take credit for, nothing we could say would cause her parents to believe it was someone else. They don't believe us to this day. By swearing on the fish, September knew I was innocent of the charge of missing our flight on purpose.

Problem is, even by the time we eventually left Mauritius our shirts still hadn't arrived. Somewhere in Mauritius there are four Bill's Burger Barn shirts waiting for a grand opening.

. . .

"You remember, of course, what I said as we were leaving Europe."

Katrina, September, and Jordan repeated sequentially as if on cue, "Yes." "No." "Maybe. I dunno. Can you repeat the question?"

"You guys need to get a life." Four people sharing another's private space for such a long time creates a weird group dynamic, including communicating by quoting sitcoms. I ignored the bait and continued, "I said we will never fit in again. That is especially true in Japan."

I have been explaining to Katrina ever since she was old enough to listen that she was just like our faithful Toyota Corolla—made in Japan and exported to America. And of course, it was while September and I were living in Japan, contemplating raising a family, that the whole World-the-Round Trip idea hatched. Being back in Japan was wonderfully comfortable.

More than a decade after we had lived there I was surprised at how much Japanese was coming back to me. It was wonderful beyond description to be able to communicate with the locals. Make no mistake—my Japanese gave me all the proficiency of the average toddler. But I found that my communication skills, no matter how crude, coupled with a credit card made a powerful statement.

Recalling our previous experiences in Japan, we were reminded of the saying that no one extorts the Japanese as well as the Japanese. When we lived in Japan twelve years prior and were making plans to explore the country, we found it was cheaper for us to fly to Hong Kong for the weekend than it would be for us to take the Shinkansen (bullet train) to Hiroshima for the weekend. So despite living in Japan for a year, we'd never made it to two places we really wanted to visit: Kyoto and Hiroshima.

Thus, visiting these places was a priority and we braced ourselves for the most expensive two weeks of our entire trip. But first, after twelve years of being away, we returned to Kamakura where the idea for the World-the-Round Trip began.

Kamakura is about an hour and a half south of Tokyo by train. An easy day trip from Tokyo, it's a popular tourist destination and, as an important cultural and historical center, was spared damage during the war. The giant Buddha that is frequently seen on postcards from Japan is just a few blocks from our former apartment.

Visiting places where we have such fond memories was even infectious for the kids, who were as enthusiastic to walk by where we used to buy groceries as September and I were.

"There it is guys. Groceries. American groceries. You can get almost anything you want in there." We were in front of Kinokuniya, which specialized in imported foods. "I'll buy you Kraft Macaroni & Cheese and if you're extra good, I'll get some peanut butter." Which was a lie and they knew it. Peanut butter just isn't available to the general population outside the United States and we were going to get a jar no matter how good or bad the kids might be.

We entertained ourselves by perusing the aisles of Kinokuniya for a bit. The look and feel of English words is exotic to the Japanese, so many things are spelled out in Jinglish. Where else can you find "Tissues of Kittens" (a box of tissues with kittens pictured on the front) or "Glutinous Starchy Substance" (corn syrup)? Even though I don't consider it food, we picked up a few boxes of Kraft Macaroni & Cheese along with our "Paste Essence of Peanut."

One morning, we started near the apartment where we had once lived and walked past the Daibutsu (the Great Buddha) then continued up into the hills above Kamakura to a shrine called Zeniarai Benten. A sign near the entry proclaims that in a year of the serpent (1185) a

Shogun had a dream of the location of a spring and that he should find the spring and build a shrine there. Access to the shrine is through an opening dug into the side of a mountain, but after a short distance, the walkway opens up into a courtyard with blue sky above. A steady stream of people from all over Japan come to the Zeniarai Benten shrine to wash their money in the spring that flows from the side of the mountain. The practice is said to bring good luck.

The courtyard was bustling during our visit with people drying their newly washed bills and coins over burning incense. We had good luck the day we visited:

> *John's Journal, November 17*
> *Since discarding her crutches, Katrina has walked with a severe limp, but week by week, her stride has improved. I decided that I would classify her as "completely healed" when I saw her run spontaneously just for the fun of it. That finally happened today, eighteen weeks after her accident. She was running down a steep hill from Zeniarai Benten shrine. She still has a wee bit of a limp, but if you weren't looking for it, you wouldn't notice it.*

Of course, we sent our bikes home before we left Switzerland in mid-September. Now in mid-November, Katrina had just passed my litmus test for returning to cycling. We discussed sending for our bikes a few times, but there was always some reason why we couldn't do it "this month." Over the remaining months, it just never happened.

www.360degreeslongitude.com/concept3d/360degreeslongitude.kmz

On Being Stupid. I had been terrorized as a little boy by my older brother, Dale, at Anaheim's Disneyland. Thirty-five years later I was finally able to talk about it. Unfortunately, I talked about it with Jordan.

I love Japan and almost everything about it—the people, the culture, the wonderfully weird mannerisms, and especially the gadgets. But I can do without the food. I mean, come on. Who eats fish and rice for breakfast?

Through our travels we had hopes that the kids would learn to expand their diet of plain pasta for dinner and toasted waffles for breakfast. Katrina had come a long way in trying new and different foods, but Japan would be a test. More than anything else I had been looking forward to introducing squid and corn pizza to Jordan. However, in a not-so-subtle way, September let me know I was a wimp when it came to eating beyond *my* comfort zone.

After leaving the Zeniarai Benten shrine, it was time to rustle up some grub. "I remember a McDonald's near the end of the pier that leads out to Enoshima Island," I said.

September patted me on the hand. "We're going to be here for two weeks. You are going to have to face the fact that eventually, you will have to eat Japanese food."

I thought of George Bush senior making the excuse that he was president of the United States and shouldn't have to eat broccoli if he didn't want to. Then I recalled the image of the same George Bush puking and passing out in the lap of Japanese Prime Minister Kiichi Miyazawa. "If I puke in some sushi restaurant," I said, "it'll be on your conscience."

"I'll sleep soundly," September replied.

Enoshima Island is just a few hundred yards off the mainland, connected by a pier. We walked right past the aforementioned McDonald's and onto the island in search of lunch. I remembered the vendors along the main walkway on the island selling what the fishermen had caught that very morning. We would find lunch, but it would squiggle, of that I was certain. As we ambled along, Katrina noted one sidewalk vendor making what looked liked thin, crispy waffles. Mmm. Lunch!

We watched the woman pour batter onto a griddle and then tightly close a lid, cooking the waffle. But I knew that a plain waffle in Japan was too good to be true; there would be a surprise inside. In retribution for inflicting years of plain pasta for dinner on me, I thought the kids deserved a surprise in their lunch. I pointed to the waffles and said, "Why don't we get waffles for lunch?"

Unfortunately, Katrina was paying too much attention. "She put something inside," she said.

"Probably apple filling or something else yummy."

Katrina moved a little closer and to her horror, saw the woman place a little squiggling octopus in the middle of the griddle, pressing it flat with the lid and cooking it into the waffle.

The kids weren't interested in waffles anymore.

Katrina started talking fast and excitedly about how she wanted to rescue those little octopuses. This was more or less expected, since we've known that we've had a Greenpeace recruit in the making since she was about two. I still envision her as a young woman in her twenties in a rubber dinghy trying to cut off the path of a nuclear-powered aircraft carrier.

I tried to sneak off but September was on to me. "I know what you're trying to do, but you're going to eat with us. Into this tempura shop you go."

Tempura is usually pretty safe for the American palate; it's simply prawns or vegetables dipped in batter and fried, then served on a bed of rice. The shop had a picture menu, and when we ordered the food we pointed to the four dishes that looked the most innocent.

When we got our rice, Katrina started to inspect it closely, wanting to avoid any surprises. Being a quick learner can be a handicap.

"Katrina," I said, "you know that inspecting your food too closely is never a good idea."

Katrina reminded me of the first time I ever told her that and then summed up, ". . . so every time I hear you say that, it sort of grosses me out."

September had been on a business trip and I hadn't been to the grocery store in ages. The refrigerator was nearly empty, so I told the kids to go out to the garden and pick some broccoli. Later, when the broccoli was on their plates, Katrina said, "Didn't you wash this? It's covered with aphids!"

I replied, "Oh, you're exaggerating. Any vegetable is bound to have some tiny bug on it. It's cooked. Pick the aphid off and eat the broccoli. You should never examine your food too closely; otherwise, you wouldn't ever eat anything."

Problem was, the broccoli was *covered* with the critters. I found myself forcing a smile because I had already eaten a big plate of it. That's how I earned my reputation of "eat first and ask questions later."

Now in the tempura shop, Katrina was examining each individual rice kernel in her bowl.

"Eewww! Some of these rice kernels look like tiny fish! I am not eating this!"

"For heaven's sake, Katrina, they're just bean sprouts. They won't kill you. Starving children in China would be happy to have that."

"Since when do bean sprouts have eyes?"

"They are not eyes! It is a bean sprout, and that is the seed."

"I am not eating it!"

"Fine. Pick out the bean sprouts. I'll eat them."

With that, I ate a couple of bean sprouts to prove my point. They were too little to taste like anything. As the meal progressed, Katrina started to assign imaginary fish parts to her bean sprouts. She could see fins and a mouth and a spine through each transparent little body.

"Give me a break!" I finally said. "Show me the gills!"

So she did. I took the tiny bean sprout and with my 45-year-old eyes tried to focus on it. "No eyes, no tail, no gills. Bean sprout."

"It is a fish!" she persisted. "You need your reading glasses!"

Ahem. I reached for my glasses and sought out the best light. To my surprise, I found I was holding a tiny, narrow fish, no more than a quarter of an inch long.

Youth triumphs over experience. This was a new concept for me, and I wasn't too keen on it. Katrina made note of future "I told you so" rights.

As an island nation, it's logical that the dietary staples in Japan come from the sea. In the twenty-first century other options than getting breakfast off a hook are available, but the Japanese culture is arguably more steeped in time-honored tradition than many others. The British might argue otherwise, but how many British teenagers have you seen bowing while speaking on a cell phone? Anyhow, I suspect tradition is a big reason why fish consumption remains high, as it couldn't be because of taste.

But, the times they are a-changin'. We found a Baskin-Robbins and Mister Donut at nearly every train station. That certainly wasn't the case twelve years ago.

• • •

"Japanese society," I explained, as we were checking into a traditional Japanese inn, "lives by a complex set of time-honored customs, and everyone we meet will be courteous to a fault. As a *gaijin* (foreigner) we don't stand a chance of ever learning what is expected and all of the rules that govern society. Luckily, we're given a lot of slack and we're more or less expected to use the wrong fork with our dinner salad. It provides them with a lot of entertainment."

"Dad, Japanese don't use forks," Jordan countered.

"It's just an example."

"I didn't know you were supposed to use a special fork for eating salad," Katrina added. "How is it different from a normal fork?"

"I could never figure that one out," I said, "but you're missing my point—there are really only two things you must never do in Japan: no footwear on the tatami mats and no soap in the bathtub. It's well known that shoes are not allowed in the house and that once inside, you wear slippers. What is less well known is that the slippers must not be worn inside a room whose floor is covered with a tatami mat. Tatami mats are worthy of bare toes or stockinged feet only."

Unfortunately, the thrill of huffing four overstuffed suitcases up two flights of stairs in our traditional-style inn left my sense of recollection in a bit of a fog.

"*Please*," our host said firmly, "do not wear slippers on the tatami mats."

Oops. Fatal etiquette rule number one had gone "poof."

After accidentally wearing my slippers on the tatami mats, I had earned the privilege of getting a tutorial on Japanese etiquette at every turn, as I constantly found our host at my elbow.

"Have you seen Hosono-san?" I asked September when she returned to our room.

"No, why?"

"He's been following me around. Now that I'm off to take a bath, the last thing I want is for him to follow me in."

I slipped quietly into the hallway, but Hosono-san had his radar locked onto me. He followed me into the bathing room to give me instructions on the proper procedures. The Japanese are obsessed with the bathing experience.

"The traditional Japanese bath," Hosono-san explained, "is preceded by first soaping yourself up outside of the bathtub. Then you must rinse off completely by taking this bucket and pouring it over you."

I knew all this, but smiled appreciatively while simultaneously suppressing the urge to drop my towel and crack it locker-room style to get rid of him.

"Only when all the soap has been rinsed away are you to get into the bath. No soap is allowed in the *o-furo*."

The reason for this process is that the water in the tub is shared by the entire family, or if you are at a Japanese inn, by everyone in the inn. This method ensures that the water stays clean. Or at least it doesn't get revolting.

To facilitate the bathing ritual, the bathing area is much different than it is in the United States. Every bathroom has a drain in the floor so you can pour buckets of water over yourself as you rinse yourself free of soap. A modern Japanese house may have a shower right in the middle of the room, but there is no dedicated stall. The bathtub itself is off in a corner, usually with a cover over it so the water stays warm and nothing nasty, like soap residue, makes it in.

I prefer this to the American system, particularly since a Japanese *o-furo* has no overflow. You can sit in a Japanese tub and have the water come up to your chin: If water sloshes over the edge, *shikata ga nai* (Japanese for *c'est la vie*) because the drain is in the middle of the floor. When we remodeled our master bath back home, we did it Japanese style.

Which is unfortunate. Because even though the master bath back home is Japanese style, the kids' bathroom is plain vanilla. This meant that Jordan had spent the previous eight and a half years of his life being told not to get the floor wet when he took a bath; in Japan, that's what you are *supposed* to do.

So despite being told to be sure not to get soap in the bathtub, Jordan refused to stand in the middle of the bathroom and take a shower ("Mom might get mad if I did that") and instead hauled the shower hose over to the bathtub, climbed in, and took his shower standing right in it. I suspect Hosono-san resorted to cleansing the tub with acetone. Or maybe he had the tub removed and replaced. I dunno. I do know we are not on his Christmas card list.

. . .

Kyoto is famous for its fall colors and the Japanese will book tours of the area months in advance, hoping to guess the precise week when the colors peak; by luck, we stumbled into the peak autumn colors, which were stunning.

More than its fall colors, Kyoto is famous for copious shrines and temples, which we seemed to be visiting simultaneously with every citizen of Japan. I marveled when visiting to learn that such-and-such shogun had a dream here in the year 1152. When we visit historic places in California the kids go bug eyed when something dates to 1852. It casts the term "historic" in a different light.

While visiting the various shrines, Katrina and I were standing on a crowded street corner waiting for the light to change before crossing the street. We were shoulder-to-shoulder with other pedestrians, so per our custom, we held hands so we wouldn't get separated by a sea of people sweeping us in opposing directions as soon as the light changed.

Suddenly I felt someone squeezing into position between Katrina and me, with elbows in my thigh pushing us apart. Looking down to scold Jordan, I was shocked to see a head of gray hair at about my waist pushing its way between us so it could be in front of the pack when the light changed. No matter that we had been pressed together by the throngs and had been holding hands. With a sharp jab, the gray head separated our hands and was last seen parting her way, Moses-like, through the sea of people in an effort to reach the head of the line.

"I thought you said people in Japan were courteous," Katrina said.

"They are, but every rule needs an exception, I suppose, and little old ladies are exempt from everything."

We were making our way to the Kyoto main train station. There was a beautiful Christmas tree at the top of a set of escalators. Japan is completely gadget crazy and perhaps nothing is more revered than the cell phone/camera/PDA/MP3 player. Hours later I was still able to close my eyes and see spots from all of the flashes of wannabe cell phone photographers snapping pictures of the tree as they were going up while I was going down. On the average subway at least fifty percent of the people are furiously working the keypads of their cell phones with their thumbs, smoke curling from the tiny screens.

What's worse is that they don't put the blasted things away when they hop off the subway. I had gotten used to seeing people bowing while talking on the phone in the pre-cell phone era. Entering the cell phone into the dynamic was a mistake. Anyone who has a bumper sticker on his car that says shut up and drive should try walking on a sidewalk in Japan while he's in a rush to get somewhere. Where's my water cannon when I need it?

• • •

Hiroshima is a huge and bustling city, and apart from the notable exception of the Atomic Bomb Dome, there is no evidence of the destruction that befell this city some 60-plus years earlier.

After arriving on the *shinkansen*, we celebrated Thanksgiving Day in Hiroshima at the Memorial Peace Park. As we made our way to the museum, Jordan protested most emphatically, "I've already done my lifetime quota of museums!" We made him go in anyway. We are such meanies.

After 30 minutes in the museum, I whispered to September, "All things considered Jordan seems to be absorbing quite a bit."

"Yes, but not as much as Katrina," September said. The museum was easily understandable by children and Katrina had been studying the captions on every display and was the slowest progressing through the exhibits.

"I suspect that's because she just finished two books about World War II." One book had been written from the perspective of a Japanese girl, and the other by a Korean girl—both autobiographies of living through that era. Each painted a grim portrait of the "other side," and made you sympathize with the main character's plight. Of course her reading list had been planned that way for a reason.

Watching Katrina for a few moments I said to September, "I'm glad to see this is having such an impact. After Auschwitz, I thought the kids might be too young to empathize."

> *Katrina's Journal, November 24*
>
> *Today we went to the Hiroshima Memorial Peace Park, which is a museum that told us all about the atomic bomb, and about what people experienced after it was dropped. Outside there is an eternal flame, a flame that will only be extinguished when all the nuclear weapons in the world are destroyed. After that we went to see a memorial to a girl [Sadako Sasaki] who died years after the bomb was dropped, and during her eight months in the hospital tried to fold one thousand paper cranes, expressing her desire to live. We had studied about her at school.*

Out of all the World War II–related museums we visited, from Utah Beach to Auschwitz, the Memorial Peace Park had the most emotional impact on me. Nothing was sugarcoated. Not that anything was sugarcoated at Auschwitz, but this was much more visceral.

The Japanese presented a balanced viewpoint, even acknowledging that they were the aggressors in the war, used slave labor, and did some bad things to the Koreans and Chinese. It surprised me to see implicitly mentioned that dropping the bomb probably saved lives in the long run.

Also presented was a thorough account of the horrors of being a survivor of a nuclear blast, including the saga of the lives and premature deaths of those who came through the initial blast seemingly uninjured, leaving no question that the luckiest were those who died instantly.

When you walk through the museum, the first exhibit area is about the war itself, and what life was like for people in Japan during that time. A lot of floor space was devoted to Japan readying itself for invasion, and calling on its people for "One Hundred Million Honorable Deaths." It surprised me to see this in print because it acknowledged that they knew they were going to lose, yet they weren't gong to surrender. More importantly, it acknowledged that those in power would toss away so many lives to uphold their idea of honor.

This first exhibit area leads into a succession of displays about individual stories of those who died instantly, and those who thought they survived. One of the most memorable was a blackened stone wall that had been brought into the museum. It was an "inverse shadow" of where someone had been standing when the bomb dropped. The intensity of the heat blackened the wall, but where that person had been standing shielded the wall from the heat and permanently created the human form of an "inverse shadow." It was creepy to stand in the outline of the shadow.

From the creepy to the horrifying were the vivid pictures and the video of the burns that people suffered over their entire bodies. There were also descriptions of melted fingernails and how they grew back black, embedded with blood vessels, which were painful to trim. There were pictures of what looked like melted skin hanging off backs and faces. It was truly horrifying.

On to the heart wrenching, the museum showcased stories of people who came through with no obvious injuries, but who suffered in the coming weeks and years. One of these was the story of a brother and sister, both of whom died within several weeks of the bomb, but who appeared uninjured in the initial aftermath. This description gave a week-by-week account of their deteriorating health, and culminated with the description of how they vomited up what appeared to be their internal organs, dying shortly afterward.

We quietly stepped out of the museum. The cool autumn day pulled us into the present, giving us emotional whiplash. No one spoke as we made our way to the train that would take us to our hostel.

• • •

Western culture has seeped into every corner of Japan from language to movies—it's even making inroads into the food. It's enough to make a Yank feel right at home. Yet before you start filling out Japanese immigration application papers, you should know that a *gaijin* will never be able understand the Japanese mind. For example, there are no swear words in Japanese; if you *really* want to insult someone, you merely neglect to mention that they are honorable. Continuing with this example, if your boss's name is Fred, without fail you call him Fred-*san* (Honorable Fred). Calling him Fred without the *san* could put him into a murderous rage. Of course, wearing your shoes on his tatami mat or using soap in his bathtub would also do the trick.

www.360degreeslongitude.com/concept3d/360degreeslongitude.kmz

Nuclear Powered Toilet Seats. The Japanese are to be credited with probably the most endearing, yet useless invention known to mankind— the heated toilet seat. But it doesn't stop there. Oh, no. It doesn't stop there.

14.

The Cruise Ship of Pain

November 26–December 15
The People's Republic of China

First impressions can teach you a lot about a person or a place. They can also be terribly deceiving. China was more different from what I had imagined than any other place we visited during our 52 weeks abroad. That impression started upon our arrival in Beijing. I saw a vibrant and modern city with wide streets. Its citizens were dressed no differently than, say, those of Seattle. Perhaps I was expecting a dirty, gray city whose citizens dressed in drab clothes and scurried about going to political party meetings? Despite the cosmopolitan veneer in Beijing and other major cities, by the time I left China I realized it was a world so different from mine, visiting was like interplanetary travel without the inconvenience of leaving Mother Earth.

We had laid out the route for the World-the-Round Trip prior to our departure so we would experience perpetual summer. That was the plan. Later, when we realized we would be arriving in Beijing in late November, September asked, "How cold do you think it'll be?"

"Probably a wee bit," I said, "but it isn't officially winter until the end of December. We should be okay."

Not. It was bitter cold. "If we're going to see Tiananmen Square and hike the Great Wall," September announced after our arrival, "we're going to need some winter clothes."

Our hostel in Beijing was in its own little world, known as a *hutong*: a black hole of a neighborhood. A *hutong* is bounded by a large city block, but once inside there is an absurd maze of "streets" intended for pedestrian traffic with the occasional car snaking through, simultaneously scraping paint off both sides of the mortar work. Rumor has it that people live their whole lives in a *hutong* and never leave. Truth is, they just can't find their way out. A casual visitor to the city may see the wide streets and the dazzling lights, but you can't understand the soul of the city without stepping inside a *hutong*. It's a metaphor for China as a whole.

If you knew the way without getting lost, our *hutong* was a few minutes by foot from Tiananmen Square. In those few minutes there were no fewer than three KFCs and enough North Face counterfeit outlets to outfit the army of a medium-sized country. Of course that is where the tourists shop and eat. Beijing residents shop and eat in the countless markets and nameless shops that make up the soul of the *hutong*.

On our way to Tiananmen Square, we filled the gaps in our cold weather gear for about what one would expect to pay for lunch for one. On the flight from Japan, we had a long discussion about, of all things, copyright infringement, intellectual property, and counterfeit products. Yet, while shopping for cold-weather gear it was evident that we simply couldn't purchase verifiable genuine name brands. Items were priced too low to be genuine. Most were similar in form and function to the name brands, with a slight misspelling of the name.

"We should be warmer now," September said after our quick shopping trip. We then made our way to Tiananmen Square and the Forbidden City to pay our respects to Chairman Mao.

The Forbidden City has an interesting past, to say the least. To protect the emperor's bloodline, aside from the emperor himself only eunuchs were allowed into the inner courtyards of the palace where the imperial family and harem lived. Even the emperor's male children were exiled once they hit puberty. The life of a eunuch is fascinating in a macabre sort of way. Poor families provided young boys to the emperor as a way to elevate the status of their family. Once accepted, the young boys were castrated and then dedicated their lives to serving the royal family. Since all but the eunuchs were forbidden in the inner courtyards, some wielded great power. This practice began in the 16th and lasted until the 20th century. Sun Yaoting was a mere nine years old when his family placed him into the service of the emperor Pu Yi just months before the Manchu Dynasty was overthrown in 1911, ending the practice. The eunuch era fully died when Mr. Yaoting passed away in 1996.

Tiananmen Square was built in 1420 and opens up to a plaza of over a hundred acres, and has been a gathering place of political and social importance for centuries. More recently it is where the People's Republic of China was proclaimed a state by Mao in 1949, and 40 years later was ground zero for the student protests where a lone student stood his ground against an advancing tank.

When we visited, the sky was brilliant blue, but a fierce wind and the bitter cold bit our exposed skin. Although we had come to peruse the site, after just a few minutes we were looking for any place that had four walls and a heater. Suddenly I felt a tug on my sleeve and a whisper in my ear, "Psst. Hey buddy—I have the latest *Harry Potter*! DVDs. Only eight yuan" (about US$1). The young man opened his ankle-length coat a bit to reveal a decent selection of late-release movies on DVD. Never mind that the latest *Harry Potter* was still in its debut weekend in local theaters.

"You come my shop. I show you. Very quality! I have very more at my shop!"

September and I cast a wary eye at each other but the icy cold had impaired our judgment, and his shop promised warmth. We started to follow him as he darted into an alternate *hutong* entrance and zipped off down a narrow alleyway and turned left, right, left, then went straight for a while then left, right, right, then down to the dead end of a dark and narrow alley.

By this time alarms were ringing in my head, "Danger! Danger! Danger, Will Robinson!" If the guy was setting us up to be mugged, he certainly did it right because as soon as we passed over the event horizon, we were lost. In his "shop" there were several harried-looking folks in a small room containing bunk beds, a one-burner stove top, and the smallest refrigerator I had ever seen.

Past the cramped living quarters was a small warehouse with copies of every DVD known to mankind, and some not yet known.

"These movies are COUNTERFEIT!" Katrina protested loudly.

"Yes, they are," I replied. "So are the winter clothes we just bought."

"But why are we even here?"

That was a good question, to which there wasn't a good answer. We had just watched the latest *Harry Potter* in the theater the night before, but curiosity—and the desperate desire to warm up—had got the best of us, and now we found ourselves in a place we didn't really want to be.

I couldn't make my mouth form a meaningful answer and Katrina knew it. After a moment, she pointed out, "If you buy that DVD, you're encouraging people to copy movies illegally."

As Katrina was dialing in the guilt, I was silently justifying making a quick purchase and then leaving. After all, what was the difference between buying the clothes and buying the DVD? At that moment, I just wanted to get outside as soon as possible. It seemed buying something was the path of least resistance.

Jordan's Journal, November 29

Today we went to Tiananmen Square. Some people told us to go to the art museum and buy their paintings because it was the last day you could buy them. I said, "Hey Dad, if I put my toe in one more museum I'll explode." That made them go away. We bought a counterfeit copy of Harry Potter *on DVD. When we went to the hostel to watch it, it was in Chinese but it had funny subtitles in English. Like when Mr. Malfoy said that Hermione's parents were Muggles it said "Melons the dishonorable parents are?" And when Mr. Malfoy was saying "red hair" to Ron it said "stupid hair." Katrina wouldn't watch it with us.*

Hiking along the Great Wall near Beijing was Jordan's wish for our trip. As we made our way toward Jinshanling it was clear that the affluence of the city didn't extend to the countryside.

"We've made a friend," I said, after a few moments of hiking along the wall. Each of the Western tourists was being followed by a local villager.

Our new friend followed us for the duration of our five-hour hike, every so often seeing if we might need a new bracelet or a bottle of water. We named her the Water-Bottle Lady. She didn't speak a word of English. She seemed to be pointing out her village on the horizon of the barren December landscape.

Late in our hike we stopped for lunch. The Water-Bottle Lady lingered a safe distance away. "We have an extra sandwich," September said. "We should see if the Water-Bottle Lady wants it."

The Water-Bottle Lady was delighted at the prospect of such a treat. Derek, who was traveling in our group and could speak Chinese, told us she had never seen a sandwich before. She closely inspected the contents between the two slices of bread. When she discovered it had a bit of meat in it, she was astonished.

After our brief lunch, we prepared to finish the last leg of our trek along the Great Wall. "Katrina, go throw away these water bottles," I said. The Water-Bottle Lady reacted with a mixture of surprise and horror. She started speaking a mile a minute and took the water bottles and placed them in a bag.

Derek interpreted for us: "She's explaining that thirteen empty plastic bottles can be traded for one bowl of rice."

It's hard not to feel guilty for the relative luxury of being able to eat at will.

Katrina's Journal, November 30

Today we went to the Great Wall. We had to get up early to catch a bus that would take us there. After a couple of hours of reading our books on the bus, we arrived at the Great Wall. First you had to walk up to the top of a mountain to get to the wall. It was really cold.

Mom thought hiking along the Great Wall would just be like walking down a cobblestone street, but it wasn't. The wall stretched as far as you could see, on the ridge of a mountain, twisting and turning. And because it was along a mountain ridge, hiking along the wall was up, down, up, down, sometimes so steep it was like climbing a ladder. Sometimes there wasn't much of a wall and while going up to the towers there weren't steps. You had to pull yourself up, using one of the wobbly stones placed there. In other words, it was SO MUCH FUN. One time I was pulling myself up a steep section of stairs with my hands and I wasn't watching where I was going and I almost fell over the edge.

At the end of our hike there was a zip line over a river. Jordan and I did it. You were harnessed in, and then you went over a river, way high up, maybe a hundred feet or more. WHHEEE!!!

Later that evening, safe in our *hutong*, we were looking at a menu posted in front of a small restaurant. English subtitles that accompanied the Chinese characters read "sweet meat," but there was picture of a dog at the bottom of the Chinese side of the menu. Pointing at the picture, I remarked, "Almost every place we've visited since leaving Europe has had a dog problem. Have you noticed that there are no feral dogs here?"

Katrina was horrified. "Ewwww!"

I learned on a previous visit to Hong Kong that the California variant of Chinese food I am so fond of is distinctly different from the real deal. It wasn't therefore a complete surprise when crunchy bovine intestines, goat's penis, and other fascinating entrees appeared on restaurant menus. The picture of Spot was unnerving, though.

John's Journal, December 3

We have been taking turns reading some of Katrina's books, which are fascinating. Red Scarf Girl is set in the Cultural Revolution that started in the late 1960s. I had heard about the Cultural Revolution, but never understood what it was. The

Great Proletarian Cultural Revolution was little more than Mao Zedong trying to retain power. What it meant to the guy on the street though, was that anyone with an education was persecuted and anyone who fancied Western goods was arrested.

A stroll around Beijing in the early 21st century makes it clear that the Cultural Revolution failed. There was a Rolls-Royce dealer at the same shopping complex as the movie theater, for crying out loud!

Another memorable book we've been reading is The Diary of Ma Yan, *written by a young girl about Katrina's age. How her diary came to be in the hands of a French journalist is remarkable. Her story is about the struggle of life in rural China and her resolution to rise above the poverty and chronic hunger she faces. Showing maturity well beyond her years, Ma Yan determines that she needs to continue her education, but her parents can't afford it. It surprises me that people in rural China are hungry and can't afford an education. Wasn't the idea to spread the wealth?*

"I have an action item for you."

September was looking too relaxed in our hostel room. She looked up and responded dryly, "How can I serve you?"

I tossed her our guidebook and said, "We have to be in Hong Kong in about three weeks. Find some place we can go that's warmer." Beijing was good to us and we stayed longer than intended, but even with the mittens, hats, and sweatshirts we had acquired it was just too darned cold.

An hour later September said, "We should go on a cruise down the Yangtze River through the Three Gorges."

"I thought they built a dam and it was flooded."

"Almost. It goes up in stages, and isn't quite completed yet."

"I'll take it under advisement. It has got to be warmer than Beijing. That is my only requirement."

The idea of a "cruise" down the Yangtze River was highly appealing to the kids, who had learned about cruises from their friends. We overheard them talking about the prospect of our Yangtze cruise.

"Jenny told me their cruise ship had, like, five different restaurants where you could just go eat as much as you want!" Katrina said.

"Hunter told me their cruise ship had three different swimming pools, one just for kids!" Jordan responded.

It didn't take much research to learn that we could expect it to be 20 degrees warmer along the Yangtze River than in Beijing, so we caught a flight to Chongqing, a tiny city with a population of a mere four million.

Since it would be almost midnight before we could get on our boat, we went to a restaurant to kill time as well as fed ourselves. After we ordered, we found ourselves briefly alone. "I wish you wouldn't do that," Jordan complained, trying to melt into the seat of his chair. He was objecting to my method of ordering chicken.

"Our waitress will go home tonight and tell her parents that some American came in and ordered by clucking and flapping his arms," I said. "Probably doesn't happen very often."

Our waitress returned with our order as well as the entire kitchen staff. "Why are they all standing around our table, watching us?" Katrina asked.

"We're the evening's entertainment," September said. "As your father well pointed out, how often does someone order by flapping his arms?"

"I was only trying to ensure that we wouldn't dine on Spot!" I said in defense. No fewer than six staff members gathered around our table. I consider myself pretty expert with chopsticks, but I never before had to use them to retrieve noodles from a hot pot. Every time one of us fumbled with the choppers, it drew laughter from the sidelines.

"I guess in a country of 1.3 billion people," September mused, "there is no such thing as privacy."

To a Westerner it is rude beyond words to point, gawk, or otherwise observe strangers in their personal space. Such behavior is accepted, even expected, in China. As outsiders, we were fair game and it was open season. Everywhere we went it was as though the entire family was being patted on the head.

After dinner we passed a grocery store on our way to the pier. "We don't know what we'll find on board," September pointed out. "We should be ready with enough food for the entire four days."

We ducked inside and found a very modern store that in many regards wouldn't look out of place as your corner supermarket, except it was packed cheek to jowl with about ten employees for every seven or eight customers. Noting the staff-to-customer ratio, I commented, "This must be a curse of overpopulation and cheap labor."

"Perhaps," September replied. "It surely doesn't seem to be driven by any economic principle I studied in school."

We made the acquaintance of the Cruise Ship of Pain just before midnight. ❧ We had splurged for the deluxe cabin with the ensuite bathroom.

Opening the door to our cabin, September stood still in silent disbelief. Being a bona fide guy I usually don't notice the décor of my surroundings, but I couldn't help it in this case. The water-stained walls and ground-up chips of paint in the carpet gave it that homey lived-in feel, as did the half-consumed cups of tea left from the previous occupants. I broke the silence. "I'm glad we got the deluxe cabin!"

"We've slept in worse," September replied. "We'll survive." Then after a pause she seemed to change her mind about surviving. "I can see my breath in here! Can you please find the heat?"

We had, of course, escaped Beijing to get out of the cold. I walked over to the heater and switched on the fan; it dutifully blew cold air. "It'll probably take a minute or so to warm up."

Twenty minutes later I removed the cowling so I could attempt to coerce some heat from it. "It's no use," I said. "The fan works fine, drawing in air through a radiator. Problem is, the radiator is completely disconnected from any hot water source. Or any source at all. The pipe is just dangling." Over the next four days we took turns blow drying our feet with September's hair dryer to remove the blue tinge. It was our only source of warmth.

Even though it was after midnight, Katrina and Jordan were happily making tents out of moldy blankets in the top bunks. It gave them something to do while I was dismantling the heater. I admitted defeat with the heater and said, "Okay, guys. Bed."

Jordan had the misfortune of being the first to use the ensuite bathroom. "AAAGGGGHHH!"

"Jordan, keep it down! You don't want to wake up our neighbors!"

"All I did was flush the toilet and this ice cold water squirted me all over!"

The next morning at 6:00 a.m. we were all sleeping deeply, only to be awakened by the sound of fingernails on a chalkboard with violin accompaniment. The PA speaker, *right in our room,* was pumping out Chinese Muzak.

"It can't be Ramadan or time to pray!" September cried out. "Make it stop!"

Later that morning we were in the dining room eating Cheerios with the boxed UHT milk sludge that is ubiquitous in the developing world. The kids were doing their morning homework and in came an American couple, one in a wheelchair.

"Name is Jeff. Where'd you get Cheerios in the PRC?" the man asked.

"John," I said, shaking his hand. "We got them in Chongqing at a grocery store, before we got on the boat. How did you enjoy the wake-up service?"

"Jeff practically exploded out of bed," the woman in the wheelchair explained. "I thought I was going to have to peel him off the ceiling."

"I can help you there," I said. "Remove the molding off the speaker and you can unplug it." I figured we couldn't understand the announcement to abandon ship anyway. It worked so well that I did the same thing to the two speakers in the hall outside our room. Of course the staff didn't look too thrilled with what I was doing, but they didn't stop me.

Jeff and Muffy were from Utah. Muffy had been on the U.S. Ski Team until a misguided tree ended her career. Now she skis with the Paralympic Team.

"So, do you have any heat in your room or hot water in your shower?" Jeff asked.

"Zip. But we did pay extra for the ensuite bathroom."

"Don't feel too bad," Jeff replied. "We paid extra for an English-speaking guide."

"Yes," September said, "it's not worth getting hung up over. You don't know what you really agreed to anyway. A lot could be lost in translation. The important thing is to roll with it and enjoy the spectacular scenery."

"You're right, of course," Muffy agreed. "But with no hot water, only the strong of constitution will be showering during the next four days."

About that time a nice grandmotherly woman came in and sat next to us. She smiled broadly and I returned the smile. She then pulled a garbage can close to her and proceeded to hack into it for a good minute or two. We had been exposed to this in Beijing, as the Chinese are infamous for their hacking and spitting. When she stopped, I started to feel the knot in my stomach relax. She then proceeded to blow her nose, sans tissue, into the trash can as well.

"I'm glad I don't have to empty the trash," Jordan remarked.

We spent the next two days floating through the Yangtze River Gorge. The river was calm, betraying the rugged terrain that rose high above us on either side. Floating through the gorges should be a "must do" for any visit to China—even after the dam is finished. During our cruise we noted markers on the cliffs and mountains clearly showing the expected water level upon completion of the dam. There will be plenty of stunning scenery after the dam is finished. Just be smarter than we were, because there are other boats marketed to Westerners!

Our "cruise" reminded us of how miserable travel can be. Typical of the kids, they forgot to notice. They were even disappointed when our boat broke down and we were rescued by another boat, because the new boat didn't have a toilet that shot jets of water when you flushed it.

Wuhan was where we had expected to disembark. Several hours before Mr. Singy-Person would have been trying to test my reflexes mid-REM, a loud banging came on our door. Mr. Grumpy opened it and shouted at us in Chinese. I did what any other sleep-deprived consumer would do. I yelled back and put a pillow over my head and went back to sleep.

Mr. Grumpy didn't give up so easily. Twenty minutes later, he was banging on the door again, only this time he came prepared with someone who could speak English. "You have to get off the boat now."

"I usually like my boats to be at the dock first. That's supposed to be after 7:00 a.m. A full night's sleep is a plus, too," I said.

"We are approaching Wuhan now. Everyone must be off the boat in twenty minutes!" Then Mr. Grumpy and his English-speaking assistant left to bang on more doors.

"Hmphf!" I grunted, as they slammed the door shut. "They'll have to throw me off. I paid for a full night's sleep."

They called my bluff. Twenty minutes later the boat had docked and Mr. Grumpy was taking our luggage down the ramp to shore. If we wanted to see it again, we were obliged to follow. Before I could say, "Gee, this doesn't *look* like a big city," our luggage was being loaded onto a bus. Mr. Grumpy's sidekick announced, "This bus will take you to Wuhan."

"You said we were *in* Wuhan!" I countered, but they simply walked away. That was the last I saw of Mr. Grumpy and his sidekick. We sat on the bus a long time, and that was before it ever started moving. The seconds seemed like hours in the predawn fog. Finally, off in the distance, we understood why we were waiting when we saw Jeff pushing Muffy in her wheelchair.

Jeff poked his head in the door. A few moments later someone was shouting at him in Chinese. September said to no one in particular, "Gee, what is that all about?" A moment or two later, Jeff was carrying Muffy on his back down the aisle of the bus. I noted that Muffy's knees were clipping people in the head as he carried her to the back of the bus; it didn't look as though he was trying to prevent it.

"What was that about?" September asked Muffy when they got settled near us.

"There was one empty seat up front," Muffy replied. "Jeff asked the man sitting next to it if he would move so we could have two seats together up front. They guy wouldn't budge and the only other seats were in the back of the bus."

September thought for a moment and then said, "I guess in a place with 1.3 billion people, you stake your claim and don't budge for anything."

Four hours later we watched the sun rise above Wuhan as we drove into the city.

Independent travel in China means getting on a bus or a train and hoping that it takes you where you want to go. You just wait until you are told (or forced) to disembark, and are left scratching your head while you watch the dust settle from the departing bus (or train). We felt gratitude to a higher power when we found ourselves deposited in the correct time zone.

We said good-bye to Jeff and Muffy in Wuhan and spent the next several hours at a bustling train station. Dazed and confused from lack of sleep and communication skills, we were hoping to beat the odds and actually make the correct connection to yet another unfamiliar place. After some head scratching, we boarded an overnight train to the southern city of Guilin and arrived before sunrise. It was colder than it had a right to be, being a scant three degrees above the Tropic of Cancer. It was time to flex our economic muscle and get a real hotel with central heating. A short walk from Guilin's train station was a hotel that looked like any other business-class hotel I had stayed in when someone else was paying the bills.

"It is *freezing* in here!" I exclaimed in disbelief upon entering our hotel room. The windows were wide open, creating a stiff breeze when the door was opened. "Let's get those windows closed and find the thermostat!"

September closed the windows and I started a search for a thermostat. After a few moments I had to conclude there was none. "Nowhere in the lobby was it posted, 'Warning! This hotel has no heat!'" I protested. "At least not in a language we can read."

"Okay, the way I see it we either have a bonfire in the middle of the bed, or go shopping for a space heater. Right after my shower." It had been four days on the Cruise Ship of Pain with no showers, then another twenty-four hours making our way to Guilin. I don't think I have ever been so happy to feel hot water come out of a tap.

. . .

We began our quest for a space heater, quickly locating a large department store a few blocks from the hotel. It was a large, modern glass and chrome building and as we walked in it appeared dark and deserted; yet the sound of Christmas carols beckoned us up the escalator to the second level. Arriving on the second floor, we found a store stocked and decorated for Christmas that would have fit right in in any sub-urb back home. Except that it was deserted. "It's freezing in here, too," September said. "Maybe they're closed."

"It can't be closed," I said. "The doors are wide open." After walking around the store for a bit, we found a group of five employees. We startled them when we brought over a space heater we wanted to buy.

"Interesting," September said, as we were taking our treasure back to the hotel. "Same thing as the grocery store in Chongqing, only different."

"How's that?" Katrina replied.

"This store had more employees than shoppers, even though there were only five employees. At that grocery store in Chongqing, there were also more employees than shoppers, but it was packed."

Guilin is a large, modern, bustling city. The surrounding mountains have been described as the Switzerland of China, although it doesn't look anything like Switzerland. The towering geological formations are as beautiful as they are bizarre and look like they were designed by Dr. Seuss. I would call it a green version of Cappadocia, but that doesn't spin as well.

The weather had been gloomy, but one afternoon the sun broke through the clouds. We took the opportunity to stroll along the elaborately landscaped walkways along the Li River. We sat on a bench overlooking a large pagoda and watched the river slip quietly by. Behind us traffic was bustling.

Suddenly there was a horn blaring and squealing tires. We all turned and saw a woman picking herself off of the pavement and shaking her first at a shiny Mercedes.

"That car almost hit that lady!" Katrina exclaimed.

"I've been watching how drivers interact with each other as well," I replied. "If I didn't know any better, I'd think the fancier cars have the right of way. Perhaps those who have no car at all are at the very bottom of the social ladder."

"That's dumb," Katrina said. "What we own shouldn't matter."

"I'm sure there are parts of our society these people would find dumb," I replied, "but you're right. What kind of car you drive, or whether or not you wear nice clothes, doesn't define who you are."

"That's a very Western sentiment," September countered. "Perhaps in this culture what you own really does define you."

We started back to our hotel, discussing social status and material possessions, including a top-level summary of Road Rage 101. When we returned to our room we found that the cleaning staff had kindly switched off our space heater and opened the windows for us.

One of the things I wanted to do on this trip was to try to understand different cultures, but I just couldn't fathom the lack of heat. Months later, safely in California, I asked a Chinese colleague at work about this. He explained to me: "It is well known that heat is not permitted in dwellings south of the Yangtze River, although that wouldn't apply to a Western hotel or river boat. You traveled too much like a local."

• • •

The woman behind the Internet café's counter was frantic. It took a moment, but I realized that she was blocking Katrina and Jordan from entering. September turned to me. "Are you sure this is *just* an Internet café?"

"It seemed to be that and nothing more when I was here yesterday." Just then the young woman handed me a card written in English that stated: CHILDREN UNDER 18 ARE NOT ALLOWED TO USE THE INTERNET.

Katrina and Jordan were affronted, but that didn't matter. "I don't care how dumb you guys think it is, it's their country and their law. You have to follow it."

"But I want to check my e-mail!" Katrina implored.

Of course I did, too. My mother was a bit frantic about us being in China and had e-mailed me a news article about an outbreak of bird flu. If you were to believe CNN, every chicken in Southeast Asia was infected with avian flu and looking at them cross eyed was enough to contract the disease. I wanted to reassure her that we were in the city and the only chicken we had interfaced with was extra crispy. "Not to worry," I told Katrina. "I'll download your e-mail to my e.brain and you can answer it back at the hotel. I'll then come back here to send it."

The next morning provided another break in the gloomy weather. We headed for the town of Yangshuo for the day. It was an easy bus ride from Guilin and a bike ride along the Li River sounded like a great way to keep out the chill and see the bizarre Seussian landscape. The nice lady at the bicycle rental place seemed to know just what we wanted and she gave us a map in English and pointed us down the road. She forgot to mention that if we were paranoid about bird flu, we shouldn't ride bikes beyond the town limits.

Making our way out of town, we discovered first-hand that bicycles ranked just above pedestrians in the right-of-way tug of war. Gradually the bustling cars gave way to wooden carts and mopeds.

It was liberating to be cycling again and we took our time cycling the dirt roads around and between the Dr. Seuss-shaped mountains. We stopped to look around and munch on apples we had brought with us. A man zoomed by on a moped. He was holding two live ducks by their feet in each hand so that the ducks were dangling upside down from the handlebars. The ducks did not look happy, but I strongly suspected that they wouldn't be unhappy for long.

"Did you see that?" September asked.

"I've been seeing that a lot the last few miles," I replied. "Except those were the first ducks I saw. Every other time it's been chickens dangling upside down. There are chicken farms all over the place." It became clear the Yangshuo countryside is chock-full of chicken and duck farms, but this realization came when it was too late to do anything about it.

"Why do they carry ducks and chickens upside down dangling from the handlebars like that?" Katrina asked. "It's not very nice."

"It's nicer than what will happen next. Those chickens will be McNuggets before the day is over."

Katrina looked thoughtful and I wondered if she was making a plan to free all the chickens in the area.

"Maybe riding our bikes in the traffic isn't our number one concern today," I said.

"What do you mean?" September asked.

I whispered so that the kids couldn't hear. "Bird flu." Of course whispering is the surest way to hold a public conversation in our foursome. "What?! What?! What are you guys whispering about?"

September frowned. "You can really be a half-empty kind of guy."

Thinking of everything that can go wrong, and how to avoid it, was once a big part of my job. "Some habits are hard to break."

www.360degreeslongitude.com/concept3d/360degreeslongitude.kmz

A Very Harry Experience. Without a doubt, the largest language barrier of any place we visited was in the People's Republic of china and finding a theater showing the latest Harry Potter movie in English was Priority One in Beijing.

15.

Immigration Purgatory in the PRC

December 15–December 21
The Special Economic Zone of Shenzhen and Hong Kong

After traveling through China for the better part of a month, we were making our way to Hong Kong where we had a flight to Bangkok in a few days. Officially, Hong Kong has been part of the People's Republic of China since the British Crown transferred sovereignty to the PRC in 1997. That may be, but coming from mainland China, one still must clear passport control to enter the Hong Kong Special Administrative Region. We found ourselves in the Special Economic Zone of Shenzhen, as it is the portal for passing to Hong Kong from the PRC.

I was poring over our guidebook, while September was trying to book a place to stay in Hong Kong. "It says Shenzhen is 'not interesting enough to warrant more than passing through on the way to Hong Kong.' Maybe we should just take the subway to the end of the line, pass through the border, and hope for the best."

"Every place I've tried is full," she said, placing our cell phone down. The GSM cell phone we had bought in London was serving us well. Whenever we got to a new place, we simply popped in a new sim card. "The WTO is meeting in Hong Kong and demonstrators from all over the world are in town. The problem is, demonstrators are like us—cheap. The last person I spoke to said all the budget places are full."

While we sorted out our lodging problem on the other side of the border, we made Shenzhen home for a couple of days. Contrary to our guidebook's description, we found Shenzhen fascinating. In 1980 Shenzhen was a sleepy fishing village of 30,000. A generation later it was four million strong. Shenzhen, and its "Special Economic Zone" is where China officially announced its experiment in "capitalism mixed with socialism and Chinese characteristics." Any visitor would be awe-struck by the modern city and conclude that the Chinese had succeeded with their experiment.

Despite the veneer of success, I can't help but wonder if it will unravel. It hadn't been that long ago when we had been the only shoppers in a large department store. Growth for growth's sake isn't sustainable. Nor had it been that long since we had been followed by the Water-Bottle Lady, trying to gather thirteen empty plastic bottles so she could trade them for a bowl of rice. Despite all its flaws, I couldn't help but conclude that capitalism serves its citizens, even its poor, better.

• • •

As we approached the immigration officer on our way to Hong Kong, passersby were being scanned with a heat sensor for anyone with a fever, quarantining anyone who might have bird flu.

"Did we forget anything important?" September asked. "As soon as we pass through here, there's no returning."

"Why not?" Jordan asked. "Why can't we come back?"

"Our visas are for single entry. To get new ones will take longer than we have."

"We've never had to worry about that before," Katrina noted. "Why is China different?"

"China is uptight about foreigners," I replied. "Just like America is."

After passing through the checkpoint, we boarded the train that would take us to central Hong Kong. "We'll enjoy the outer islands for a few days," September explained to Katrina and Jordan as we boarded a ferry an hour or so later. We simply were not able to find accommodations in Hong Kong proper. "Then when Paul and Derek return, we'll stay with them in the city." Derek had been our on-the-spot interpreter when we hiked the Great Wall and had offered to let us stay at their place in Hong Kong.

Lamma Island was a short ferry ride from Hong Kong Island. We stopped at a tourist office that specialized in finding apartments for short-term stays. After a bit of paperwork, a woman from the office led us into the dark recesses of a *hutong*. After a few quick turns we were standing in front of a furnished apartment that would be home for two days.

"Have you seen the power cable for my e.brain?" We had been in the apartment only an hour, but our suitcases had already exploded, leaving no horizontal surface uncovered.

"No," September answered. "When was the last time you used it?"

"At our hostel back in Shenzhen."

"Maybe it's still there."

A cold chill swept over me. It was just on the other side of the PRC border, at most twenty miles, but a world away for me. I grabbed the cell phone and ran outside, away from the noisy chatter of the kids. A few moments later I returned.

"What's the story?" September asked.

"I, uh, they, uh. The hostel in Shenzhen has my power cable."

After weeks of being cold in China, we were finally warm. The sun was bright and the ocean spray kissed the hiking trails that beckoned across the island. But I had only one thing on my mind: our guidebook said that "sometimes" one can obtain a special one-day visa to visit Shenzhen just by showing up at the border crossing.

So, I did what any unreasonable person in my situation would do. I started toward the PRC in a dead run. I left September and the kids and ran straight toward the ferry terminal. The last ferry back to the island was in about six hours and the round trip to Shenzhen and back would be at least six if not seven hours. So I ran faster.

After catching the ferry, then connecting to the subway, I found myself nearing the PRC border about an hour and a half later. I was making good time and started to relax and watch the TV monitors in the train. Not being able to understand what was being said, or read the captions, it was nevertheless clear that somewhere in the world the police were clashing with rioters in the streets of a big city.

Suddenly a wave of gasps rippled through the car. The look on my face must have given away my bewilderment because someone leaned toward me and said, "The police have closed all access back into Hong Kong."

The big city I was watching on the monitors was Hong Kong and the rioters were WTO protesters. I was cut off, and there was no way to return to September and the kids, at least not that night. I smiled, knowing that there was no longer any reason to rush to make the last ferry, as I couldn't go back anyway. I had my priority, and that was to get my power cable. Once I accomplished that I would worry about where to spend the night.

As I left the Hong Kong Special Administrative Region, the man behind the glass examined my passport and then gave me a smirk. What was that all about?

Hong Kong was now in my rearview mirror, but I was also not yet in the PRC. A hundred or so yards away I could see lines forming for entry into the PRC.

There was a long wait in line to cross the border. I talked to a couple of European passport holders who were going in the same direction I was. They had come to Hong Kong without a Chinese visa and found themselves wanting to visit Shenzhen for a day. I only wanted to visit for an hour, but it still required crossing this line in the sand that someone had drawn on a map more than a hundred years ago.

I watched as my new European friends got to the immigration officer and crossed over into the PRC. They turned to me and smiled and waved. Cool. If they could do it, why couldn't I?

When it was my turn, the nice lady flipped through the pages of my passport. Slowly at first, then faster. "Where is your visa?" she asked.

"I don't have one. I was here this morning and forgot something important. I thought maybe I could go back for an hour or so to retrieve it."

The smile slid from her face and was replaced by a grim expression. It turns out that *most* people can get a special day pass to visit the "Special Economic Zone" of Shenzhen, but Americans can't. No way, no how. It seems that the Chinese are a bit grumpy about how their citizens are being treated by the U.S. immigration authorities post-9/11, and in a tit-for-tat hissy fit are making things a bit difficult for Americans at their borders.

"This is not possible," was the firm and grim reply of Ms. Immigration Control. She confiscated my passport and I was escorted to immigration purgatory between the two borders and into a room of bleary-eyed people who looked like they had been there a long time. I sat down. On my left was an older gentleman with a flowing beard and robes who was clearly Muslim. He looked as though he had been there at least a day. On my right was a young Asian couple dressed in tight black leather, covering as little skin as possible without being arrested for incident exposure. They looked really nervous about something. I couldn't help but think, "Oops."

As I sat there, I found myself wondering about room service. After I had long concluded there was none, a uniformed officer walked into the room with my passport in his hand. Without uttering a word he ushered me back across the border into Hong Kong. As I left the room, I smiled and waved to the bearded Muslim gentleman and the mostly naked Asian couple. Nobody waved back.

On the train back to Hong Kong I silently cursed the U.S. Patriot Act and those uppity U.S. immigration officials who are so successfully annoying the rest of the world. My e.brain was dead for lack of power and it was all their fault.

While I was languishing in immigration purgatory, the police had arrested hundreds of rioters and the routes back to Hong Kong Island had been reopened. I rushed to the ferry terminal only to watch the last ferry sail away.

"An extra ferry has been added tonight," the ticket agent said, "because lots of people have been stranded."

An hour later I was back on Lamma Island. The smugness from catching the last ferry was quickly replaced by the disquiet of the formerly proud. I had only been to our apartment once and that was after blindly following a chattery tourist office employee for several minutes through a *hutong*.

Oops again.

I rambled aimlessly throughout the *hutong*, shattering the stillness of night. *"Katrina!"* I called out at the top of my lungs. *"Jordan!"*

Maybe I'll stumble into our apartment and September will be up waiting for me, I thought. (I would have called out for September, but I have found by experience that when I try that, people look at me funny and then call back, "October!")

Calling out for my kids garnered nasty looks from people I would never see again. It was only after deciding to return to the pier and spend the night on a bench that I noticed a sign with my name on it, taped to a light pole. It was in September's handwriting and read, JOHN: GO THIS WAY with a big arrow pointing the direction I should go. At the next corner was another sign, and then another and another until I finally reached our apartment's front door. Bless her pointy little head. If I wasn't already married to her, I would propose all over again.

．．．

The following morning was the Sunday before Christmas. One of the things we had been enjoying on our travels was attending church whenever we could. Not only did it help us not to confuse our Thou Shalts with our Thou Shalt Nots, it was a great way to meet local people not affiliated with the tourist industry.

We found a 1:30 p.m. English-language service in the Wan Chai district of Hong Kong Island near the home of Paul and Derek, who were returning that day. We would bake cookies for Santa, and they would eat them. We all thought it a fair trade for a few nights' accommodation. As we boarded a ferry to make our move to Hong Kong Island, I told September and the kids about my adventure the previous night.

"After all that, and you still don't have your cable?" Katrina asked.

"Nope."

With glee in his voice, Jordan asked, "Will you miss your brain, Dad?"

I didn't want to talk about it. That's when I changed subjects and told them that for a while I had thought the WTO riots were going to keep me from returning at all.

"Those people are so STOO-pid!" Katrina exclaimed, talking of the rioters.

Jordan, however, was quite intrigued. As we had learned at the Blue Mosque when he made his naughty tally of nonscarf-wearing women, Jordan was fascinated with the concept of civil disobedience. The thought that someone could be so naughty made his whole body pulsate with excitement.

"What do the police do to the rioters, Dad?" Jordan asked.

"Well, sometimes they arrest them and haul them off to jail."

"How many are there?"

"Hundreds, I think."

Jordan started pacing up and down the ferry aisles with excitement. "How can the police arrest hundreds of people? I mean, that's too many people, and the police can't fit them all in one car to take them to jail." Jordan was talking a mile a minute, and his little body shivered with glee. This was an entire world of defiance of which he'd previously been unaware; it made tallying women without head scarves at the Blue Mosque mere child's play.

"In cases like this," I explained, "police might subdue the rioters with tear gas or water cannons and then cart them away in buses designed to hold dozens of prisoners at a time."

Tear gas and water cannons were something Jordan could identify with, as poison gas was an essential element in most Batman movies and practically every video game he had ever played. Jordan sat down and retreated into his private world, ballistic sound effects occasionally escaping his mouth.

We got off the ferry and went a couple of subway stops to the Wan Chai district, where we dropped off our suitcases at Paul and Derek's house, then started out on foot toward the church building. Being the Sunday before Christmas, it would probably be our only chance to sing Christmas songs in a congregation, something that is a family tradition dating back at least one year.

Still several blocks away from the building, we started to see some ominous signs of civil unrest. As we drew closer, it was clear the WTO riots were located exactly where we were headed.

Parked along the side of the road were a series of bomb-removal vans and SWAT vans. The ordinarily bustling pedestrian traffic had given way to legions of bleary-eyed police in bulletproof vests. When we got within sight of the church building, there were hundreds of police in riot gear surrounding a few dozen protesters. The WTO meetings were in progress right across the street from the church building. Blocking access to the church were layers upon layers of riot police in full-body riot gear with tall plastic shields, standing shoulder-to-shoulder.

"Church must be cancelled," I said. "There's no way to even cross the street without cutting through rioters and police."

"There's a pedestrian overpass," September pointed out. "We can use that to cross."

"Perhaps this isn't a good idea," I protested, nevertheless following her up the steps. We wove through clumps of journalists and the delegation from Uganda, who were on their way down. They gave us a wary eye. I knew what they were thinking: "Aren't the police supposed to keep the riffraff away?" I gave them a cheery smile and a wave.

When we got to the overpass above the street, we encountered a line of plastic tape emblazoned with big bold letters blocking the path: POLICE LINE—DO NOT CROSS.

"Okay, we tried," I said. "Forget about church. Let's get out of here."

September was not deterred. "This is too cool!" she exclaimed. "How often do you get to go to a riot before church? Stand up straight," she said quietly to the kids, "look confident and just act like you know what you're doing." She lifted up the police tape, dragged the kids under it, and started marching them across the overpass.

I couldn't believe it. Well, actually I could. September's mother had spent a day in jail a few years earlier for crossing a police line when she tried to drive down her own street, which had been blocked for a parade. I hadn't known that a defective gene could cause one to disregard a police line. "You can't do this!" I protested, trailing along. "You want to get pepper sprayed?"

"I'd like us to sing Christmas hymns as a family in a congregation," September began to pontificate as she led our children over the overpass. "It's the only connection we have with home during the holiday season. History was built on small acts of civil disobedience—the Summer of Love, Rosa Parks, and so on. It's a worthy cause."

"But there's no church today. Do you see anyone else crossing the police line?"

September was not showing any signs of turning around. I figured I couldn't let the three of them go alone, so I followed. As we descended the steps on the other side of the street, we saw dozens of protesters being herded onto police buses, each with an armed escort. I found myself wishing I had brought my camera, but who brings a camera to church?

As we approached the church building, several police in riot gear were sitting near the front door. The entryway was littered with food boxes and bottles. Clearly, the police had been using the area all night long as a place to eat and rest, but by the looks of them, they hadn't been getting much of the latter.

September approached the door confidently and smiled at the police, who were sitting by the entrance as she tried to open it. Several pairs of bloodshot eyes were giving us quizzical looks.

The door was locked, but from inside came a nervous, heavily accented voice. "Who is there? What do you want?"

"We're here for the 1:30 service," I replied.

There was a long pause. I could only imagine what the man was thinking: "These people are clearly not the sharpest tools in the shed." Finally the voice said, "There is no church today. Please go away."

I've never been told to "go away" at church before, but decided to take his advice without offense. We turned and hadn't taken two steps before an official-looking woman approached us, saying, "You are not supposed to be here. How did you get here? What are you doing?"

September smiled. "We were just trying to go to church. Merry Christmas!"

We strolled away and wound back through the scores of bomb-retrieval vans, SWAT vans, police motorcycles, and prisoner transport buses. Jordan paused to pick up something from the ground. His eyes grew wide and he exclaimed, "Look what I found!" as he handed me a tattered brochure.

"Jordan's radar has gone off," I said to September, looking over the brochure. "It looks like there's a Disneyland right here in Hong Kong, and it's only a few subway stops from Paul and Derek's house. Did you know that?"

"That's news to me!"

And with a hopeful look in his eye, Jordan said, "You just never know what's going to happen on the World-the-Round Trip."

* * *

"You just never know what's going to happen on the World-the-Round Trip," September repeated the next day to a feverish Jordan. "We'd like to take you to Disneyland, but if you still have a fever in the morning, we can't go."

Missing Disneyland was the least of our concerns at the moment. We had just passed, albeit accidentally, right through Bird Flu Central a few days earlier. We had just put down our tent stakes, so to speak, in the home of our friends Paul and Derek, who we were now potentially exposing to a nasty virus. We were also to fly to our rendezvous with September's mom in Bangkok on Christmas Eve.

"I remember when we were in England," Katrina offered, "that Jordan got a fever and we just gave him Tylenol."

"You can't pass him through a goat," Derek said. "With the bird flu scare there are checkpoints everywhere. The stakes are too high."

"Pass him through a what!?" we asked simultaneously.

Paul chuckled. "It's a saying around here. A goat will eat anything. You can feed a goat a bunch of fake coins, for example, and when they come out the other side, they look aged—quite authentic looking. But the saying is a metaphor for anything that has been altered for the purpose of deception."

Miraculously, the following morning Jordan's fever was gone. Katrina was quick to point out the benefits of going to church even if we were blocked entry, correlating it with Jordan's sudden recovery, and then summed it up with, "So now we can go to Disneyland!"

I knew she had been praying for some sort of divine intervention, although I wasn't sure if her motives were out of concern for her brother, or out of her desire to go to Disneyland.

Nevertheless, I marveled at her childlike faith . . . and wasn't that what the whole World-the-Round Trip was about? If September and I hadn't had childlike faith, we wouldn't have left California.

"I suppose we can," I said, agreeing with Katrina's analysis. "You just never know what's going to happen on the World-the-Round Trip!"

16.

Nipple-Nibbling Fish

December 21–January 2
Thailand

ne day the Human Genome Project will discover the mutation that causes people, such as my dear wife, to ignore Mother Nature's self-preservation impulse and do things like cross police lines during WTO riots. I knew September had inherited it from her mother, with whom we were now rendezvousing, for Christmas in Thailand. Marie, aka Granny, would apply her own special blend of nurture to our group dynamic. Adding a counter to the eccentricity was September's law-abiding cousin, Melissa, who needed a break from her high-stress job.

We hadn't been in Bangkok an hour when Granny and Melissa showed up at our hotel. The kids spent the next several hours telling Granny everything we had done in the last six months, in one long run-on sentence without breathing once. Luckily, Granny had been able to score a power cable for my e.brain before she came and I had to endure Jordan's taunts that I was "brain dead" no longer. No sooner than I could charge my e.brain than we were on our way to the island of Ko Tao, in the Bay of Thailand.

> *Katrina's Journal, December 23*
> *. . . after we got off the ferry to Ko Tao, we rode in the back of a truck to our beach bungalow. Actually, all the taxis are like that here—you just hop into the back of the truck. There are no seat belts or anything. It's a little bit dangerous, but I like it a lot. Our bungalow is right on the beach and has big boulders by it. We climbed the boulders with Granny.*

It was Christmas Eve and we bought a potted palm tree and decorated it and our rooms with tinsel and garlands that Granny had brought. "I also brought a treat!" Granny said, as she revealed the ingredients for s'mores hidden within her suitcase.

As the sun was setting over our beach bungalow we made a bonfire, burned piles of marshmallows, and started singing Christmas carols as loudly as we could with mouths stuffed. "Would you like to join us?" I asked some Australians who happened by. They curled their noses at the sight of chocolate mixed with marshmallows.

"We could get some Vegemite for these marshmallows, if you'd like," I offered.

But they declined in a very Australian sort of way, which consisted of a graceful taunt and a put down about our country, which we interpreted as "We would be happy to join you if you had beer and sang different songs." They kept moving along the beach to be with the rest of the young backpacker types who pretended they were too cool to notice that it was Christmas Eve.

• • •

Ko Tao was to be a relaxing vacation from our travels, meaning no structured activities. We sort of failed on that, chartering a boat to take the six of us snorkeling one day. The captain brought his wife and two-year-old son as well as a bunch of squished, overripe bananas. "I hope that's not lunch," Jordan whispered to me, pointing at the bananas.

At our first stop, I quickly donned my fins and mask and jumped in while the rest of the group were still on the boat sorting out equipment. The water seemed to boil over with a kaleidoscope of colorful fish. I could clearly see the bottom, about 20 to 30 feet down. We were in a city of huge sea urchins and I went down to get a closer look at them.

When I surfaced for air everyone on the boat was squealing with delight. Only then did I notice why the water was roiling with fish; the captain was tossing the overripe bananas into the water, driving the fish crazy.

These were the varieties of fish you might see in an average saltwater aquarium, about four to six inches long and brilliantly colored with all shades of the rainbow, and utterly harmless. Fish are pretty stupid, yes? I thought so, too. It turns out that fish are stupid, but not as stupid as I am.

I decided to lure the fish over to me by pretending I had food. It worked. Soon I was surrounded by hundreds of eager mouths, each about the diameter of a soda straw, looking for a handout. It was about this time that I noted the captain was feeding the fish from inside the boat; whereas I was pretending to feed them while *in the water*. All the little fishies were very cute when viewed from far away, but less so when they were brushing against me with their mouths working furiously to find something to fill them.

A little voice in my head told me it was time to stop pretending I had food and to get the heck out of there. No sooner had I decided to obey the voice when one of the little fishies found something to munch on. Not to be too graphic, but the water was a bit cold for a warm-blooded mammal such that my, er, "headlights" were on high beam. So this fish took a mouthful of the one thing that was poking out—my right nipple.

A blood-curdling scream ripped through the air. Or it would have, had I not been under two feet of water at the time. My scream just sort of gurgled out pathetically, unheard. It was now clear why September had refused to breastfeed after the kids had sprouted both upper and lower incisors.

While making my getaway from the nipple-nibbling fish, all I could think of was how in some future scenario I would be lying in a morgue while someone was trying to identify my remains:

"Scar on knee—check. Scar from appendectomy—check. Right nipple missing—check. Yup—that's him all right."

It's funny how your brain works when flooded with adrenaline.

I spent the remainder of the day snorkeling with my arms folded resolutely across my chest, hands tucked under my armpits. Everyone else in the group spent the day snickering conspiratorially, sneaking bits of food into the water wherever I happened to be.

Jordan's Journal, December 27
> *Today I ordered lemonade from a restaurant. It tasted horrible! Mom said they must have accidentally put salt in it instead of sugar. We sent it back and the new one tasted the same. We sent that one back, too and told them it was salty. The new one had even more salt! Apparently, they like salty lemonade in Thailand. When we asked them to make one with sugar, they looked at us like we were from Jupiter.*

Before we knew it, we had spent a week accomplishing nothing. September's cousin Melissa had that thing called a "job" where she did something called "work." This all sounded vaguely familiar, but we tried to talk her out of returning anyway. Initially she considered ignoring this "job," but something called "guilt" came into play and she was off to Bangkok to catch a flight back home. Granny was going to travel with us for a while longer.

After we bid Melissa adieu, September announced, "I'm bored here."

"Boring can be good," I said. "I'm boring, and I'm good."

"Yes, be that as it may, I have something else in mind."

"Don't tell me. You want to find a nice police line and cross it to keep ourselves entertained."

"Sort of. It's just that the line I want to cross is the border into Cambodia. I want to go see Angkor Wat."

I didn't know much about Angkor Wat, just that it's a huge temple complex, known to be one of the world's premier archaeological sites and considered a "must-see" on the Southeast Asia circuit. I was happy just to watch the sunset from our beach bungalow and work on retaining my one remaining nipple. I lobbied against going to Cambodia (the ruins of Angkor Wat being our sole reason to go there) because we had seen countless ruins and temples.

"If I have to put one toe inside another temple, I'll explode!" Jordan cried when I leaked the information about his mother's plans at lunch.

That's my boy! I was completely willing to let Jordan take the blame for us not going to Cambodia.

Unfortunately, September has the exasperating trait of being one step ahead of me, and she really wanted to go. "Jordan," September casually commented, "I'm not sure children are allowed to go to Angkor Wat."

Jordan, Katrina, and I all sat up straight in our seats. I knew darn well kids could go to Angkor Wat. What was September playing at?

"Why, Mom?" Katrina asked, bewildered. "Why aren't kids allowed to go to Angkor Wat?"

"It's too dangerous. Cambodia still has thousands of buried land mines left over from the war. Plus, it has poisonous snakes, including king cobras. If you go to Angkor Wat, you have to be really careful not to stray off the marked paths."

"Really, Mom?"

"Why can grown-ups go?"

"We can stay on the path!"

"How old do you have to be?"

"What kind of snakes are there? How poisonous are they, really?"

"How big are the explosions from land mines if you step on one?"

"Can you look it up in the guidebook? When will we know if we can go?"

In one stroke of genius, September had sold Jordan and Katrina on the idea of going, warned them of the small, but real, dangers, obtained their promise not to wander off as they are prone to do, and scuttled my plans for hanging out on the beach in Thailand for another week.

In short, we were going to Cambodia.

www.360degreeslongitude.com/concept3d/360degreeslongitude.kmz

The Saga of the *Exxon Valdez*. If you are ever tempted to replace the engine in your car with one from "overseas" have a peek here.

17.

The Ugly Side of Humanity

January 2–January 9
Cambodia

Cambodia shook us. We had seen abject poverty in Tanzania and the Chinese countryside, but it did little to prepare us for what we would experience in Cambodia. Months after we left, I couldn't get the images out of my head.

• • •

"*Lonely Planet* says don't take the bus. They state this most emphatically," I said.

"Why? How else are we going to get to Siem Reap?" September asked.

"Fly. The roads are supposed to be horrid. Unfortunately, judging by the price of a ticket, it appears that the airline is aware they have a monopoly."

"Well," September said, "we've survived bad roads before. Nothing can be as bad as the roads in the Serengeti, could it?"

We found a bus company operating at the main train station in Bangkok that could take us to Siem Reap. The ticket agent assured us it was only three hours to the Thai-Cambodian border, then another four hours to Siem Reap. "You'll enjoy the ride in our air-conditioned Mercedes-Benz bus," she told us.

As promised, we started our trip in style, but once we arrived at the Thai-Cambodian border we would never see that bus again. Our driver simply pointed vaguely in the direction of the border, saying, "Someone will meet you on the other side and take you the rest of the way."

Three hours and 300 yards of sidewalk and 300 yards of red tape later, we were in Cambodia. "So now what happens?" I asked no one in particular.

"I guess we wait," September replied.

So wait we did. We waited with a group of Europeans who were traveling with us, and we talked amongst ourselves. Katrina and Jordan had become savvy travelers, but the mixture of the heat and not knowing when or how we were to depart was trying for all of us. Luckily, Granny was able to keep the kids occupied looking for food and snacks while September and I tried to sort out our next move. We queried the other travelers. "Anyone know who we're waiting for?" "Any idea how long we need to wait?" "Does anyone have any documentation, like a travel voucher?" Unfortunately, no one did.

Even though we had all paid for a full bus ticket onward to Siem Reap, many people ultimately hired private taxis for what was believed to be a four-hour drive. More than an hour later the 27 of us who remained were herded into the back of a dual-axle cattle truck.

I could easily see the road ahead from where I was perched in the back of the truck. The truck approached a bridge that went over a small river. As the bridge came into focus, I grabbed the sides of the truck in a panic, braced myself for a collision, and let out an expletive.

"Watch your language!" September demanded.

"Did you see that? There were planks missing on that bridge wide enough to swallow a tire! The driver didn't even slow down!"

We were following a river and switching banks every so often. Everyone gradually relaxed as we became desensitized to the state of the bridges. Then the driver zipped over a bridge composed of no more than two wooden planks, each just wide enough to accommodate a tire; I wouldn't have walked across it for fear of falling off. All the passengers collectively held their breath for a moment, but the driver zipped over as if nothing were amiss. Halfway across the bridge I found that I had unconsciously lifted my feet off the floor as if the action would somehow make me lighter.

After several hours of bone-jarring roads, September finally admitted, "Okay these roads are worse than the ones in the Serengeti."

"I beg to differ," I replied. "True, this is more miserable, but the difference in the Serengeti is that we traveled in a rugged Toyota Land Cruiser that was up to the task. I swear this truck has no shocks and its tires are square."

Katrina and Jordan took this journey stoically, having had several months' experience with uncomfortable travel. Granny, on the other hand, was having the time of her life. My mother-in-law has traveled extensively around the world, often alone on a bicycle, her favorite destination being rural Yemen. The dust, heat, and noise, and nonstop near-death bridge crossings seemed to provide exhilaration such that she commented several times, "I'm so glad we didn't fly!" Fourteen hours after leaving Bangkok, in the wee hours of the morning, heads buzzing, we were in Siem Reap, Cambodia.

· · ·

Siem Reap, literally translated, means *Siam Defeated*, in honor of the Khmer defeating the Thai in a bygone era. It is a now a town of seventy thousand people with an international airport and an endless row of glitzy hotels with rooms that can be as high as $500 per night. For $13 we landed in a clean, comfortable guest house with much-needed AC.

I paid close attention when school was in session that first morning. September explained, "In Khmer, a *wat* is a temple. The entire area surrounding this town is known as Angkor Wat and it was built during the height of the ancient Khmer civilization, which lasted from the 9th through the 15th centuries. Angkor Wat is often cited as the largest religious complex in the world. Being so deep in the jungle of Cambodia, it was unknown to the outside world until the 1860s when Europeans colonized the area."

After the early morning history lesson we found ourselves walking down the main street that is lined with restaurants and gift shops, all catering to Western tourists. One place caught our eye because it advertised fruit smoothies made with "commercial" ice, meaning the ice was clean. As it was humid and stifling hot, an ice-cold drink sounded wonderful. We walked into the open-air restaurant and all ordered a smoothie, along with breakfast.

I'm always the first to finish eating, having grown up in a large family. Enjoying that contented, full-stomach sensation, I leaned back in my chair and watched a truck pull up in front of the restaurant. The driver hopped out and brought in a massive block of commercially made ice. He shooed away the feral dogs that were resting in the shade on the floor of the restaurant and placed the ice on the floor in the same shade that had been occupied by the dogs. As he began to hack away at the ice with an axe, large chunks of ice broke off and went skidding across the concrete floor. His assistant chased after the ice chips and dutifully placed them in a chest.

Suddenly my fruit smoothie wasn't so refreshing.

Something I had read in *Lonely Planet Cambodia* suddenly took on a fresh perspective: "If you see anything being done incompetently, remember that all the educated people in the country either fled or were exterminated in the late 1970s."

I had grown up hearing about the Cambodian genocide. But watching two people break ice on a concrete floor for fruit smoothies where dogs had been lying while the words *anything being done incompetently* echoed in my head gave the events of 30 years ago a gut-wrenching clarity.

. . .

We took a "tuk-tuk" to the ruins of Angkor Wat. In Cambodia and Thailand a taxi is known as a tuk-tuk, which is a trailer pulled by a small motorcycle—a Chinese counterfeit of a Honda Trail 90. I had a Honda Trail 90 as a kid, and put a few thousand miles on it zooming all over the desert and mountains of Southern California before I even got my first zit. Now, as the five of us piled into a trailer behind one tiny motorcycle, I hoped that the brake system had been upgraded since the original 1960's-era original. And off we puttered.

Arriving at the largest temple of Angkor Wat, we hired a young man in his early twenties to be our guide for the day. When we crossed a bridge over a moat that surrounds the largest temple, our guide had an important factoid for us.

"This is the view from the scene in *Lara Croft: Tomb Raider* as they enter the hidden chamber."

I had no idea what our guide was talking about. "Is that a movie?" I asked.

Our guide was only too happy to fill in the gaps in our knowledge about such an important cinematic touchstone. Clearly smitten with the movie's heroine, Angelina Jolie, he pelted us with every little detail about her and what she did while filming in the area. Such was his fervor that we watched *Lara Croft* months later when given the opportunity. I can honestly say I've seen detergents that leave a better film.

Angkor Wat cannot be absorbed in a few days. It had not been too many months since we had been touring cathedrals and castles in Europe. We had visited many examples of exceptional craftsmanship, from the Vatican to the Charles Bridge in Prague. None of these can compare to the scale and detail of Angkor Wat. Individual temples are spread over several square miles and enormous pagodas top every shrine. While the vastness of the complex is impressive, it is the detail that is most remarkable and the intruding jungle that gives it its character.

Clearly, the entire complex of Angkor Wat was a labor of love for an ancient civilization; every square millimeter of stone is an intricate storyboard toiled over by generations of craftsmen. As the *Tomb Raider* trivia dried up, we were left with an endless stream of data about what all the bas-reliefs and dancing devas etched in stone meant. As the place is immense, there was far more story than we could absorb. Think France's Bayeux Tapestry on an exponential scale.

To make matters worse, my mother-in-law, curse her wretched Mensa cranium, has an infinite capacity for just this kind of mind-numbing detail. By the time I had heard the umpteenth story of how this elephant-headed goddess had a tug of war with a seven-headed serpent and landed in a bath of milk and sealed her power for eternity, I knew it was our turn to make up a story.

The walls of the temples are covered in carvings that tell a story. It has been my life ambition to create my own enduring urban legend and be immortalized on www.urbanlegends.com. Whoever came up with the one about the blind date that went bad where the guy wakes up in a tub of ice with one of his kidneys missing is a genius. Now that we were in Angkor Wat, I realized my opportunity was before me.

While Granny was entertaining our tour guide, the rest of us came up with a plan to carve our own legend into stone. We would place it out of sight in some obscure temple to be miraculously "discovered." But what story to tell?

After much discussion, we settled on a storyboard carving that has a flying saucer with the Microsoft Windows logo on one side and the number 666 on the other. Then we'd show legions of people bowing down to the flying saucer and worshipping it. We would have to some-how pass our stone storyboard through a goat so that it would have that "aged look."

Too bad our stone-carving skills weren't up to snuff; our carving's discovery would have made a great news story. It may yet. I may not know about stone carving, but I can use Photoshop.

The tour guide was detailing one of the storyboards while Katrina and Jordan took refuge in the shade. Seemingly out of nowhere a mon-key approached Katrina and started grooming itself. Katrina sat still and smiled at the monkey. The monkey responded by showing her its many teeth. I didn't know if the monkey was threatening her or simply returning the smile. Then I realized that monkeys probably don't have the social pattern of smiling.

Oops, I thought. One wrong move on Katrina's part and that monkey is going to use those teeth and take a divot out of her arm.

What happened next was either sheer brilliance on Katrina's part or dumb luck, but Katrina responded by simply raising her eyebrows. The monkey responded by raising its eyebrows. Slowly, the monkey came right up to her and started to brush its hand on her thigh; it was grooming Katrina for lice.

The monkey must have thought that Katrina had a terrible case of the mange and had lost all of her fur. It started to inspect the (very fine) hair on her thigh, and proceeded to pinch the little hairs and pluck them out, one at a time, and then eat them.

Katrina tried very hard not to scream out in pain. Always having my children's best interests in mind, I told her to stay still so I could take pictures. After a minute or two, just as suddenly as the monkey started to "groom" Katrina, it turned its back to her and pointed to its back as if to say, "Okay, I did you. Your turn to do me."

So, Katrina dutifully started to brush through the monkey's fur. Every time she tried to stop and get up and walk away, the monkey would look up at her disdainfully and point to another area it wanted groomed. I don't think Katrina found any lice. And I really doubt she would have eaten any if she had. Katrina quickly decided it was time to start shaving her legs to avoid being mistaken for needing a good lice grooming in the future.

Exiting one of the temples, the sound of playful music beckoned us. As we approached the source, we found several landmine survivors playing music with a donation box prominently displayed. The lesson of seeing a group of amputees was not lost on Jordan, who from this point forward soberly reminded us all to stay on the path every time one of our toes happened to so much as touch a blade of grass.

No sooner were we reminded of the dangers of the landmines than Katrina found an enormous snakeskin that had been recently shed. It was intact in every detail, so that the holes for its eyes and mouth could be clearly seen. Suddenly we all became a little more careful where we placed our hands as we climbed the steep stone steps, or when we stepped into a darkened chamber.

* * *

Our tuk-tuk driver became an honorary member of the family, taking us everywhere we went. On the back of his tuk-tuk was posted an advertisement for a restaurant. Prominently displayed on the ad was the internationally recognized symbol for online addicts who need to get a quick fix: Wi-Fi.

Our driver asked where we wanted to go, and I pointed to the advertisement on the back of his tuk-tuk.

"I would like to go here," I said.

"No, you don't want to go there," he said. "I can take you to a nice place. You will like it."

He didn't understand. I needed an e-mail fix. "I want to use their wireless network," I said, pointing to the Wi-Fi logo to make my point. He had good English skills, but I've met native English speakers who don't know what a wireless network is.

He said, "Wee Fee? You want Wee Fee?"

Wee Fee sounded close enough to me, so I nodded enthusiastically. We all piled into the tuk-tuk and were on our way to get Wee Fee. The others might be going to get food, but I had one goal.

At the restaurant we were shown in by the maître d'. I was logging into their network before we crossed the threshold of the door.

"I'm in! I'm in! I'm in!" I sang, doing a little dance.

"We are all in," September said.

"No, no, no," I said, as the maître d' showed us a seat in the waiting area. "Their network. It's wide open and fast." I settled into a plush armchair and was downloading e-mail and looking at the news—the world was mine and I could go anywhere I pleased.

"This is an interesting place," September commented.

I glanced around quickly, not wanting to take my eyes off my two-inch-by-three-inch screen. "Looks nice to me. Kind of fancy for

Cambodia, though." The purpose of the soft light with the reddish glow hadn't sunk in yet.

"Interesting artwork on the walls," Granny commented. "What kind of place have you taken me to, John?"

I glanced up for a moment at a painting. "Hmmm. It's a neo-expressionist nude. Big deal."

"I see you learned something about art while at the Louvre," Granny continued, "but what will your children think?"

I knew she was goading me. Didn't she know I was mainlining a steady stream of 1's and 0's? Without looking up I said, "Not much. You can't swing a dead cat in Europe without hitting a painting of a bare breast. In the Vatican Museum, statues of naked men missing their penises are all the rage."

The maître d' brought us a menu. Annoyed that I had to stop what I was doing, I quickly looked through the menu and picked something out. I proceeded to go back to reading about important world events, such the scandal in Orlando where a bunch of high school boys on a Disney World field trip were put in the same hotel with a swingers club. Just then Katrina and Jordan started snickering and pointing their fingers at the artwork.

"Pointing isn't polite—what's so funny, anyway?" I then looked at what they were pointing at. The nude was Rock Hudson: his feather boa strategically covered his anatomy. Across the room from Rock Hudson was Chairman Mao with earrings and red lipstick. Another wall sported a painting of a very overweight guy wearing a tutu, a smile, and little else. His hairy chest would have made Bigfoot jealous.

I glanced at September. "Nice restaurant," she said, giving me a wicked smile.

It isn't as though I wanted to raise Katrina and Jordan in a hermetically sealed mayonnaise jar, but the restaurant's décor was a little over the top. In less time than it takes to explain it, I realized that my own eccentricities entitled me to a lifetime of teasing for my restaurant selection. But while my eccentricities may have been learned, September's are genetic. A couple of weeks traveling with my mother-in-law made me realize that. Regardless, the deck was stacked against Katrina and Jordan, as they were losing out on both sides of the nature-nurture thing.

For a moment I considered leaving, but hey, we had already ordered, and the restaurant had a big serving of Wee Fee. "Yeah," I said, "I like it, too."

I *was* careful to sit next to September throughout dinner and to put my arm around her. As the walls were plastered with paintings of men in high heels and corsets, there was no sense in giving anyone the wrong idea. Through dinner I contemplated the bigger picture of Cambodia's recent history and what it meant to be able to display a painting of Chairman Mao in drag in a public place. I think Cambodia will not only survive, it will thrive.

. . .

We had considered taking a boat down the Mekong River to Phnom Penh until we learned that one full of Western tourists recently capsized, *Vasa*-style. It seems that tickets for seats on the boats are for Western tourists, and the locals are put up on the roof. My best guess is that the captain keeps taking passengers and loads them onto the roof until water is near to lapping over the sides of the boat.

As we had already covered inverted pendulums and Archimedes' Principle after the *Vasa* museum, I resisted the urge to have another science moment on the subject and we simply decided to take the bus to Phnom Penh. We met a nice Australian family that was spending a few months traveling around Southeast Asia. They had come to Siem Reap the day before we had via the same route from Bangkok.

"So," I asked, "how about those bridges? They must not have been too bad or you wouldn't be here now."

The father spoke up. "When we came through, one bridge was totally out and had apparently collapsed only minutes before we arrived. We were stuck for hours until it could be repaired, and then all the crew did was lay wood planks across the river. The planks were no wider than the width of a tire."

"Ah, yes. I think our driver hit that bridge at 40 miles per hour. I nearly wet myself. And yet, here we are doing it again."

"Well, a fair measure of crazy is doing the same thing twice and expecting a different outcome," my new friend snorted, "but I suppose you need to be a bit crazy to be on a walkabout for an entire year with your kids."

I had either been insulted or praised. Perhaps both.

Once in Phnom Penh, all the horrid traffic we had previously witnessed worldwide suddenly seemed sedate and orderly in comparison. In China we observed that the fanciest cars seemed to have the right-of-way at intersections. In Phnom Penh this was no longer subtle, putting the average person at a huge disadvantage, because the average person was on a moped. Rather, the average *family* was on a moped. At the same time. I never knew that a 50cc moped could carry a family of four and their shopping all at once, but I have the pictures to prove that not only can it be done, it's common.

I don't think anyone could ever really be prepared for Phnom Penh. From the insane traffic to the child beggars sans clothes and sans the occasional limb, it is not for the faint of heart. It is also a city full of beautiful people.

On one particular Sunday we meet Prak. He had very good English skills and became our guide around Phnom Penh. We learned a lot about Cambodia and its people from Prak. "My wife is very lucky," he said. "She has a good job making clothes in a factory owned by the Chinese."

So the Chinese were outsourcing their manufacturing to Cambodia, and the jobs were considered high-paying work. That put a lot of things into perspective.

In Siem Reap I had purchased a biography, *Stay Alive My Son,* from a seven-year-old amputee who was going from restaurant to restaurant selling books. Over the next several days I read Pin Yathay's captivating-in-a-horrific-sort-of-way experience of the brutal Khmer Rouge genocide in the latter half of the 1970s. Now I had the opportunity to ask Prak about this period. He matter-of-factly itemized the number of family members he had lost in those years.

"No one was safe from the horrors of that time," Prak explained. "Everyone over 30 years old has many family members who died." The juxtaposition of being in a nonthreatening environment, say a bustling marketplace, and gazing into someone's eyes and having them calmly discuss their harrowing experiences with openness and frankness was very unsettling.

I can recall Walter Cronkite reporting the Vietnam War's daily body count on the evening news. After the war ended, strife in the region continued for a number of years. Half a world away, I fretted about getting my driver's license as Phnom Penh fell to a Communist-inspired faction called the Khmer Rouge. In later years, stories about Pol Pot and atrocities at a place called the Killing Fields gradually began to be told on the world stage. But I understood little about how the fabric of an entire culture was torn apart until I visited Phnom Penh, spoke with Prak, and read Pin Yathay's story of how he lost first his parents, then his siblings, then his children, and finally his wife.

In the years Pol Pot was in power, the Khmer Rouge tried to establish a purely agrarian form of communism where the entire population worked on collective farms. To accomplish this they tried to eradicate all traces of modern life. In a matter of days after the fall of Phnom Penh, all cities nationwide were permanently evacuated at gunpoint and the people herded into the countryside. With no planning or infrastructure in place for such a dramatic change, the resulting chaos and famine were inevitable.

To control the population, the Khmer Rouge marked anyone with an education as an enemy, as educated citizens were the most capable of overthrowing the new government. The Khmer Rouge cannibalized its own citizens by systematically exterminating doctors, engineers, teachers, skilled technicians, and the like. Some escaped into neighboring countries, but most were ruthlessly killed, often by starvation, as it was the most economical method. In the most extreme examples, simply carrying a pencil was proof enough that one possessed an education, and hence the carrier was sentenced to "re-education," which could mean being quietly taken out into the jungle and bludgeoned to death, another economical method of execution.

The net result was that during their reign, the Khmer Rouge took a functioning and prosperous society and thrust it back to the Stone Age, destroying an entire culture in the process. By some estimates, during the Khmer Rouge years of 1975 through 1979, approximately one-third of the population of Cambodia was exterminated or died of starvation or disease.

For me, the experience of visiting the sites of the Khmer Rouge killing machine around Phnom Penh was a world apart from other places we visited where misery and death had been inflicted on a mass scale, such as Poland's Auschwitz or Japan's Hiroshima. I think that in part this is because time has erased the visible wounds in Europe and Japan. Time has not yet been able to work its magic in Cambodia.

For example, we visited Phnom Penh's Genocide Museum, which is housed at the site of the former High School 21; this school was converted into a prison and torture facility during the Khmer Rouge years and was referred to as simply "S21." As we approached the gate of the S21 compound where the Khmer Rouge coerced "confessions" from its enemies, we were greeted by a beggar. This was not an ordinary beggar, but a survivor of the compound we were visiting. He had been tortured by having acid thrown in his face, and his crooked arms and legs looked as if they had been broken but had never properly healed. His horribly disfigured face was little more than dislocated clumps of flesh and his eyes were vacant windows of milky white scar tissue; you simply could not look into his face and not gasp out loud.

At the S21 Genocide Museum we spent time in classrooms that had been converted to places of torture. Graphic photographs that hung on the walls were yellow and fading, but enough detail remained to communicate the intent. A sign on the wall, a relic from the prison, read ENDURE YOUR PUNISHMENT WELL.

"I can't help but compare this to the Peace Memorial Museum at Hiroshima," I said, looking at the faded yellow photos and documents.

"What do you mean?" Katrina asked.

"The museum in Hiroshima is an impressive building with multimedia displays to tell a story that needs to be told. The Japanese have invested a lot of money to ensure the story is preserved and told well.

Here, with no glass in the windows, there is nothing to protect the photographs on display from the humid tropical environment. Without investment of some kind, in another decade there may not be anything to preserve."

"Preserving history," September summarized, "is a luxury of the well fed."

It was the same situation at the Killing Fields. To see the Killing Fields, you must hire a tuk-tuk and drive for a half-hour down a rutted, muddy dirt road through a neighborhood of squatters' hovels, and when you arrive you pay a couple of dollars to a man sitting in a small wooden shack built with all the structural integrity of a child's lemonade stand. In the center of the site is a pagoda housing a few skeletal remains, but mostly the Killing Fields is simply an open space. Supposedly the human remains in the mass graves have been exhumed and the site is simply the location where bodies once lay. However, human bones and bits of clothing were protruding from hard-packed dirt trails through the fields that were the graves of thousands of victims. The many feet that have walked through have worn off the topmost layer of soil, exposing the remnants of those who perished.

Seeing the realities of Cambodia was a hard lesson for two young kids from suburban America. But finding this kind of experience is the reason we had left the comforts of California. As I reflected on our time in Cambodia, I was ashamed that September had had to coerce me away from the beaches of Thailand.

Katrina's Journal, January 7

   . . . after that, our tuk-tuk driver took us down a very dusty and bouncy road to the Killing Fields. First, we went inside a small room with a very high ceiling, where there were skulls lined upon shelves that went up, up, up. I was sad to see that so many people were killed. Once outside, we walked on a path that went by lots of empty graves. Dad soon realized that on the path there were human bones showing in the packed-down earth. They were all over. Not just one here, one there, but the bones were as common as rocks.

I overheard Jordan saying to Katrina a few days after we left Cambodia, "You know that man we saw at the museum who had acid thrown in his face? Some things you remember even though you wish you didn't have to."

www.360degreeslongitude.com/concept3d/360degreeslongitude.kmz

Cambodia suffers about two land mine accidents every day. De-mining efforts are underway, but at the current rate, it will take over a hundred years to rid the country of this scourge.

18.

The Cute One and the Danish Postal Pin-Up Girls

January 9–January 18
Thailand, Again

I once rode an elephant at a zoo, paying an enormous sum to take Katrina, then age one, in a large circle for a five-minute ride. The elephant was well behaved and even tempered. I was egregiously misled by that experience into thinking that I should take my family on an "elephant trek" in northern Thailand.

The night before our trek we had a pep talk by our guide, Toto. I'm not sure of the spelling, but I could easily remember his name because I just imagined his wife was Dorothy. We met seven others who would be on our trek with us; Jordan and I, along with a Dutch man who was there with his girlfriend, were outnumbered three to one by young, single European women. There's a message to the single guys out there. There are *a lot* of unattached single women backpacking the world.

Some of the girls—and yes, at nineteen they can still be referred to as girls—clearly looked disappointed that there were no guys to flirt with over the next few days. A couple of them took an immediate liking to Jordan, but he wouldn't give them the time of day; I noted the clueless gene does not skip generations.

"Each day will have some difficult hiking sections," Toto explained, "but there will be a hot meal and shower at the end of each day." The promise of a shower after a long day of hiking in the sun was welcome news—it was one of the things we had sorely missed on our safari in the Serengeti. For three days we would hike and raft our way through the mountainous region of northern Thailand. The touchstone was the promise of an elephant trek on the morning of the second day.

> *Jordan's Journal, January 11*
>
> *Today we went on our trek. There were lots of other people on the trek, too. First we drove to a waterfall from a hot spring that we could climb. It was really warm! I took my shoes off with the goal to not get my socks wet. I actually managed to get my whole body wet. For lunch we had fried rice. I used to really like rice but in Asia there's too much of it.*

At the end of our first day hiking we were the guests of a hill tribe near the Burmese border. There had been a lot of elevation gain and I was proud that Jordan kept up and didn't complain. Little did I know to what extent Jordan would go so he could keep up with the adults—I wouldn't find that out until we hiked the Inca trail in Peru.

The twelve of us were given the use of a large one-room hut for the night and each clique claimed a corner of the spartan room. It was clear that we would all get to know one another quite well—perhaps better than some would want.

"Where's that shower?" I asked Toto. It had been a long day of hiking in the hot Thai sun.

"There is a bucket near the river."

"Oh." You would think that by now I would have realized hot running water in the developing world is pretty much unavailable outside of a Marriott. Unfortunately, *this* river was not fed by a hot spring. Since it is unlikely any melting glaciers were in the region, I concluded the village was having the water cryogenically cooled for our enjoyment.

The bucket-cum-shower was out in the open with no provision for privacy of any kind. September threw on her swimming suit and, making the best of the situation, took a "shower" and I did the same. Katrina and Jordan resolutely refused. They would jump in any old body of muddy water, but as soon as it was labeled a "shower" they treated it as though it were lethal.

All of the European sorority babes took showers as well, in swim-suits, or failing that, their underwear. I wouldn't really know for sure. I am merely reporting what I assume to be the case.

Two of the girls worked for the Danish postal service as letter carri-ers. "We are each a mailman," Annika said. Due to their buxom appear-ance, September and I began to refer to them as the Danish Postal Pin-Up Girls. I'd failed to appreciate what a fine country Denmark was when we were there.

• • •

Night comes early and quickly near the equator. With no electricity, after darkness fell there really wasn't much to do, so we headed to our hut for the night.

During our travels we all occasionally expressed some of the things we missed about home. This particular night, Jordan started it off by stating emphatically that if he never saw a bowl of rice again it would be too soon. "What I want are garlic fries at AT&T Park while watching the Giants thump the Dodgers."

"I would be happy with a bowl of cereal with real milk from a real refrigerator, not that boxed UHT stuff that's always warm," Katrina said. September was pining for the banana chocolate chip muffins that her friend Heidi makes. For me, only Fiery Hot Flautas from Chevy's with extra jalapeño jelly could make life complete.

Before we had left for our trip, all of us, but especially the kids, counted down to the moment we would leave on the World-the-Round Trip. This started many months before we left. As I lay in a spartan hut near the Burmese border pining for Fiery Hot Flautas, I realized for the first time that we weren't counting down our return to California. Except for the occasional food cravings, there was little thought of home being any place except where our stuff was at the moment.

* * *

It was elephant time. Katrina was so excited I was worried that when the elephants started to show up she would rush up to one and give it a giant hug on the ankle. In my mind I was rereading a Tanzanian newspaper article about a little boy whose last act in this life was agitating an elephant by throwing a rock at it. Voices in my head started arguing.

"Yes, yes, yes, but that was a wild animal. These elephants are trained."

Another voice said, "Soooo. I am quite certain that the elephants have not had personality screening prior to applying for the job of hauling tourists around." While the voices in my head were busy arguing, I told Katrina to stay away from the elephants.

She didn't. I was to learn a lot about elephants that day, but even more about Katrina.

When the elephants started to arrive at the village, Katrina decided that she was going to make friends with "The Cute One." When I wasn't looking she picked an armful of grasses and flowers as an offering to The Cute One, and then climbed up the tower that was used for getting on the beasts' backs so that she was at its eye level. 🌐 There she sat, holding out her offering. The Cute One then took Katrina's bouquet in her trunk, consummating a friendship. Katrina continued by having a long conversation with her new friend.

I am not sure how all this occurred right under my nose after she was told to stay away from the elephants, but Katrina was now friends with The Cute One and *had* to ride her and only her.

Elephants are massive beasts. I never fully appreciated this until perched atop one. Katrina, Jordan, and Granny climbed aboard a bench-seat that was strapped to The Cute One's back and lumbered off into the jungle. September and I rode another elephant we nicknamed The Big Guy. Soon after we got underway, The Big Guy's handler offered me the "privilege" of trading places—I could sit on the neck and the handler could sit on the bench, next to September.

"COOL!" I enthusiastically traded places. No sooner had I maneuvered into place than I realized that an elephant's head is not equipped with a handle to grab onto. I also failed to appreciate that an elephant doesn't really have much of a neck to sit on, so I was sitting on top of his shoulders, which swayed back and forth a tremendous amount as he walked. I seemed to be sitting on top of a three-story house that was rocking back and forth in a 10.0 earthquake. "This elephant is not OSHA-approved!" I yelled.

The elephant's handler asked, "Do you want to sit on the bench where it is safe?" There was something in the way he framed the question that suggested weakness if I were to retreat. It's a guy thing, but after making a big deal out of sitting on The Big Guy's shoulders, I couldn't give up so easily, and remained on The Big Guy's shoulders for the next couple of hours.

We approached a river. The Big Guy stood at the edge of the riverbank, giving me a bird's-eye view of what it was about to do—step off what seemed to me a cliff and into the river. As he contemplated his best path, I quickly reviewed my options, which were limited to jumping off. I considered that, then consoled myself that my will was in order.

When The Big Guy stepped off the bank and into the river, I was thrown forward. I once again searched the elephant's smooth and broad head for anything to grab onto. No handle materialized and I stayed on purely by divine intervention.

Once we were in the river, the elephant directly in front of us decided it was time to relieve itself and we were given a demonstration of the sheer volume of material of which an elephant needs to be relieved. A small mountain was laid there and as the water began backing up behind it, I recalled that I had "showered" in this very river the previous night. I was overcome by the urge to drive to the nearest Wal-Mart, buy a case of Evian, and bathe in it.

Unfazed by the fact that his buddy had just pooped in the river, our elephant paused to get a drink. After four or five long drinks The

Big Guy's trunk came up to my eye level and I braced for an instant fire hose.

The Big Guy wasn't done toying with me. For the next hour or so, it seemed all The Big Guy wanted to do was remind me that he was bigger than me and that I was highly annoying. As we trundled along he kept pausing to uproot some small tree and then chew it, when suddenly a large branch thick with foliage came directly at me.

"Your elephant is trying to kill me!" I asserted to his handler, who was sitting comfortably on a bench next to September.

"His head itches, that is all," the handler assured. "He uses the branch to scratch."

The Big Guy also liked to sneeze on me. I could feel him gather a tremendous breath of air, then his trunk would come up to my eye level and I would be hit with a hot jet of air mixed with dust and droplets of goo.

Meanwhile, Katrina, Jordan, and Granny were hundreds of yards ahead of us on The Cute One and I couldn't see them any longer. When September and I finally caught up with them, I was relieved to see that Katrina and Jordan had not been reduced to the thickness of a sheet of paper and had already dismounted. Had I known what to expect, I don't think I would have agreed to the elephant trek, and I certainly wouldn't have subjected my kids to it.

As we dismounted, Katrina came rushing up to September and me. "Wow!" she exclaimed, "can we do that again?!"

"How's that? I am *so glad* it's over. Did your elephant try to knock off the trainer who was riding on its shoulders?"

"Oh, he didn't ride there most of the time," Katrina replied. "Jordan and I took turns riding on her shoulders. It was really fun!"

I was dumbfounded. I would never have allowed them to ride up there if I could have seen what was going on.

"Didn't you nearly get thrown off every time your elephant stepped off the bank to cross the river?"

"Oh no," Katrina said. "The Cute One held onto me really tight by pressing her ears to my thighs. It would have been scary otherwise."

What was this all about? The Big Guy seemed determined to dislodge me one way or another. The Cute One was holding on to Katrina.

"Didn't your elephant keep sneezing on you, or uproot a tree and try to knock you off with it?"

"No," Katrina confessed. "I made friends with her back in the village before we started. I gave her something to eat and a bouquet of flowers."

"How's that? I thought I told you to stay away from the elephants."

"Gee Dad. I didn't want to get on a big animal like an elephant without knowing it was my friend first."

John's Journal, January 15

We found ourselves traveling for a few days with two young women from Denmark. They had been working their first job out of high school as letter carriers for the Danish postal service for a whole four months. Four months of work can be so demanding mentally, it is little wonder they were taking a one-month leave of absence to travel around Southeast Asia. They had a week remaining and wondered where to go next. I suggested Cambodia.

"Where is that? What is there to do there?"

Though the girls were in a neighboring country, they weren't sure where Cambodia was, had never heard of the genocide there, and were only vaguely aware that there was once a war in a place called Vietnam.

On the one hand these were still just kids, but they were also recent products of a rich country's educational system. They were up on current world events and certainly knew much more about U.S. politics than I do about European politics. I have little doubt that the average recent U.S. high school graduate would also know very little about Cambodia.

Speaking of Cambodia, we went to church in Chiang Mai and met a local family who showed us around town. The father was an ice cream vendor. We learned that one thousand baht (US$25) bought all of his capital needs for a day. He considered it to be a lot of money.

I couldn't help but to compare my situation relative to my new ice cream vendor friend, and then to Prak whom I had met in Phnom Penh. To me, $25 per day was trivial, and while it was a significant sum in Thailand, it would have been an unthinkably large sum to Prak.

We reached a village, very much like the one we stayed at the night before. As the sun was setting, we were greeted by a toddler who acted like he owned the place. He quickly won the hearts of the Danish Postal Pin-Up Girls, who showered him with all the affection they had tried to give to Jordan.

The chief of the village had many wives and they were going to dance for us later that night. At the appointed time we sat around a fire that took the chill out of the night air. The same toddler came out to greet us and was instantly drawn to the Danish Postal Pin-Up Girls.

Little kids can get away with anything, because they're so cute. This little guy went right up to his new Danish girlfriends, pulled down his pants, and started to pee. Smiling at the dumbfounded Pin-Up Girls, he maintained eye contact the entire time he drained his bladder.

I couldn't help but think that he was marking his territory now that others were nearby. The chief had his gaggle of girls, darn it, and these particular ones now belonged to a two-year-old. While most of the village was chanting and dancing around us, they were oblivious that their youngest was making the statement that he was the alpha male.

Jordan was aghast. "Look what that little boy is doing! Don't his parents know any better? Why don't they teach him better?"

I wanted to tell Jordan that his parents had probably taught him exactly what they should have, and he was now doing it. But Jordan just wouldn't be able to grasp it, so I just smiled and shrugged my shoulders.

19.

Busted in the Ladies' Room

January 18–January 19
En Route over the Pacific

Leaving Chiang Mai, Thailand, we started a sequence of events that would include one overnight train and three long-distance flights, culminating fifty-one hours and thirteen time zones later in San Jose, Costa Rica.

I wasn't looking forward to it.

After the overnight train, we arrived at the airport in Bangkok when it was still dark and waited for our afternoon departure for Taipei, then onward to Los Angeles. From there we would catch our flight to Costa Rica. It was time for Granny to go home and we watched her board her plane. We wouldn't see her for another six months. When it was finally our turn we found that China Airlines gave the herd in economy class a wide selection of movies to choose from, everyone having their own personal screen to view it on.

Predictably, Jordan zeroed in on a recent release superhero movie. The flight was long enough that Jordan watched it twice. The moment we stepped off the plane in Taipei, he proceeded to explain the plot in detail. "Mom, will you watch it with me on the next flight? Will you? Say you will!"

"Why I'd love to!" September said, in desperation to keep Jordan from boiling over.

"The next flight is a red-eye," I said. "You sure you want to stay up and watch a movie?"

"Even if that movie is on the next flight, Jordan has been up for twenty-four hours. He'll be unconscious before we leave the tarmac."

We were all starting to get a little ragged and ripe. With six hours before our flight to LAX we were getting restless.

"Hey, did you see that?" I asked September. "There's a picture of a showerhead next to the door of the restroom." A shower sounded divine, but our luggage was checked through to L.A. and none of us had soap, towel, or a change of underwear in our carry-ons. But that wasn't about to stop us.

"You guys stay here and read your books," September said to the kids. "We're going to take a shower." Katrina and Jordan had earned a fair amount of freedom during our travels. For example, we felt just as comfortable leaving them alone in an airport departure lounge during a shower as we did in a hostel while we did laundry.

"Together?" Katrina asked.

"Not as far as you know."

No towel required only a bit of improvisation. Using a handful of soap and a wad of paper towels from the men's restroom, I was able to shower, using the paper towels to pat myself dry. Bliss. It was one of the best showers I have ever had.

Feeling refreshed, I really didn't want to put on the same underwear that had accompanied me since the morning of the previous day, so I did what any semireasonable person would do—I washed them in the sink. Hey, there's a hair dryer, I thought to myself. September sometimes dries the laundry with her hair dryer!

Imagine my surprise when the hair dryer just didn't work. What does one do with wet underwear when there isn't anything else to wear?

September was in the ladies' shower across the hall. It seemed logical that there would be a hair dryer over there, and that she could dry my underwear for me. I slipped on my trousers, damp underwear in hand, and walked over to the doorway and called out to her.

"September . . . ?"

No one echoed back, "October!" so I figured she was alone. I called again, this time with a wee bit more volume.

"I'm just getting started!" she replied. I told her want I wanted, and she replied back, "Just come in and use the hair dryer yourself. There's no one else in here."

I timidly slipped one word the ladies' shower room, glancing over my shoulder every other second, expecting a giant hand to suddenly appear and point an accusing finger at me. The giant hand never appeared and after a few moments I started to get somewhat comfortable in my surroundings. I started to blow-dry my underwear, always wary of any movement in case the Restroom Gender Enforcement SWAT team came swooping in.

Even though I had my guard up, the next thing I knew someone of the female persuasion was standing next to me giving me an incredulous look.

Pretending not to notice, I went about my business as though I dried my underwear there every day. As the seconds ticked by, I could feel holes being bored into my skull as this woman was staring at me in disbelief.

Tick. Tick. Tick.

I couldn't stand the tension any longer, so I turned to her and smiled. With that gesture, she looked a tad panic stricken and vanished as suddenly as she had materialized.

I decided that my underwear was dry enough, went back to the men's room, changed, and returned to where the kids were reading their books.

The Restroom Lady was nowhere in sight, nor was the Restroom Gender Enforcement SWAT team. Mission accomplished.

Turning to the kids, I said, "There's a lovely shower in there. The water is warm, most likely void of elephant poop. You don't have to keep putting coins in it to keep it going. Don't you want to take a shower?"

"Grmmph. Can't you see we're reading?"

I forgot to advertise it as a mud waterfall, warning them not to get dirty.

As I sat in the transit lounge, people kept giving me these awful stares like they knew I had a dark secret. Did the Restroom Lady come out into the transit lounge screaming that there was a man in the ladies' room drying his underwear, and now everyone was trying to get a look at this demented pervert?

I looked around for the giant accusing finger pointing at me, but it wasn't to be found. I felt uneasy, burdened with my dark secret.

After what seemed like an eternity, September emerged from her shower and came out to join us.

"Ick!" she said. "What's all over your face?"

"Huh?"

"You have this grayish fuzz all over your face. What have you been doing? Eating lint from the dryer?"

It turns out that I had paper towel lint all over my face. The kids have always said that my beard stubble was like sandpaper and the paper towels were no match for it. September spent the next few minutes grooming me, monkey style, picking tiny bits of towel fuzz off my face.

•　•　•

Hours later, we were boarding our flight from Taipei to L.A. It was already after midnight in Taipei and we had been on the move for more than 30 hours. I felt as though someone had harvested my eyeballs. September looked about how I felt. The kids were as perky as ever.

Jordan had the in-flight magazine out before the cabin door closed.

"Hey, Mom! Guess what! That same movie is playing on this airplane, too! You promised you'd watch it with me. Remember Mom? Remember? You want to watch it? Remember what it was about?" Jordan proceeded to rehash the plot. I gave September an I-told-you-so look.

"The in-flight entertainment won't start for at least an hour," September whispered to me. "Surely he'll be asleep by then."

As soon as the flight was airborne, I donned earplugs and was off to a blissful chemically induced sleep. It isn't as though I pack around 20 pounds of clueless with me just for conversational purposes, but hours later when I regained consciousness somehow I was in a fair amount of trouble.

"Hey, I didn't promise him I would watch it. Don't make promises you can't keep." This comment did not boost my approval rating.

September proceeded to enlighten me as to how Jordan would pause the movie and rewind it so that he could explain the implications of what was happening in the plot. I did my best to furrow my eyebrows in a concerned fashion and occasionally make an empathetic groan at a critical juncture. It seemed to help, but sometimes I wish there were a guidebook on women I could refer to.

• • •

Two hundred thirty-two days. It had been way too long since I had had a decent burrito. Even though we were only passing through LAX with a two-hour layover, I had been counting down the days for a very long time. LAX had to have a Chevy's or at least a Taco Bell.

You can imagine my disappointment when all I could find was a measly burger joint that also sold burritos. Worse, I swear the cook had trained in England.

• • •

After our second red-eye in a row, we arrived in Costa Rica, checked into a hotel by the airport, and turned in for the night. It was 8:00 a.m. When we woke up it was dusk outside. We went to the mall up the street hoping to find breakfast. To my delight, we were greeted by a Taco Bell in the mall's food court. And there was free Wi-Fi!

So, I had been reduced to getting excited by a Taco Bell. Maybe I was just excited about the Wi-Fi. I pulled out my e.brain and looked at the empty browser window and wondered where to go. It finally struck me as pathetically ironic. I didn't need to "go" anywhere.

During our travels, September and the kids loved to tease me for my obsessive searching for open Wi-Fi networks so I could scan the headlines. It had been my way to keep my finger on the pulse of the world. Over the last dozen or so weeks, however, it was becoming increasingly clear that the world as viewed through the lens of the media was a different one from the world I was experiencing through our travels.

It isn't as though I completely gave up going online for an information fix, but my compulsive behavior of searching for open Wi-Fi networks to satiate my morbid fascination with the post-9/11 news died in a food court in San Jose, Costa Rica.

I stuffed my e.brain back into my pocket, and turning to my family, said, "I love being in a new place and discovering what makes it tick!"

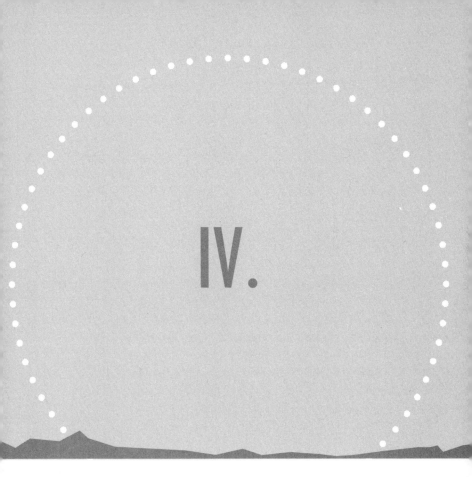

HOME IS WHERE YOUR STUFF IS

20.

Danger! Banana Crossing!

January 19–February 9
Costa Rica

Anyone who has dealt with real estate in California knows that every "Planned Unit Development" has a cutesy made-up name with an alternative spelling, like "Chardonnay Parque." This is to make it sound exotic even though it is just some place next to the BART Park-N-Ride. So it was with a healthy amount of skepticism that I went to a Costa Rican "Cloud Forest." I was blown away. Really. The wind *really* blows.

Costa Rica sits between the Pacific Ocean and the Caribbean Sea, the two coasts being only a few hours' drive apart. Between the two coasts is an impressive mountain range sporting no fewer than seven active volcanoes. One of the volcanoes, Volcan Arenal, has been active almost daily since 1968, when it wiped out an entire village.

The two coasts and the high mountain range in between create a veritable cloud factory. In the Cloud Forest you watch clouds whiz by, propelled by the impressive velocity of the wind. I have watched clouds from a 747 that don't go by nearly as fast. And the clouds are so low it seems that you can reach up and touch them, creating a kind of Timothy Leary effect.

When we left Thailand we had said good-bye to September's mother, Marie. When we arrived in Costa Rica, we said hello to September's brother, Perin, his wife Ashley, and their three children.

We had come to Monteverde because of its much-hyped cloud forests and rain forest tours that were conducted along walkways suspended a hundred feet and more in the air, or by whizzing above the forest canopy on a series of zip lines. The hype was well deserved, although Katrina and Jordan feigned polite interest. After having no other kids their age to play with for more than 30 straight weeks, what they really wanted to do was to spend time with their cousins building a fort behind our cabin.

Katrina's Journal, January 21
    When I woke up this morning, I found a big black scorpion in the shower. It was pretty cool. It saved me from taking a shower! After breakfast we worked on the fort with our cousins. But after a few hours, Mom and Dad made us stop so that we could do a tour over the rain forest on zip lines. Fortunately, there was still enough daylight left after riding on the zip lines for us to work on our fort again. It is almost finished.

When the fort was completed it was time to move on, and we descended to the beaches of Montezuma. Within the space of about 40 miles, the scenery and environment changed from pleasant temperatures in the mountainous forest to hot sun, sand, and surf.

You don't just "pass through" Montezuma. After a two-hour ferry crossing, then a couple of more hours to the end of a long and bumpy dirt road, Montezuma has that magical quality that makes you forget there was ever life at the beginning of the road.

That magical quality also has the tendency to create a population that comes and forgets to leave; it became immediately clear where all the Deadheads went after Jerry Garcia died. All those college-age kids spend their days not wearing enough clothes and lining the only street selling handmade necklaces, T-shirts, earrings, navel rings, and other rings that I don't even want to know where they are intended to go.

• • •

September came running down the worn trail from town. Trying to catch her breath, she said, "The EMT is on the way."

The waves at the beaches of Montezuma were a bit on the wild side. When I predicted someone would get hurt, September chided me, "You're such an Eeyore!" Little did I know that the "someone" was going to be one of the adults. September's brother Perin had been body surfing when a wave had used him to demonstrate a perfect pile driver.

We had already learned that health care varies dramatically throughout the world—not the quality, but the administration. For example, we couldn't even get doctors in Denmark, Turkey, and Japan to take our money. When the EMT showed up at the beach in Montezuma, Costa Rica, bearing a credit card reader that was connected to the world via satellite phone, I knew that accounts receivable wouldn't be an issue.

The EMT spoke excellent English, and surprise of surprises, he wasn't an EMT at all, but a physician. What happened next was a bit of a blur, and I'm not even the one who went into shock. There were a lot of needles and dire talk of worst-case scenarios. When it was settled that Perin's credit card was valid and that his insurance would reimburse all the expenses, a four wheel drive ambulance took him and his wife to an airstrip 50 minutes and 15 rough-and-tumble miles away. From there a private chartered plane, complete with an EMT, flew them another 50 minutes to the capital.

Poof. They were gone. And we had no way of communicating to see if Perin's injuries would require anything like amputation. The following day was dedicated to reuniting anxious children with parents. The trip to San Jose took Perin and Ashley two hours; it was 16 by car and ferry.

When we finally reunited Perin and Ashley with their three children, Perin was wearing a sling. "I see all the important bits are still attached," I observed.

"Not quite. I was administered a massive wallet-ectomy." Perin explained that the hospital staff seemed captivated by this concept of private medical insurance, and how, regardless of the procedure, insurance would "cover it." Even when it was clear that his injury was limited to a separated shoulder, the hospital insisted on an overnight stay and whipped up a potpourri of drugs and tests to keep themselves amused.

"Clearly, they've done this before," I said.

"Yeah, it seems that it has become a cottage industry for the doctor. He has his own private ambulances cruising the country looking for adventurous souls who push their adventure too far. When the hospital finally let me go, the doctor was nice enough to offer me a cash discount for services rendered. One thousand dollars."

Over the previous months we had seen evidence of multitiered health services: a public tier where services are free or low cost, and another private tier that presumably offers better and more upscale service. It would seem that the darling of the medical system in Costa Rica is yet a third tier—foreign tourists with insurance.

Perin explained to the doctor that his cash supply was a tad short of the required amount, so the doctor eagerly offered to drive him to the nearest bank. It turns out that the doctor started demanding cash after a surfer suffered a partially severed penis in an accident and then put a stop payment on a check, stiffing the doctor for the reattachment fee.

• • •

Post wallet-ectomy, Perin, Ashley, and family went home and we found ourselves in La Fortuna, known for its proximity to rain forests and Volcan Arenal. I was making breakfast at our hostel and September was doing math with Jordan. I wasn't really paying attention to what they were saying, but as there wasn't anything rattling around in my head at the time, September's voice came into focus.

"James works at a store 15 hours per week. If James works five days per week and works the same number of hours per day, how many hours a day does James work?"

"James must be French!" Jordan responded.

A wave of relief rushed over me. I had worried that our children might be too young to learn anything by traveling, but here was proof that they could absorb important information from their surroundings.

One of the big pastimes in La Fortuna is to sit in the natural hot springs, go to the swim-up bar, and order margaritas in the shadow of an active volcano spewing red lava. Using the logic that everyone else was doing it, so it must be okay, we went and let the kids order non-alcoholic margaritas.

Jordan sat at the swim-up bar and wore this huge grin. He kept talking to himself, but the only thing he was saying was, "I really like this place. I really like this place. I really like this place . . . "

I was worried he might injure his brain with all that fervor, so I interrupted. "So Jordan, why is it that you like this place?"

"I don't know." Which is, of course, the standard kid reply to everything.

The eruptions weren't tremendous, but the volcano was impressive. At one point a cloud of ash shot up several hundred feet in the air. As it got dark, we could see the glowing red quite clearly on the mountain.

Then Jordan did something that surprised me. He actually volunteered information. Usually I have to use a crowbar to pry information out of him but he became a spring of nonstop volcano facts that I never knew was inside him.

"Oh, really?" I said. "And how is it you suddenly know so much about volcanoes?"

"We studied them in first grade."

Ah. Come to think of it, all my volcano knowledge probably went back to the first grade, too. I guess Mount Vesuvius didn't do it for him when we were in Pompeii, but the red glow flowing down Volcan Arenal was enough to bring out the data that had been hibernating inside him.

Just as suddenly, Jordan blurted out, "I really like science."

Where did that come from? It didn't matter. My heart swelled. There was hope.

• • •

We came to love almost everything about Costa Rica—everything except the money. Prior to Costa Rica, the most obnoxious coins were Swedish, where the five-kroner coins are roughly the size of a hubcap and are worth a fair amount of money. If you had one in your pocket, there was no mistaking that it was there.

But the Costa Rican coins are worse. First of all, there are eight different denominations. Second, they look alike: There are four silver and four bronze, but all are nearly the same size. Their sheer bulk means if you have a pocketful you are either trying to get rid of them or you are on the way to see your chiropractor.

Trying to get rid of our coins is how we discovered that Costa Ricans are terrible at arithmetic. In Cambodia, the street kids selling newspapers could instantly calculate change and seamlessly make transactions using any combination of three currencies.

That ain't happening in Costa Rica.

I was buying groceries for 4,500 colones. I had a 5,000-colone note, but I did not want 500 colones in those infernal coins. Since I also had 500 colones in coins, I handed the cashier these plus the 5,000-colone note, expecting a 1,000-colone note in return.

The cashier looked at the money I handed him with utter confusion across his face, then handed back the 500 colones in coins, opened his cash register, and handed me another 500 colones in coins as change. Now I had 1,000 colones in coins. He acted like I was trying to rip him off. I stuffed the coins in my pocket and limped away.

If this had been an isolated incident it would not be noteworthy, but math huddles—a stumped cashier who had to call for backup support—were common.

During math huddles, we would give the problem to Jordan to solve, to see if he could beat the cashier. Typically the cashier would call for backup, and two adults would punch a calculator until they got the answer they liked best. Jordan liked being able to out-cipher an adult, and finally started to see the point of his morning math lessons.

John's Journal, February 2

I remember leaving Greece thinking that our trip had really just begun. The people in Europe are not that different from those in middle-class America. But everywhere we have traveled since then has been hugely different. "What makes us different?" is a question that lately keeps me up at night. Why are the street kids in Cambodia such whizzes at arithmetic and the clerks behind the cash registers in Costa Rica so abysmal? Why are stores in France open 30 hours a week while the stores in Turkey are open 18-plus hours a day? Why are Germans so fanatical about punctuality, and the Italians so . . . late all the time? And last, but not least, why does the entire world, other than the United States., speak more than one language and Americans just expect that one of those is English?

I certainly don't know the answers; however, it is equally intriguing how we are all the same. We all just want to raise our kids and have a few of the comforts of life. It's odd how many homes I have seen of the desperately poor that sport a color TV.

One of the best things about travel is meeting people who live life differently and think about things in ways you've never dreamed of. Perhaps no one person embodied all that was different from me more than Daruka, an American who happens to live in Uganda. He and his Arizonan girlfriend had made a rendezvous in Costa Rica.

Daruka was easygoing; you couldn't imagine an easier person to talk to. He was a merchant marine. To maintain your status as a merchant marine, Daruka explained, you have to work at least a hundred days per year. If gaps in employment span more than 300 days, you lose seniority and have to recertify your training. So Daruka worked the system. He worked 100 days and then took a 300-day vacation. His hundred days' worth of pay covered all his expenses in Uganda.

I admired the guy as someone who worked to live and not the other way around. Daruka asked, "So, what do you do for a living?"

I was at a loss for words. Back home in Silicon Valley your career defines your status in the socioeconomic structure. I used to relish the looks people gave me when I told them I was a rocket scientist. Yet, I choked on those words now, realizing it would sound hollow. All I said in response to his question was, "I'm a taking a break from being a cubicle warrior," and went on to explain that we were traveling around the world, never explaining about what had long been such an integral part of who I was.

* * *

The tiny town of Tortuguero is another haven from the world of cars. Like all such places we had visited, the quality of life just seems so much richer in the absence of cars. Access to Tortuguero, on the Caribbean coast, is by boat or plane, and like many such places, getting there would be half of the adventure.

Our shuttle driver, Juan, needed very little encouragement to talk. Juan was to drive us from La Fortuna to a place called La Geest, and from there we would take a boat the rest of the way to Tortuguero. Juan embodied Costa Rica's rallying cry of *Pura Vida!* which is literally interpreted as "pure life." Juan was full of life and love for his country and wanted to make sure his passengers appreciated his country as much as he did.

Juan pointed out every tree and bird to us on our drive, slowing down and offering to take our picture in front of, say, a coffee bush. It wasn't just toucans and coffee bushes that got Juan excited, though. I have never seen an adult get so excited to see cows before. I thought he might roll down his window and start mooing at them.

Juan told us a lot about Costa Rica, such as that the country is proud it has no army. To think that a country was comfortable enough with its place in the world to negate the need for an army was intriguing.

This was juxtaposed with what Juan said next. "Over the past several years immigrants have been flocking in from Nicaragua and Colombia, fleeing poverty and war. Over one million of them! It burdens the healthcare system and is why you see so much razor wire in San José."

I wondered how much fact there was in Juan's statements and how much was hyperbole. With Costa Rica's population at four million, it was difficult to imagine one in four people were illegal immigrants. I was reminded again about our similarities, in spite of obvious differences: Juan from a country with no army, we from the country with the biggest army, both of us from countries struggling with real and perceived immigrant problems. This was just for starters.

"Would you like to see some iguanas?" Juan asked, taking the conversation in a completely different direction.

We had seen iguanas before, so we politely declined. "No, thanks. We just want to get to Tortuguero."

"Oh, you have never seen iguanas like this before. You will love it." With that comment lingering in the air, Juan made the detour to see the iguanas.

He stopped at a bridge that was already loaded with tourists, each with a camera stuck to his face. I politely stuck a camera to my face, snapped a few iguana photos, and got back in the car.

After we left the iguanas and had driven for another half hour, Juan asked, "Are you hungry?"

"No."

"Okay," said Juan, "we'll stop at a restaurant."

"But we're not hu —"

We stopped anyway, and he led us into a small, outdoor roadside cafe. "What would you like to eat?" Juan asked.

"Nothing."

"Okay," he said, "I'll order you some pineapple."

In a previous life, I think Juan was somebody's Jewish mother.

After we were once again on our way we came to some banana trees, row after row after row. Juan came to a complete stop in the middle of the road. "Would you like to take pictures of the banana trees?"

Cars behind us started honking their horns. How was I supposed to tell Juan these weren't the first banana trees I had ever seen? I doubted I would go home and frame the picture of the banana tree and display it prominently in my living room as a memory of our visit to Costa Rica.

By this time, Juan had rolled down his window and was shouting something to some workers in the plantation. One of the workers got up, walked to a metal pole, and flipped a switch.

It wasn't until then that I noticed a long span of metal track suspended about ten feet off the ground, hanging from which every three feet or so were hundreds, no, thousands of bunches of bananas. The elevated track paralleled the road for several hundred feet and then disappeared as it wound its way through the trees.

The track sprang to life and started to move the bananas through the field, and then—surprise!—right across the road.

We were at a bona fide banana crossing.

The track crossed the road right in front of us and then on to a processing plant. When the banana track was moving it created a little train that chugged right across the road with the bananas hanging at about windshield height. I wondered how many motorcyclists had caught a bunch in the face when not paying attention.

And yes, I took a picture of the banana train. 🌀 It is now framed and displayed in my living room. Really.

. . .

La Geest is no more than a dock on a river in the middle of a massive banana plantation. We boarded a boat that instantly reminded us of the boats on the Jungle River Cruise at Disneyland, except the captain didn't tell lame jokes, and the crocodiles weren't fake.

When our jungle river cruise came to a rest an hour later, we were in the village of Tortuguero, population 690. A 30-second walk to the east of our guest house was the Caribbean Sea, and a 30-second walk to the west was the river on which we'd arrived. Sixty seconds south was the entrance to a national park and to the north was about a five-minute walk through town. Unfortunately, we arrived three months too early to observe turtles coming in from the sea to lay their eggs.

John's Journal, February 4

I have come to hate roosters. "Hate" is a very strong word. The flagrant use of it is punishable in our family, but it is applicable in this situation.

I remember my grandpa telling me when I was a little boy that when the rooster crowed, the rooster was really calling out my grandpa's name to tell him it was time to go milk the cows. Now, every time I hear a rooster crowing, I can hear the four syllables distinctly:

"MIS-TER-BLACK-BURN!"

Every time I hear one, I marvel that roosters all over the world know my grandpa's name. Then I struggle to try to remember what country I am in and why, and then there is just no going back to sleep.

Tortuguero is infested with roosters. With no glass in the windows of our guest house, there is simply no sleeping in after the roosters call out "Mister Blackburn" to tell him to go milk the cows.

Still, you can't help but like a place where the main street through town is a footpath made of sand, paved in the muddy places with coconut shells.

Tortuguero is as hot as an oven and humid as a steam room. Locally, the area is known as the Amazon of Costa Rica. Besides the giant sea turtles, which only visit long enough to lay eggs and then leave, Tortuguero is chock-full of crocodiles, sloths, snakes, and these nasty stinging ants that attack you if you accidentally touch their tree. Naturally, people flock there by the hundreds. There is something green and leafy clinging to anything and everything—from telephone poles, to the tops of picnic tables, to the ropes holding up the occasional suspension bridge.

While other Central American countries have seen much of their rain forest disappear due to slash-and-burn agriculture and other unfortunate uses of the land, the Costa Rican government, starting in the 1950s, established large national parks and reserves. Today, 27 percent of the land in Costa Rica is protected, preserving the landscape and forest habitats and setting the stage for a very successful tourist industry focusing on ecotourism. The effort shows.

It is also the kind of place where you can go through as much insect repellent as water. We stayed at a hostel with Mr. Bitey. He is the parrot who sits on his owner's shoulder looking cute and innocent. But try to stroke his feathers and he will demonstrate a parrot's ability to crack a Brazil nut, using your finger as an example.

The people of Tortuguero are fiercely proud of "their" turtles. Fifty years ago the population harvested the turtles in huge numbers for meat, but now the village is wholeheartedly engaged in turtle conservation, often deploying large groups of schoolchildren to guard nesting sites. We adopted a sea turtle for $25 at the conservation center. We are now the proud parents of Turtle 24601 and when "our" turtle is spotted in the wild we receive an e-mail update.

There are two ways to explore Tortuguero National Park. You can walk along a nature trail that is six inches underwater when it's raining, and only two inches underwater when it isn't. Or, you can canoe along a never-ending series of canals and rivers. We opted for both methods. On our canoe trip every time we saw two eyes 👁 poking up out of the water September would go rigid.

Jordan's Journal, February 5

Today we went on a canoe tour through the jungle in the canals. We had a lot of fun. I liked the smaller canals best, because we were surrounded by green, green, green. I mean, the branches had vines hanging down from them blocking the canals, and the tree trunks had ivy and other plants growing on them. It was really the jungle. And I enjoyed the animals, also. We saw a three-toed sloth, sleeping in a tree, where it looked like a lump of fur. We also saw a two-toed sloth climbing slowly around the tree. We also saw a few caiman, which are like small crocodiles, but all you see are two beady eyes and sometimes part of a snout poking out of the water. Our guide says they are

*waiting for birds to snatch. Mom freaked out when she saw the
eyes so close to the canoe. But we didn't see any blue or red tree
frogs, or poison arrow ones. Oh, well. There's always next time.*

Two days, two buses, and one boat later we arrived at Sixaola, Costa
Rica. Pedestrian border crossings can be intimidating, unlike their
sterile cousins that greet you at an international airport. At an airport,
you are behind pretty good security, and there aren't any question-
able characters floating around. At Sixaola there is a wide river that
defines the border between Panama and Costa Rica, and an old, abandoned train bridge suspended high across the river. On one side of the
bridge is Costa Rica's immigration control building, and on the other
is Panama's. In theory, you just walk across the bridge and then find
transport on the other side and go on to your destination.

But we expected a huge crush of people hoping to make a buck.
So, before we even stepped off our bus, we hired the services of one
Mr. Wile E. Coyote. Okay, that is our made-up name for him. But he
spoke good English, and we reasoned it could be handy to have a willing translator for finding ground transport on the other side.

We soon found ourselves on the old, wooden railroad bridge that
defines the border. A sign hung above the beginning of the bridge, wel-
coming us to Panama. In front of us were about two hundred feet of
weathered, cracked, wooden planks to cross before we would get to
Panamanian immigration. The huge railroad ties under our feet were
spaced far enough apart that if you slipped off the wooden planks nailed
to the ties you just might fall through to the river below. It would be
a tight squeeze for an adult, but I didn't want to test how much room
there was between the ties with one of the kids.

We worked our way across the bridge, choosing our footing with
care. Behind us was a huge semi truck loaded with bananas, bumping
its way along, parting the pedestrian traffic to the sides. We rushed to
beat the truck across the bridge and were never so happy to have our
feet on terra firma.

So, like, welcome to Panama.

21.

A Pirate in the Caribbean

February 9–February 27
Panama

Okay, everyone, hum along—you all know the tune:
Just sit right back and you'll hear a tale
A tale of a fateful trip
That started from this tropic port,
Aboard this tiny ship . . .

I used to love watching *Gilligan's Island* as a kid. I'd sit in front of our black-and-white TV and fantasize about the lifestyle of the marooned. No schoolwork. What a life! As an adult, when the pressure of the rat race would build up, I would frequently quip "We are going to sell everything and move to Gilligan's Island."

Our first stop on our way to South America was straight for what we hoped was going to be our island paradise. Bocas del Toro (literally "Mouths of the Bull" en Español) is the name of both the Panamanian province and the main town in a group of small islands off the Caribbean coast of Panama. Some of the islands support only a few families while in Bocas (as it is known locally) the town's most modern amenity is its grass airfield. It has an easygoing, laid-back atmosphere that quickly infected us to the point that we stayed much, much longer than planned.

Upon our arrival in Bocas we happened to meet Lori, who had recently moved to Panama from Arizona. After a short visit we headed straight for her B&B, Hacienda del Toro, on a tiny island nestled in Dolphin Bay. Yes, there are dolphins in the bay; watching them, one would think that they were participating in Sea World tryouts.

John's Journal, February 11

We arrived in Bocas del Toro, Panama. To get here we took a boat through canals that were made to take bananas to market, but which have long been abandoned. Now the canals are lined with shanties that look like they came from the set of Deliverance, *but the people on the porches wave rather than leer. The person who sat behind us in our boat was getting married the next day. She was holding her large wedding cake, trying to shelter it from the spray as we crossed the channel to the island of Bocas. We are now at a B&B run by Americans Neil and Lori. Wasabi, their pet parrot, whistles the theme song to* The Bridge Over the River Kwai *at the crack of dawn. He is worse than a rooster, but how can you get mad at him?*

Neil the Pirate lives on his own island with his wife and son. They have no car, as there are no roads whatsoever on their island. Every morning they watch the children of their indigenous neighbors walk out of their houses in crisp school uniforms, climb into a dugout canoe, and paddle to school.

Neil was once a cowboy who lived on his ranch in Arizona, but when Arizona became too civilized, he traded his Stetson for two gold earrings. With Wasabi perched on his shoulder, he personifies the part of a pirate in the Caribbean. "There is only one thing more dangerous to a rain forest than an Indian with a chainsaw," he told me as he leaned across the bar, "and that's real-estate developers with an agenda."

His indigenous neighbors raised cattle and every few months they would clear-cut a few more acres of their island home. Neil added, "My neighbors are coming around though. We pay them for access to their land when our guests hike or go on horseback rides through their property. They're beginning to understand that right of access is more profitable than milking Betsy the cow. Now if I could just save Red Frog Beach from developers."

Neil went on to describe how well-financed developers persuaded the president of Panama to look the other way and turn the once-pristine home for the endangered red tree frog on its head. Now with a former Miss Universe for its spokesperson, North Americans were flocking to purchase the beautiful villas at Red Frog Beach, sadly missing its namesake.

Neil went on to tell me everything he loved about his island home. "The only thing really missing here is a good boat mechanic in Bocas," Neil said. "A good one would be able to name his price and would be turning business away."

September gave me the briefest of glances. In just a few milliseconds, her subtle eyebrow raise communicated a lifetime of shared experiences. We sometimes dreamed of escaping the rat race, and this idyllic island paradise had a need. Neither of us had worked on a boat before, but she was well aware that I have turned a few wrenches in my lifetime, and we both know how to take a class.

Neil's American neighbor, Frankie, lived across the bay on his own private island. Frankie had delivered yachts for a living until he retired. Now Frankie keeps himself amused by raising cows and growing organic cocoa beans. Roasting the beans himself, using his own secret recipe of thirty-one herbs and spices, he makes his own chocolate bars to sell to tourists.

How cool is that?

With Dylan, Neil and Lori's thirteen-year-old son as our guide we went on a horseback riding trip, looking for "poison arrow" tree frogs. "I'll get one for you," Dylan said, jumping off his horse and catching one in his bare hands. He must have seen the expression on my face. "They aren't that poisonous. Unless you have an open wound and smear the frog's skin into it, you'll be fine."

Just like that, forty-odd years of playground folklore evaporated.

Jordan's Journal, February 19
Today we finally went on that snorkeling trip. First we rode in a boat and saw dolphins. Then we went to this cool place where we could snorkel off the dock. We saw a barracuda as big as me!!! The way I spotted it was scary. I was swimming right by the dock when a gigantic Godzilla fish appeared. It started swimming over to me with its mouth open showing me its half-inch razor-sharp teeth like it was going to eat me. I swam for the ladder on the other side of the dock as fast as I could. The problem was someone was getting out very slowly and I had to be too polite to save my own life.

After a few days on Neil and Lori's island, we were back on the main island of Bocas, heading to a place described to us as "as far away as you can get from anywhere." Our taxi driver parted his shoulder-length dreadlocks, smiled at us with his three remaining teeth, and said with his thick Caribbean accent, "De car. Eet iz 'ongree. Eet will need a snack b'fore eet will go oll de way to Drago."

Ongree? What does that mean? Why doesn't anyone sell a dictionary of Caribbean English? Our driver continued, "You juss geev me some o' dat mohney now an' I kin feed de car, ah-right?"

Our taxi driver drove through a neighborhood and came to a stop next to a run-down house. He got out and chatted with some people for a bit, then went inside.

"Any idea where our driver's going?" I asked September.

She laughed. "Okay, new math story problem, Jordan. James works at a store. The store is usually open before lunch and often closes before dinner. Where will you find James taking his siesta?"

A few moments later our driver came out with two Coke bottles full of the car's snack. He tipped the contents of the Coke bottles into the gas tank and off we went.

But we didn't go to Drago, at least not right away. Our driver had friends that needed chatting up. Since Drago was on the far end of the island, he didn't want to miss an opportunity for socializing along the way. We drove along slowly with the windows down so that the driver could simultaneously drive and converse with his buddies, and ask if anyone had any errands they might need to run in Drago.

We had come to Drago for one reason. September and I had been searching the world for our version of utopia—just in case we decided to never return from our trip. Lauterbrunnen was one possibility, but the Swiss immigration requirements are pretty high: The Swiss are trying to keep their country void of riffraff like rocket scientists by requiring large sums of cash and friends that will vouch for your integrity. I'd always suspected the two always went hand in hand.

Although the island of Bocas del Toro was a world apart from the Alps, its laid-back Caribbean lifestyle was tremendously infectious. The few cabins that made up the village of Boca del Drago, or simply Drago, were at the end of a long road on the far side of the island.

Approaching Drago for the first time, I noted the last section of road ran across the beach and was submerged. Our taxi driver waited for the precise moment for the tide to recede then made a dash before the surf submerged the road again.

There are no hotels or inns in Drago; the only place to stay is at a cabin owned by the Biological Research Foundation, which does sea turtle and other marine research. Since it wasn't sea turtle season, their cabin was available. The caretakers were even kind enough to run the generator from dusk until 10:00 p.m. so we would have electricity part of the day.

Aside from a couple of cabins, there is absolutely nothing at Drago. Nothing, that is, except for an azure lagoon and a narrow, deserted white-sand beach lined with coconut palms as far as the eye can see. It was what the eye *couldn't* see that made us leave our dream of settling on Gilligan's Island behind us.

"Something bit me!" September exclaimed. She reached down and pinched . . . nothing. At least that's what it looked like.

Ever heard of a "no-see-um?" Neither had we, until our arms and legs were covered with itchy scabs. I am sure that "no-see-ums" have a proper Latin name, but the locals' description of these pests seemed pretty accurate. After several days in idyllic Drago, Jordan, the tastiest of our bunch, looked like a teenager without a dermatologist.

September was quick enough to pinch one of the culprits between her fingers and held it up for me. To my 45-year-old eyes it looked like a cross between a salt grain and a sugar granule, only blurrier. I had learned that I had to trust Katrina to be my eyes when it came to stuff like this. "Katrina," I called, "can you tell what this is?"

"Of course," she grinned. "It's a bean sprout. Try it and tell me what it tastes like."

When we arrived in Africa, we were ready for insect warfare. We knew that we would be traveling in a malaria zone, and so in addition to malaria medication we had the insect warfare equivalent of a thermonuclear bomb. We had REI "Jungle Juice," with 100-percent active ingredient (DEET) and had been carrying it with us ever since we left California. Funny thing is we didn't really need it in Tanzania. We were there in the dry season, and there just wasn't much of an insect problem. Five months later in Drago, and what I wouldn't give for a bottle of Jungle Juice. No-see-ums are tinier than a flea and mightier than a mosquito, able to withstand Deep Woods Off! with a single breath.

Drago was almost everything we could hope for in a reality escape. Unfortunately, the no-see-ums drove us mad. The folklore is that the no-see-ums only bite newcomers and leave you alone after a month or two. We couldn't wait that long and did a Ctrl+Alt+Delete.

As we were to depart Bocas and make our way to Panama City, we happened upon one of the homemade candy bars made by Frankie, Neil the Pirate's neighbor, at the airport café. We bought one and it felt hefty in our hands. The candy bar was wrapped in an odd-shaped piece of aluminum foil that had been torn from a roll, and the outer packaging was plain white paper that Frankie had clearly printed on his own laser printer and then taped with good ol' Scotch tape.

We were eager to taste it. I mean, we were looking at homemade chocolate where the beans were grown on a tropical island and roasted on the spot, and made with milk that was milked that very morning by hand. It's gotta be good, right?

September took one bite of the chocolate, got a horrified look on her face, and spit it out in her hand. It was as dry as chalk and tasted like burnt ashes mixed with sand. The reality of making one's own chocolate directly from home-harvested beans was not up to the romance of it. It was a perfect metaphor for living the alternate lifestyle in paradise: Things aren't always what they seem and it's what you can't see that will drive you mad.

. . .

Before we left California we had purchased several flight segments for our trip: San Francisco to London, Istanbul to Tanzania, Tanzania to Japan, Hong Kong to Bangkok, then Bangkok to Costa Rica. Many of those segments had meaningful layovers, such as Mauritius between Tanzania and Japan. Now that we were in Central America our itinerary was like the blank pages of a new diary: We had no more prepurchased flight segments.

"We've been looking forward to moving at a slower pace," I said to the kids as we arrived in Panama City. "Now we can have that. We won't have to rush through a place in order to catch our next flight, because we have no next flight."

We settled into Panama City while we were making plans for South America. There were lots of things we wanted to see and do there—visit Machu Picchu and the Amazon Basin to name just a few. The Straits of Magellan and Torres del Paine at the southern tip of the continent were both considered musts. We wanted to savor the experience, which for us meant to go overland as much as possible.

While we prepared to go south, I took the chance to enroll in a three-day intensive course in Spanish. Granny had brought us Spanish lessons on an MP3 player when she visited for Christmas, but this was unsatisfactory; when we needed the phrase for say, buying bus tickets, we had to search for a file somewhere in a device the size of a cigarette lighter. Finding the exact phrase when at the ticket counter was really frustrating.

We had also picked up a Spanish phrase book, which was only marginally better. I opened it up and started to browse through it randomly, coming to a section called "Trouble with the Police." It had such useful phrases as: "These drugs are for personal use." "Can I speak to a lawyer in English?" "Can I pay the fine on the spot?" "You are being charged with murder."

We made it our goal to not need these phrases.

My Spanish teacher's name was Javier. "How long will you be staying in Panama City?" Javier asked.

"A few days. Just long enough to make arrangements to go south."

"South? Through the Darién Province to Colombia?"

"That's the plan, although we are having difficulty finding a route description."

"You cannot do this." Javier was emphatic. "The Darién Province is rugged and there are no roads. More important it's a wild and lawless place. People turn up missing there all the time."

The description of no roads was frankly a powerful attraction. However, two guidebooks and now Javier were starting to spook me.

● ● ●

"We are going." I was getting impatient. "How can we spend time in Panama City and not visit the Canal Zone?" The Panama Canal is not only cool, there is a lot of important history tied up in it. It was, in effect, begging for a Science Moment. I was eager to go, but Katrina and Jordan had just received a new shipment of books.

"But I'm in the middle of a chapter!" they exclaimed in unison. I decided right there that books were overrated. At least a nice sitcom comes in thirty-minute chunks. Books, on the other hand, always have the next chapter.

On our way to the Panama Canal's Miraflores locks, I told the kids what everyone knew about the canal. "The two oceans are only 50 or so miles apart, but a ship going through the canal saves thousands of miles compared to going the long way around. The coolest part is that the two oceans are at different levels so boats that go through the canal have to use water elevators. Which is what we are going to see."

Out on the observation deck I was mesmerized by the Miraflores locks. I could have watched the ships transiting through and being raised and lowered for hours. I tried to leverage a discussion of the locks into a Science Moment, but some people just don't get emotional about great engineering. Deflated, I accepted that in the eyes of a nine-year-old, Archemides' principle of flotation just wasn't as cool as the glowing lava of a live volcano. We left the observation area and headed for the canal's exhibits. I was in for a nasty shock.

"Dad, you are *wrong!* The Pacific and the Atlantic are at the same level. It says so right here!" Jordan was pointing to one of the displays with a description that stated most emphatically that the two oceans were at the same level, and that a common misconception about the canal was that the two oceans were at different levels.

In the space of only a week or so, two long-held and cherished pieces of playground folklore went poof. Next thing I would be informed that *F* no longer equaled *ma*, or, shudder, a human's mouth really is dirtier than a dog's behind.

However, as with most things, a simple answer is not always the most accurate. Months later, I read online that the maximum tidal range on the Pacific side is from +11.0 feet to -10.5 feet, and that the tidal range on the Atlantic side is no more than 24 inches. By comparison, the mean sea level at the Pacific end of the canal is on average about 8 inches higher than at the Atlantic end.

Suggesting yet again that things are rarely what they seem.

• • •

We went to Flamengo Island for a day of sunshine. The island is connected to the mainland via a manmade causeway. There is a good cycle path all along the causeway and you can watch the ships sail under the Bridge of the Americas on their way to or from the Canal. It was a beautiful summer day and we were doing nothing in particular.

"Katrina," I asked, "what book were you so interested in that you didn't want to come out here and enjoy the sunshine?"

"It's called *Secret of the Andes.* It's one that Mom bought before we left and is about the Spanish conquest." Katrina was quick to point out how evil the Spanish were, wiping out an entire culture.

"Not so harsh, Little One," I said. "Things aren't always what they seem. The Spanish thought they were doing the right thing."

"How can you say that? They were so mean and downright evil!"

"Perhaps, but they were also mothers and fathers who loved their children. If you had asked them, they were doing God's will, taking resources from a wild people and distributing them to the righteous. The United States did basically the same thing in the 19th century with the American Indians, moving them from their heritage lands to reservations. Many Indian nations died because the United States wanted their land. The nations that survived still lost their land and were moved to places no one else wanted to live."

Katrina gave me a slack-jawed look. I knew I had hit my mark. Even Jordan was paying attention.

"We can look back and judge the people of history and what they did, and a lot of it looks pretty stupid from our perspective, because we 'know better.' But really, we are tomorrow's stupid people because we don't know what we don't know. Future generations will understand things we can't even comprehend now. From their perspective, we will be ignorant and they may judge us just as harshly as we would the Spanish conquistadors."

Walking along the causeway from Flamengo Island back to the mainland with ships exiting and entering the Panama Canal, I had Katrina and Jordan's attention in the manner I had thought would be mine every day of our trip. I turned the conversation to a Science Moment without alerting the kids to it, explaining all sorts of things supposed "learned" people did hundreds of years ago, such as the practice of "bleeding" a patient, that we think are pretty stupid now.

At the apogee of my smugness for gaining the kids' rapt attention in such a lovely setting, I was walking into a first-rate example of how I can be pretty stupid in the here and now.

When we reached the mainland the nice pedestrian sidewalk along the causeway just sort of evaporated. We pulled out our map and made our way through El Chorrillo, a poor neighborhood that took the brunt of Operation Just Cause when the U.S. invaded Panama in 1989. We hadn't been there a 120 seconds before two people came rushing up to us, telling us we weren't safe.

"Um, sure," I replied, and kept walking. We were, after nine months on the road, seasoned travelers. We thought we were being spooked into hopping in a taxi we didn't want. Within seconds the police showed up and were pretty clear that we should leave. Immediately.

A taxi driver whisked us away. "That neighborhood is not safe for you," the driver told us. "Most parts of Panama are safe, but there are places you should not go. A missionary couple went missing in Darién just a few days ago. They will never be seen again."

That was the third strike against going south overland.

The next day I asked my Spanish teacher, Javier, about the neighborhood we found ourselves in and if we were really in danger.

"Yes," Javier replied, "the people in that neighborhood are hungry and have been ever since the United States left the Canal Zone."

"That doesn't make sense. If they were better off when the United States was here, why are they mad at us?"

"They are not thinking clearly as you or I. All they know is their hunger and that you are well fed."

Javier went on to explain that the entire middle class in Panama collapsed when the United States left. He used the example of his friend who was a butcher. "My friend made $2,000 a year when the United States still controlled the Canal Zone. But since they left, he can no longer find work as a butcher. He now makes much less doing odd jobs as he can find them. Many in Panama preferred the United States being in control of the Canal Zone. The promise was that the citizens of Panama would prosper when the United States left, but the opposite has occurred. Of course, you will never read that side of the story in any newspaper."

I went on to explain how our experience in El Chorrillo helped us realize that going overland to Colombia through the Darién Province was probably not a good idea. "So we will be extending our stay in Panama City until we can find a flight south."

"Then you *must* experience Carnaval. It starts this Saturday. We have the best festival in all of Central America! It will be a delight for your children!"

• • •

"Carnaval?" September said, when I returned from Spanish class, passing along Javier's recommendation. "I dunno about that . . . Carnaval can't be very appropriate for the kids."

"I said the same thing, but he swears it is *for* kids."

Carnaval is, of course, the four-day-long festival that is celebrated before the beginning of Lent. It is celebrated in the streets with a daily parade and dancing until the wee hours of the morning. It isn't the first activity that comes to mind when thinking of something that is kid oriented.

I had a mental image of Carnaval: There would be a crush of people who had been drinking too much, and essentially naked women gyrating in the streets. Brutal, yes, but I would risk it for the sake of the kids' cultural enrichment. Everyone we had talked to always used one word to describe the festivities. Wild. Okay, fine. Wild what? We were about to find out.

September gave each of the kids a business card with the hostel's name and address on it and two dollars so they could get a taxi home if we got swept apart by a sea of unruly partyers. We then bid adieu to the new stack of books in our hostel and set out to discover what the fuss was all about.

The police had set up security checkpoints so that the only way to the festival was to pass through them. They checked us and our backpacks for weapons, then let us in. Once through the security checkpoint, we were almost immediately offered the chance to buy a bag of confetti.

This was a bit unexpected. Gee whiz . . . I didn't really feel the need to throw confetti, so I politely declined. The vendor gave me an amused look, like he thought I was a bit of an idiot.

People were milling about with their kids and pushing strollers. We ventured into the throng, heading in the general direction of the music. I took note of the police in their olive-green fatigues and oversized weapons strolling up and down the street ensuring the peace.

No sooner had I started to wonder when we would see the scantily clad women, than we passed a middle-aged woman holding hands with her husband, who was pushing a stroller with his one remaining free hand. They looked a little too old to have kids in a stroller, so I assumed the child in the stroller was their grandchild. The woman looked at me and gave me a smirky sort of smile. Just as I returned a quizzical look she took a handful of confetti and threw it in my face.

I was stunned, rooted to the spot and sputtering in confusion. Where was that blasted confetti vendor when I needed him?

This repeated itself about five more times in the 60 seconds that followed. Clearly adult males are the preferred targets and it was pretty obvious I was unarmed. Plus, I was a genuine gringo, which was probably a triple-word score or something.

Even though September and the kids weren't the focus of aggression as I was, soon enough they too were targeted. Within a few minutes after entering the battle zone, we had all been plastered with handfuls of confetti. It didn't take us long to formulate a plan of retaliation.

"Okay," I said to Katrina and Jordan. "Here's what we'll do. People want to get me and Mom more than anything and you can dart in through the crowd easier than we can. So you kind of hide behind us, then when someone gets us with confetti, run after them."

For 20 cents a bag, we could keep Operation Blitzkrieg going for a long time. We just kept feeding Katrina and Jordan bags of confetti when their munitions supply got low.

As can happen with this kind of play the tactics quickly escalated. We hadn't gone through too many bags of confetti before the Super Soakers started to come out. Jordan, armed with a bag of confetti, had crossed enemy lines. The target was a woman in her sixties who had dumped a bag of confetti over my head. Jordan had locked onto his target when she suddenly grabbed him and held him while two of her girlfriends, both also in their sixties, doused him with their Super Soakers.

I watched, mouth agape, as the scene unfolded. I was worried that Jordan was going to return from his mission in tears, but when he did return, all he wanted was a Super Soaker and revenge.

I could understand that.

A vendor was ready with high-capacity water guns, preloaded and ready to fire. Suddenly Jordan was transformed into a little Rambo.

With his Super Soaker at Carnaval, Jordan was going to get revenge for every pat on the head, every pinch on the cheek, and every poke in the ribs that he'd received in the previous nine months. His target was anyone over 30, and he could strike with impunity. He was in his element.

After several street battles where Jordan could avenge all wrongs inflicted on the family, we made our way back to the hostel.

Not much more than 24 hours later we would be receiving a 1:45 a.m. wake-up call so we could catch our 4:00 a.m. flight to La Paz, Bolivia. We didn't know it then, but in La Paz we would be walking into a Carnaval war zone that would make Panama City look like a stroll through the Hundred Acre Wood.

www.360degreeslongitude.com/concept3d/360degreeslongitude.kmz

Red Frog Beach has quite a background. Of course there are two sides to every story, but the locals feel strongly that favoritism and corruption gave the developers the license they needed to build here. All I know is what I saw.

22.

Please Pass
the Armageddon Pills

February 27–March 6
Bolivia

"Just keep your head down and make a run for it," Arthy, the owner of our guest house in La Paz, advised. We had met him three seconds earlier and it seemed we were already trusting him with our lives. Reviewing the situation from inside our taxi, we could see that the odds weren't in our favor. It was the third day of Carnaval and a huge parade was in progress. The crowd had already been whipped into a frenzy.

The only way to the guest house was through the crowd and the parade. Our taxi driver gave us a sympathetic look and a gentle shove out the door. What else could we do? Wait for the crowd to go away? Our experience with Carnaval in Panama told us that wouldn't happen until the wee hours of the morning. We dove for daylight between a group of Quechua traditional dancers and a brass band, and raced across the wide street, pulling our suitcases behind us. At the halfway mark the crowd realized fresh meat had just been delivered.

At first it was just one water balloon. The barrage that followed was not unlike what happens to a chicken being pecked to death by its peers. The first little peck is totally harmless. But then the other chickens sense blood and a mob mindset ensues. Totally defenseless, we were pelted with all sorts of mayhem from water balloons to spray foam to buckets of water dumped from the second-story balconies above.

We arrived in the reception area of our guest house covered in foam and soaked completely to the skin. We spent the rest of the day drying our clothes, nursing our wounded dignity, and plotting revenge. 🌑

Jordan's Journal, February 28
   Today me and Katrina went out and got bigger squirt guns and a bucket full of water balloons. After we were done throwing water balloons, having water gun fights, and being squirted with foam, we were soaked even though we wore our rain jackets. Today is the last day of Carnaval. It was a lot of fun.

At 12,007 feet, La Paz is the highest capital city in the world. Having flown in from Panama City at sea level, we were making a huge change in our environment. It took three days to recover from the effects of altitude sickness: fatigue *and* insomnia (is there no justice in the world?), headaches, nausea, and loss of appetite. Even after three days when we started to feel "normal" again, a flight of stairs would still leave me clutching my chest and gasping for air.

The entire greater La Paz metropolitan area, and by extension, the corner of Bolivia into which it is stuffed, is the highest of almost everything imaginable. Bolivia has the highest commercial airport, the highest capital, the highest salt flats, the highest ATMs . . . You get the picture.

The statistic that we didn't see quoted was that it has the highest people. Chewing coca leaves in Bolivia is as legal as chewing gum (unless you are doing your chewing in Singapore). A casual glance up and down the street confirms that *everyone* in "traditional" dress is chewing something, and I don't think it's Wrigley's.

So what do you do in La Paz while recuperating from altitude sickness? You go to the Coca Museum, of course. 🌑 A staggering percentage of Bolivia's economy is based on the cocaine industry, and the Coca Museum proved to be fascinating, albeit in a disturbing way. The Coca Museum explains anything and everything about the coca leaf, from its uses among indigenous peoples more than 500 years ago to how to chew it, how to refine it into cocaine, and how to smuggle it out of the country. Did you know that Dr. Sigmund Freud was the first documented user of cocaine? Or that the successful outlawing of the active ingredient of cocaine in Coca-Cola in 1914 was the beginning of the lobbying efforts that resulted in the U.S. Prohibition Act in the 1920s?

One of the most titillating "facts" at the Coca Museum was that the Coca-Cola company imports over two hundred metric tons of coca leaves every year into Atlanta, Georgia—not to use the active ingredient that gives the coca leaf its infamous reputation, but as a flavoring.

This "fact" is according to the Coca Museum in La Paz, Bolivia. I found this information a bit difficult to believe—if the Coca-Cola Company is really using coca for any reason, you would think the general public would go nuts. Half of the population would be trying to snort Diet Coke and the other half would be bombing vending machines. However, for the record, if this news breaks—I'm a Diet Pepsi guy.

As soon as we hit the ground in La Paz we visited several travel agents to explore our options for crossing over the Andes into Chile and to the southern part of the continent before the southern winter set in. We planned to circle back to Bolivia and Peru after going south.

Patrick was recommended by Arthy, the owner of our guest house. Patrick ran a small tour agency in La Paz, and claimed to be a transplant from Switzerland. His passport might say Switzerland, but I had him pegged for an Italian in three syllables. After talking with him for a few minutes, I discovered he was a former banker from Lugano, the capital of Italian-speaking Switzerland. He came to Bolivia on vacation ten years ago, met a beautiful Bolivian woman, married her, and took her home to Switzerland. A few months before I arrived in his La Paz office, he had given up his predictable life of advising wealthy Italian clients as vice president of a Swiss banking firm to start a travel business in Bolivia.

Patrick's infectious enthusiasm for his adopted home caught me off-guard. We just wanted to get to Tierra del Fuego.

"No, no, no," said Patrick. "That just won't do! Right now is the very best time to visit the Salar de Uyuni. From Uyuni *then* go overland to Chile, and south from there as you wish. You must not miss the Salar at its most beautiful time."

I hadn't heard of this "Salar" thing. The Salar de Uyuni, Patrick explained, is a giant salt flat. (Of course, you already knew it was the highest in the world.) I have driven from San Francisco to Salt Lake City many times, crossing the salt flats in western Utah in the process. Too many times—I was willing to pay extra to drive *around* the Salar.

But Patrick's Italian gesticulating and enthusiastic superlatives started to break though my outer defenses. "The Salar is now covered with just a few inches of water!" exclaimed Patrick. "In a few weeks the salt flats will be dry."

I found myself thinking, " . . . and why do I care?" I recalled the floods of the Salt Lake Valley in the mid-1980s. Utah taxpayers had paid millions to create "Bangerter's Bog," the ill-fated project named after the governor of the time to defer flooding by pumping water onto the salt flats. It had been twenty years, but I still had to stifle a snicker at the thought of visiting a flooded salt flat.

I tuned Patrick out while recalling my experience with salt flats, so I wasn't quite catching everything he was trying to say. His Italian-ness meant that he spoke way too fast when he got excited, and in his animated, over-excited state, Patrick tended to gloss over details like driving through salt water.

"I'm sorry," I said, "are you proposing we *drive through* the salt water? Isn't it a long way? Won't it ruin your car?"

"Yes."

"Yes? Which yes? Yes it'll ruin your car?" I asked a few more questions and as the picture came into focus, I was utterly flabbergasted. No sane person would drive 60 miles across highly concentrated salt water, would they? I mean, salt on the roads during the winter is bad enough. I shuddered to think what that salt water would do to a car if you drove through it.

But Patrick isn't sane, in a loveable sort of way.

Not only was he proposing that we drive through the Salar de Uyuni from north to south through salt water, he was proposing a five-day overland trek on dirt roads, much of it over uninhabited terrain, right over the Andes dropping into San Pedro de Atacama, Chile, which garners its fame from never having received measurable precipitation.

Patrick was so enthusiastic about describing all the fabulous things we would see along the way that he was unable to calmly discuss such pedestrian details like where we would eat and sleep. Whenever I pressed him for such information, the conversation invariably turned back to what stunning scenery we were going to see.

Patrick had that charismatic quality that made you instantly like him. He also gave me an oddly uneasy feeling—something like a close relative you admire in spite of his quirks that surface at inappropriate times.

After meeting with Patrick I felt absolutely confident we wouldn't be taken out on the Altiplano (high plains), robbed, and left for buzzard food. This was a real concern: We learned from various sources that many overland tour operators in the area are primarily engaged in the business of smuggling cocaine over the border into Chile, using hapless tourists as cover. As I didn't want to test-drive any of the "Trouble With Police" phrases from the *Latin America Phrase Book*, I booked the trip with Patrick.

Back at our guest house, I informed September we were going on a five-day adventure over some of the remotest country in the world with Patrick as our guide. As I explained our itinerary, I could sense her anxiety quotient increase.

"Okay," she asked, "where will we sleep and what will we eat?"

"Uh, I asked that a couple of times, but he didn't really answer me. I think it sort of depends. Food is supposed to be included, though."

"Depends, on . . . what?"

"Every time I asked that, he ended up explaining what a beautiful country this is. This is his business, though. What could go wrong?"

"I thought you said he was a Swiss investment banker."

"Yeah, in a previous life."

"If I need to place a sell order for one thousand shares of Microsoft, I'll call him. In the meantime, I'm going shopping."

September wasn't taking any chances. Since it can be freezing on the Altiplano, even in the summertime, she went out into the streets of La Paz, and for about 30 dollars, bought us all a complete set of warm hats, gloves, socks, and sweaters.

She returned, and dumping a pile of winter clothes onto the bed, announced, "I'm going to get some extra food, too."

"Oh come on," I said. "Food is included on this trip. Patrick told me he was going to buy groceries."

"You said yourself this was some of the most remote terrain in the world. If we break down, I want to be prepared." And she was out the door again.

Unfortunately for September, while it's easy to buy, say, a kilogram of lentils from a lady selling sacks of legumes on the street, easy-to-prepare food that you can consume on the road is difficult to come by in La Paz. Peanut butter, for example, is nonexistent; I didn't know what September was going to come home with if our staple food was not to be found.

An hour later she returned with an enormous sack of Pringles potato chips and peanut M&Ms. "Sorry," September muttered. "Not much to choose from."

Pringles has the dubious honor of being the most ubiquitous food item in the world. If you could call it a food item. She also had a few apples and some cheese and crackers. But it was the Pringles and M&M's that got Jordan's attention.

"Hey, Dad! Did you know that Mom bought two whole giant bags of M&M's? Want some?"

Jordan knew that to protect himself, he had to get me to eat them, first. I was immune to Pringles cravings, but the M&M's were another matter entirely. But I'm not quite that dim. I knew Jordan's methods.

"You can't have any," I replied, trying to conceal my sarcasm. "Mom is saving them for our trip and some end-of-the-world scenario." That's how all the extra food and winter clothes became known as our Armageddon supplies.

The day of our overland journey to Chile via the Salar de Uyuni arrived. Patrick picked us up at our guest house in a giant truck called a Unimog, a huge 4x4 army wannabe sort of thing built by Mercedes-Benz. Strapped to the roof were two 20-gallon barrels. I was surprised to learn that there was an extra person on board. Ciprián, a native Bolivian, was to be the driver and chief mechanic, and Patrick the guide.

An on-board mechanic. That's a good sign, right?

We piled our luggage and Armageddon supplies into the back of the Unimog. Patrick took note of our food supplies. "But meals are included. I went to the grocery store myself."

Not wanting to reveal that September was skeptical or cynical or both, I simply said, "September wanted to bring a few snacks."

We had the entire back of the Unimog, about the dimensions of a good-sized moving van, to ourselves. It was nicely upholstered and we had lots of room to spread out for our long journey. Patrick and Ciprián sat in the cab up front. If we had any need to communicate with them, we stuck our heads out the window and screamed, hoping they heard over the roar of the engine.

After several hours on a wide dirt road, the Unimog started to sputter and groan. September and I gave each other quizzical looks. The kids had months to fine-tune their eavesdropping skills to the point that they could do it even when September and I weren't actually speaking.

A chorus of "What?! What?! What?!" started up.

Ciprián pulled the Unimog over to the side of the road. Sauntering out of the driver's seat, he stuck his head under the hood. I hopped out so I could stand around and act concerned.

Jordan got very excited. "Can we have the Pringles now?" Katrina lobbied to dig into the M&M's, which, for the sole purpose of annoying September, I had since named Armageddon Pills.

September stuck her head out the window and asked, "Do they know what the problem is?"

"Water in the fuel line," I said. "Ciprián is flushing it out now."

She pulled her head back inside and faced the children. "Water in the fuel line does not qualify," I heard her say.

Ciprián got the Unimog running again and soon we came to the town of Oruro, where we turned off the main dirt road and onto a small dirt track. The narrow road started out innocuously enough. A bounce here, a jiggle there. But before long it seemed that we were strapped on top of a jackhammer. A glance out the window told the story succinctly enough. The "road" was only a road inasmuch as you could tell someone had been along this way before and had taken the trouble to push the tank-stopping boulders aside.

The engine sputtered again. It appeared that we were still suffering from water in the fuel lines. A few moments later Ciprián had flushed the lines and we were again bouncing our way to the horizon.

Breaking down, flushing out the fuel lines, and then starting again became more or less a routine for us until it was way after lunchtime. During one of our stops, I asked Patrick about lunch.

"We have all the makings for a great feast, but we have no way to cook it until we find an inn to bed down for the night."

And so it was that we started dipping into our emergency food rations. To Jordan's dismay, however, September declared the Pringles and Armageddon Pills off limits.

As we continued to bounce toward the horizon, steam started to emanate from under the hood of the Unimog. We pulled over once again; a casual glance told me this time it was serious. "Now we we're stuck in the middle of nowhere!" Jordan gleefully exclaimed.

Steam was pouring out from under the hood and water was spurting from under the engine. Ciprián was a blur of action. He drained the radiator fluid into a bucket, all before I could have figured out what size wrench I needed. Then he pulled off the bottom radiator hose; it was split.

This was it. We were toast. A hundred miles from nowhere.

With Patrick acting as interpreter, Ciprián explained that all the jostling of the rough road had caused a fatigue rupture of the radiator hose.

From his toolbox of magical supplies, Ciprián produced an old bicycle inner tube and started to tightly wrap it around the radiator hose.

I was beside myself with disbelief. A cooling system is pressurized to 15-pounds per square inch; there was no way an old bicycle tire wrapped around a four inch-long split could make the radiator hose watertight with that kind of pressure behind it.

September took one look at the radiator hose and went back into the Unimog and dug through her suitcase, emerging a few moments later with a roll of black electrical tape and dental floss and handed it to Ciprián. Ciprián looked at the electrical tape and dental floss with true love in his eyes. The ruptured radiator hose was expertly repaired with a bicycle inner tube, tied off with dental floss, and sealed with electrical tape, and I was proven to be a doubting Eeyore.

And so the sputter-line flush continued until the sun got low on the horizon and we pulled into the tiny village of Satuario de Quillacas. We had been on the road for eleven hours, and with six to feed, we had gone through a significant portion of our emergency rations. In that time we had seen the landscape change from big city to the barren Altiplano.

> *John's Journal, March 4*
>
> *What a ride. There was no road too bumpy or river too deep for Patrick and the little Unimog that could. We are sooo in the middle of nowhere. All the buildings in the little village are made of adobe and the roofs are thatch, if they have a roof. All windows seem to be bricked over.*
>
> *There is no phone service here so the inn had no way to know we were coming. During dinner we met a Cuban doctor, a gentleman about fifteen years or so older than I am. He kindly gave up his room so we could have a place to stay and is now sharing a room with others. He was in Bolivia for "pleasure travel" is all I could understand. He is the first "real" Cuban I have ever met. Oh, how I wanted to talk to him! But the language barrier was huge.*
>
> *We were communicating a little bit, but what I really wanted to know was how Elian Gonzales was doing. He said he didn't know who Elian Gonzales was, and I said Elian was all over the U.S. news several years ago when he turned up in Florida drifting at sea. Oddly, after this my new Cuban doctor friend couldn't understand me anymore.*

· · ·

Jordan's Journal, March 4

Today we started our trek in the back of something called a Unimog. It was bumpy and I risked my life to get an Armageddon Pill, but mom caught me. It was dangerous to pick your nose also, because it was so bumpy.

At the crack of dawn Ciprián had the gas tank off the Unimog. He had drained it in hopes of getting all the water out, and was now in the process of putting Humpty Dumpty back together again.

We took the opportunity to walk about the village. The landscape was dry and desolate, and it seemed that the townsfolk live on the very edge of existence. As we walked around the village, we were ushered over to the local church and given an impromptu personal tour. By the end of the tour several of the townspeople were making a fuss over us, all immensely proud of their community and wanting to show it off.

Eventually the day unfolded like it had the day before. We bumped along a primitive road, stopping once or twice an hour to flush the lines. For lunch, we dipped into, yet again, our emergency food supplies because there were no facilities to cook the food that was "included" on the tour.

Around midafternoon we rounded a mountain, and what lay in front of us was astounding. As far as we could see stretched a white horizon of salt, covered in shallow water. The Unimog plunged purposefully into the water. September looked out the window, concerned. "With all the water in the fuel and the trouble we seem to be having, are you sure this is a good idea?" She seemed to be talking to the thin air as much as asking a real question.

"I think these guys know what they're doing."

"Can you give me an example?" September asked pointedly. "They're adventurous, yes, but that isn't the same thing."

We drove several miles into the Salar de Uyuni and stopped. I had crossed salt flats before, and had been skeptical of this excursion, but now that I was here, I had to admit it was beautiful in an other-worldly sort of way. From horizon to horizon the surface of the water was perfectly flat, and gave a mirrored refection of the sky above.

The result was that it looked like we were standing in the clouds, and out toward the horizon, you couldn't tell where the earth ended and the sky began. The horizon was utterly lost in the reflection, yielding a disorienting surreal effect. Patrick's enthusiasm for the place came into focus.

We waited for the sunset, as the colors promised a spectacular show.

Spectacular it was. Over the next 30 or so minutes the sky turned from red to orange then to yellow, green, blue, and finally purple. We climbed out of the Unimog and waded in the water, marveling at the reflected colors as the sky grew darker. I don't think I have snapped so many pictures in one place in my life.

As dusk gave way to dark, I wondered where we would bed down for the night. "There is a small village, Jirira, on the northern edge of the Salar," Patrick said. "It's about an hour away. In Jirira there is a small inn run by a woman named Doña Lupe."

"Is she expecting us?" I asked naïvely.

"No, they have no telephones in Jirira."

We turned our backs on the now-black sky and splashed our way back into the Unimog, to start our last push to Jirira.

But the Unimog wouldn't start. Patrick and Ciprián climbed back down into the ankle-deep water and cajoled and coaxed the beast for a very long time in the dark, peering into the bowels of the engine. September peered into the bowels of her suitcase and pulled out a flashlight. But even with the aid of September's flashlight, no amount of fuel line flushing and coercion from Ciprián would make the truck go. Patrick and Ciprián were looking more and more grim as time passed.

It was now very dark, we were in the middle of a freaking lake, we had eaten the last of our emergency rations, excepting one item, and best of all, no one knew we were here. The wind picked up and the night grew colder. September passed around our new winter clothes.

As September handed out the scarves and hats, I turned to Jordan and said, "Would you please pass the Armageddon Pills?"

With a huge grin and a cheer, Jordan dutifully retrieved the M&Ms.

23.

Armageddon Pills—Don't Leave Home Without Them

March 6–March 12
Bolivia/Chile

Panic hadn't quite set in yet, but we had already made a fair dent in our M&M supply when Patrick and Ciprián emerged, anything but victorious, from under the hood of the Unimog. They were speaking earnestly in Spanish, but I motioned for them to come have a treat. Ciprián quickly wiped his hands and cupped them, and I poured out several peanut M&M's for him. He looked as though he had never seen a peanut M&M before and he bit into one. Ciprián's face brightened and he nibbled the chocolate away from a peanut. He and Patrick then started speaking in Spanish. Ciprián's native language is Quecheua and I could tell he was struggling to make Patrick understand something as he was making a sucking sound with his lips while holding the peanut. Ciprián ducked under the hood again.

A few moments later the Unimog roared to life. I asked Patrick what happened. Ciprián, our Latin MacGyver, repaired a vacuum leak with a peanut from an Armageddon Pill and a bit of electrical tape. Jordan, and to a lesser extent Katrina, were genuinely sad that we wouldn't be spending the night in the Unimog.

It was oh-dark-thirty when we rolled into Doña Lupe's inn. Of course Doña Lupe had no idea we were coming, but when you have an inn at the edge of the Salar, you learn how to throw open the doors and get something good to eat on the table in nothing flat.

Doña Lupe was a large, grandmotherly sort dressed in a traditional brightly woven skirt and bowler hat. As soon as she saw us pull in she came running out of her one-room adobe house to welcome us. It was clear from the warm greetings between Ciprián, Patrick, and Doña Lupe that they all knew one another, and held each other in high regard. But when our family of four came tumbling out of the back of the Unimog, Doña Lupe gave Patrick and Ciprián a withering look and started to scold them like school boys.

Doña Lupe spoke to Ciprián in Quechua, and although we didn't understand a single word, the message was pretty clear. She spoke rapidly in a scolding voice as she pointed first to the salt flats, and then to the pitch-black sky, and then to our children. When she was finished berating Ciprián for endangering two young children, she gestured imperiously for all of us to follow her inside.

The Spanish title "doña" is an honorific, bestowed only upon those few who, after a number of years, have attained a certain stature within their communities. Doña Lupe had the only inn in town, the largest fields of quinoa (the grain grown high in the Andes Mountains), and most importantly, a herd of nearly a hundred llamas. It was clear from her manner that she was used to being obeyed.

Doña Lupe immediately took the children under her wing and sat them in front of the warm wood-burning stove. Pulling pots and cooking utensils from the kitchen shelves, she muttered to herself in Spanish, shooting Patrick a "look" from time to time, as I picked up a few of her Spanish words such as "children" and "hungry."

I thought about stepping in and coming to Patrick's rescue and telling Doña Lupe that we had a great dinner consisting of peanut M&M's,

but then I thought it was best to play the part of "victim" rather than "perpetrator."

Doña Lupe was preparing a meal of quinoa soup, which smelled divine, but we decided that given the late hour Jordan was in no condition to try something new. September quickly went to the Unimog and retrieved the last box of macaroni and cheese that we had purchased at Kinokuniya in Kamakura, Japan many weeks prior. September handed it to Doña Lupe.

Doña Lupe looked at the box as if it had just arrived special delivery from Jupiter and turned it over and over as if by so doing it would reveal its secret. September tried to take over and explain what it was and how to make it. Doña Lupe waved September off with her hand and proceeded to take the box and dump the entire contents, cheese sauce and all, into a pot of boiling water, and that was that. What came out some minutes later was a bit of a watery mess, but Jordan was so sleepy he didn't notice.

· · ·

Doña Lupe had built her first guestroom more than 25 years ago and has been adding on ever since. In the tiny village of Jirira, she had a monopoly on the tourism industry, but at $1.25 per person, she didn't seem to be interested in capitalizing on it. Her inn was very basic: Its few rooms were constructed of adobe with ceiling joists made of dried cactus. Despite being made out of dirt, it was incredibly spotless.

The next morning Ciprián was once again under the hood; the entire engine block looked like a giant salt lick. He was taking apart all of the electrical connections and cleaning them, then sealing them with grease in preparation for crossing the Salar.

Our $1.25 per person included a hearty breakfast of bread and scrambled eggs. When we were nearly finished eating, Doña Lupe brought in cups of tea made from coca leaves. I personally had no issues with drinking coca tea; without an alkaloid catalyst, the drug is benign. Katrina was another matter; to her, moral issues are black and white. To drink coca tea would be a crime against humanity, much like buying a black market DVD—and I had already made that mistake. I had had a discussion about coca tea with her previously, but as every parent knows, sometimes you have to choose your battles. I was in the uncomfortable position of declining the coca tea that was offered.

"No, gracias," I replied meekly.

Doña Lupe gave me a surprised, quizzical look. Perhaps we had not understood. She said in Spanish, "I have brought you some coca tea to drink after your breakfast." I could actually understand what she was saying. It was a bit of a language breakthrough.

I didn't have nearly the Spanish vocabulary to explain myself, so I simply flashed my biggest thank you (but no thank you) smile and repeated myself.

She put her hands on her hips, frowned pointedly, and proceeded to clearly enunciate three distinct syllables in Spanish, as if talking to a small child.

"CO-CA TÉ!"

I answered again, "No, gracias. Solo agua, por favor."

Doña Lupe's expression was a mixture of surprise and indignation. Surely we were imbeciles in need of a translator.

She marched away, muttering to herself, returning a few moments later with Patrick to interpret. He explained that coca tea is a standard breakfast drink in these parts. By Doña Lupe's audible "hmmph!" you would think she was Bill Gates trying to give away all his money, but these stupid people just wouldn't take it.

John's Journal, March 6

Bolivia is dirt poor. Then again, so were Cambodia and Tanzania. Somehow, this is different—"content in spite of poverty" is how I would describe it. Bolivia's poverty is a legacy of the Spanish explorations. The saying here is that Bolivians had the cow, and Bolivians milked the cow, but the Spaniards got all the milk.

In the 16th century Potosí, Bolivia was the richest city in the Western Hemisphere. The Spanish were mining the silver from the surrounding mountains to pay debts related to their infamous inquisitions. Initially Catholic influence forbade the natives from chewing the coca leaf, but when they realized that production in the mines fell, it was once again permitted. This was about 50 years before Jamestown was first settled in Virginia. Potosi has since gone bust, the riches having been drained away centuries ago.

We were still a long way from the Chilean border. Fortunately, after Ciprián had repaired the Unimog that morning at Doña Lupe's inn, it ran flawlessly. Bolivia is as big as the state of Texas and the parts we were now entering were some of the most remote and desolate on the planet. It is one of the reasons Butch Cassidy and the Sundance Kid chose to try to hide here.

That day we crossed the entire Salar de Uyuni without incident, and the next day we pulled into the town of San Cristóbal. I pointed out the window and said, "It looks like we fell out of Bolivia and into a Norman Rockwell painting." Gone were the adobe houses and in their place were modern, yet simple homes that looked as if they had come right out of the American Heartland. We pulled into a café for breakfast; it seemed that it had been airlifted from Route 66.

Patrick explained the recent history. "San Cristóbal started out as a small village seventeen kilometers from this place. The 350 villagers made a living from growing quinoa and raising llamas, and the village was identical to every other in this region, except for one distinguishing feature: It was the location of a small, historic stone church, built in the late 1600s." Patrick gestured toward the church.

San Cristóbal may have once been seventeen kilometers away, but it was certainly right there at the moment. Patrick continued. "The church contains intricate carvings in its interior and elaborate frescoes painted on its plastered walls, and is much beloved by the people of the region roundabout."

A few years ago a Canadian mining company had been doing some exploration in the area, and discovered some astoundingly large deposits of silver. The company was delighted and wanted to start mining the silver, but the problem was, the silver was underneath the village of

San Cristóbal. So the Canadian company met with the village leaders. Would the residents mind moving the village?

The end result was an entirely new village seventeen kilometers away, complete with a school, a small hospital, and a sports center. The company built modern houses for the villagers, and then deeded the land and houses to them so that they would have full ownership of the new property. Most significantly, the company hired Italian art experts to move the historic church stone for stone to its new home. Even the frescoes that were painted on the plaster walls were preserved.

The mining company's investment in San Cristóbal gives the village a strong contrast to other communities of the Altiplano, as it has paved roads, electricity, modern communications, and an actual sewer system. Yet, as we walked through town, I noted that behind many of the new, modern homes, there were traditional adobe mud dwellings in the backyard. "Patrick," I asked, "what gives with the in-laws' quarters?"

"Most people don't like the modern homes as they are too cold. They like the convenience of living in one room, where the cook-stove or open fire warms the entire house."

Aha. Residents were eschewing their brand-new company-supplied homes in droves. This was an epiphany—not everyone wants to live like we do! From our brief experience in Doña Lupe's kitchen, we knew that a wood-burning stove warms an adobe house smartly. The thick mud walls hold the heat in, ensuring a nice environment, even through the cold nights. I had naïvely thought that everyone was envious of the North American lifestyle and would jump at the chance to trade places with me. Surprise!

· · ·

The roads had much improved since we crossed the Salar, but they were still dirt. I could tell September was thinking about the town of San Cristóbal, which we had just left. "Interesting place," I commented. "All nice and shiny."

"I can't help but wonder what it will look like in 20 years," September replied. "Who 'owns' the infrastructure? Patrick said that the citizens own the houses. But what about the sewer, or the power lines, or the roads? Does the mining company own them? If so, what happens when they eventually leave? If not, who maintains the infrastructure?"

I had been wondering about similar issues. Some of the social problems we had witnessed in our travels and how they varied from country to country kept me awake at night. Something clicked in my head, but I was uneasy saying it, because once said, I couldn't take it back.

"I can't help but wonder if that's one of the problems we saw in Tanzania. As long as the colonists were there, the infrastructure was in fair shape. When they left, the roads and rail lines and power grid disintegrated. Perhaps because the outgoing government didn't set up a system of maintenance and the incoming government didn't know how to act until it was too late."

September looked thoughtful for a moment, and then said, "I don't know. Sounds too simple. Complex social problems are never so simple that they can be wrapped up in a nice little packaged description."

"True enough."

• • •

We had been climbing slowly ever since we had left La Paz five days earlier. As we reached the continental divide we peaked at 4,980 meters (16,340 feet). The high Andes were dry, barren, and bitter cold—nothing to break up the monotony of dirt and rocks as far as the eye could reach— no trees, no vegetation. Zip.

www.360degreeslongitude.com/concept3d/360degreeslongitude.kmz

Mars on Earth. The stark landscape reminded me of the Martian crater Gusev that, thanks to the NASA rover *Spirit*, had been on the front page of every newspaper years earlier. Then Patrick told us, "NASA comes down here every so often doing long-term habitation tests."

Recalling the scene from *Capricorn One*, I then started to scan the horizon to see OJ. They wouldn't do that, would they . . . ?

After crossing the continental divide and performing the border ritual into Chile, we found that the roads became paved and descended sharply. Within an hour we arrived at our destination of San Pedro de Atacama. We had moved from dry and bitter cold to dry and unbearable heat in less than an hour.

We had successfully made it over the Andes mountains. It was Ciprián, by his sheer grit, who had gotten us there, and September's paranoia that had kept us fed. The groceries Patrick had purchased lay virtually untouched because when we really needed them, there was no way to cook them.

However, the vision that had inspired the trek to begin with was pure Patrick. If he were my investment banker, I would give him my life savings. In spite of his unorthodox methods, or perhaps because of them, with Patrick as our guide we had seen some of the planet's most fantastic scenery and made it out of one or two rather harrowing situations. Nothing compares to the Salar when it is covered with a few inches of water. It is desolate and beautiful and there isn't any other place on earth quite like it. And I wouldn't have had the events unfold any other way.

• • •

We arrived in San Pedro de Atacama, Chile, on the eve of our 15th wedding anniversary, sharing the four bunk beds in the room of our hostel with our two children. San Pedro is a backpacker's paradise on the edge of the Atacama desert with lots of attractions and activities, most of which were similar to what we had already seen and done with Patrick in Bolivia. We spent our time in San Pedro making arrangements to travel south and debating if it was hotter here or in Dubai.

The following day, Katrina asked, "You guys aren't going to do anything for your anniversary?!"

"We can't just get a babysitter," I answered.

"We don't *need* a babysitter!" Jordan said defensively.

"No, I suppose you don't. But Mom and I couldn't just leave you and Katrina alone while we celebrated."

"You're only allowed to leave us alone when doing boring stuff like laundry. You aren't allowed to leave us alone to celebrate," Katrina said with a tone that reminded me that the teenage years would soon be upon us. "We do everything together!"

"Just about everything," September agreed. "But we just had a big adventure in the Unimog, didn't we? That was our anniversary celebration. What we need is to get some laundry done and make arrangements for moving on."

"How about that Unimog adventure?" I asked. "You guys didn't seem too worried, but you know if it wasn't for Ciprián, we might still be in the Salar."

"Why worry?" Katrina responded. "We could have slept in the Unimog, and we had enough clothes to keep us warm."

"But we didn't have much food," I said.

"How about all those groceries Patrick had that we couldn't cook?" Katrina asked. "We could have eaten them uncooked. Something always works out."

"We didn't need Patrick's boring old food!" Jordan exclaimed. "We had Armageddon Pills! We should be sure we take Armageddon Pills with us wherever we go."

Months earlier when we were cycling in Europe, there was almost always a fair amount of anxiety about finding a campground every night. Now it seemed all we needed was a pack of M&M's to remind us that all we really need is something to eat, something to wear, and somewhere to sleep. We were half a world away from Europe, but it was pretty clear we had come much farther than that.

• • •

"Did you get the bus tickets?" I asked.

"Yes. It's 23 hours to get there," September replied.

"*23 hours!* Holy cow!"

"That's just to Santiago. Puerto Montt is another 17. We have reservations in business class."

"Business class? Really?"

"Sort of," September explained. "It's referred to as 'Salon-Cama,' but they let me sit in one of the seats and it feels just like business class."

With Chile being a Twiggy-shaped sort of country, the north/south distances from various points on the map are huge. The country is 2,700 miles from top to bottom, and since we wanted to make it to the southern tip of South America, we'd have to travel just about every inch in between.

We had been on long bus rides before, but nothing like this. When we first stepped on board I was impressed. The accommodations were better than business class on an international flight. The kids immediately reclined their seats all the way back and started using the seat-back as a slide. I smiled at our neighbors and pretended I didn't know who the kids were. It would be a longer ride for some than for others.

24.

Roll, Puke, and Yaw

March 12–April 9
Chile/Argentina

We didn't know it when we arrived, but Puerto Montt, a port city in central Chile, was to be a place where Katrina would cross a big threshold from being a little girl to being, well, not so little anymore. She got her ears pierced.

Katrina claims no interest in such things; at least that's the story that she offered to her parents. By comparison, Katrina's friend back home had been begging to have her ears pierced since she was old enough to form a complete sentence. Much to the chagrin of said friend, her parents actually liked having a little girl and hoped to keep her from growing up too fast. There would be no ear piercing until her twelfth birthday, which would fall after we returned home.

In a pact of solidarity, Katrina and her friend decided that they would have their ears pierced simultaneously. I had been vaguely aware of this, in the same sort of way that I am vaguely aware that walruses mate.

That was until an e-mail showed up in my inbox from Katrina's friend, asking me to please pass along a message to Katrina that her parents would now allow her to get her ears pierced, so that meant Katrina could, too. I was confused. Had Katrina's friend had her birthday moved? I thought this ear piercing thing was on schedule for her twelfth birthday, still several months away.

As I read the words of the e-mail from Katrina's friend, an eleven-year-old girl thousands of miles away, I was getting waaaaay TMI-ed. Apparently there was a clause to the "wait until you are twelve" rule about getting her ears pierced that I was previously unaware of. Katrina's friend had crossed a certain biological threshold that is much anticipated by prepubescent females, creating a loophole in the "wait until you are twelve" rule. I would have preferred to remain clueless about all this, but the words on the computer monitor had already been seared into my retinas.

Without much fanfare September marched Katrina to the local mall in Puerto Montt to have her ears pierced.

"How do you know they have ear piercing at the mall?" Katrina asked in a mild and ineffective protest.

"You haven't been noting the accoutrements adorning the Metro Gen-Xers, have you?" I said.

"Huh?"

September translated. "What your father is trying to say is that most of the kids your age around here have more than one nose ring."

After September and Katrina spent the necessary amount of time twittering about which shade of purple earrings would best offset Katrina's brown eyes, it was time to load the earring gun with what they had picked out. Miss Ear-Piercing Person put the gun to Katrina's ear, fired, and with a squeal of pain, it was over.

Except it wasn't.

The gun had jammed. After jabbing a metal stud through Katrina's ear lobe, the gun jammed and remained attached to her ear. Miss Ear-Piercing Person tugged and twisted and probably swore at the gun in Spanish, while discounting the fact that it was attached to a living person's ear lobe.

The thing wouldn't budge. After several minutes Miss Ear-Piercing Person went to get Mr. Ear-Piercing Person. One look at this guy and there was no question he had had a *lot* of experience with an ear piercing gun, albeit on the receiving end. There wasn't a square millimeter of his exposed body that wasn't pierced or studded—fourteen individual piercings on his face alone, Katrina reported, not counting his ears. I had always sworn that if one of these pencil-necked geeks ever got near my daughter I would disassemble him with a pair of vice grips and a serving spoon. Now, here was a mouth-breathing Neanderthal inches from Katrina's face taking apart an ear-piercing gun with a small screwdriver, and I was feeling gratitude.

After ten minutes or so, Mr. Ear-Piercing Person had taken apart the gun and Katrina was now free to go through the piercing ritual all over again, using the other ear as a test bed to see if Mr. Ear-Piercing Person knew how to put the gun back together again, too. He did, and she did, and we left with a daughter one step closer to being a teenager.

• • •

"I never knew so much rain could be absorbed in one small region," September said, shaking off the cold after returning from the tourist office. We were making arrangements to book passage on a cargo ship called the *Navimag,* to take us to the southernmost reaches of Patagonia. The days were cool and wet in the late March autumn.

"Our boat doesn't leave port for over a week," I explained to the kids. "What do you say we go get some chocolate?" I don't remember who tipped us off that Bariloche, Argentina was a "must-see," but it was a short bus ride from the *Navimag's* home port in Puerto Montt, Chile. Bariloche had been settled by Swiss-German immigrants about 150 years ago who thought the place looked like home, and who had gone about the task of making this nook of Argentina as Swiss as possible, right down to the cow bells and some local chocolate-making.

Bariloche is in a spectacular alpine setting of towering granite peaks and deep blue mountain lakes. It does resemble Switzerland with its breathtaking beauty, but without the breathtaking prices. We were pleased to find that while it isn't far from Puerto Montt, since it is on the other side of the Andes, it has a much more arid climate. So we were blessed with beautiful blue skies.

"Today," I announced that morning after homework was completed, "is dedicated to the task of trying several different kinds of chocolate. Let's get to it."

Walking down the main street of Bariloche is enough to make a dedicated chocoholic swoon. The smell of chocolate hangs heavy in the air and every other door seems to lead to an inviting little boutique selling all kinds of chocolate.

We stepped into one boutique on the main street, just a stone's throw from the shores of Lago Nahuel Huapi. With our limited Spanish vocabulary we couldn't make out the labels behind the glass counter telling us what the many different offerings were. It was very much like being offered a piece of chocolate from a boxed set, not having any clue what you were picking out.

When oenophiles go about tasting wine, the process is to take a small sip and swirl, savoring the flavor, and then spit it out. This is so one can taste as much wine as possible without getting hopelessly drunk. We were adopting a similar strategy.

"Okay, guys," I said, "remember the plan, just one piece an hour."

We spent a great deal of time choosing the perfect piece of chocolate and then hurried out the door to try it. Jordan promptly picked up his carefully selected chocolatey mound and took a bite. He let out a yelp and his face twisted with disgust. What unspeakable horror was stuffed inside his beautiful chocolate? He struggled to find something to do with the putrid mass in his mouth. He couldn't speak as he flailed his arms and searched frantically for somewhere to spit it out. September took a nibble and discovered the awful truth: Jordan had bitten into a chocolate-covered prune. I pondered the motive for manufacturing such an abomination. I thought that prunes were universally abhorred, to be consumed only by the infirm in an act of desperation. Maybe this was the local answer for a chocolate-flavored laxative, but who would unleash such culinary terrorism on an innocent child?

Jordan was almost in tears. This was his one shot at chocolate heaven, and he'd blown it on a prune. I couldn't abide such injustice. To recover from the prune disaster we all went back into the store for seconds, abandoning any pretense of pacing ourselves in an effort to put the Prune Incident behind us.

Despite the unfortunate trauma associated with the chocolate-covered prune, I can now look anyone in the eye and tell them that Bariloche has the best chocolate in the world. Everyone and anyone should come to Bariloche just to stop in a different *dulceria* every day and try something new, but the little nugget of joy you are looking for is a chocolate-covered *dulce de leche,* which is commonly known Stateside as Danger Pudding. If you haven't been initiated to Danger Pudding, just enter it into the Google search box and click, "I'm Feeling Lucky." You'll learn all sorts of trivia you never knew you needed, such as manufacturer liability and the temperature at which sweetened condensed milk caramelizes.

It wasn't long before it was time for us to return to Puerto Montt to board the *Navimag* for our journey south. Typical of such journeys, we had an early morning departure.

The pier can be an interesting place early in the morning. This particular day, the sky was a brilliant blue and a young man approached us. He looked as though he hadn't found his local vertical in years, even though he appeared to be in his early twenties. The young man tried to look at us, but opening his eyes in the dazzling sunshine seemed to be causing him pain. He spoke to us in German, the words accompanied by a Niagara-ish flow of spittle out of the corner of his mouth and down his chin.

With some effort on our part, and a switch to the English language on his part, we were able to determine what he was trying to ask us—he had no idea where he was, and could he please borrow a phone? We told him he was in Puerto Montt, but that was no help to him as he had never heard of it before.

Katrina and Jordan were collecting plenty of examples of seeing drunk people around the world—from Czechs dancing in canoes to the young German before us who was in a city he had never heard of.

"How could he not know where he is?" Jordan asked.

"He probably came off a boat that came to port last night," September replied. "People can forget what they do if they've been drinking too much."

"Then why do they do it?"

"Why indeed. People do lots of things they shouldn't and later regret. We are a funny breed. The key is to not have any regrets."

We were at the pier to board the *Navimag*; I couldn't help but be impressed by its sheer size. We walked across the dock and into the ship's massive cargo hold. An enormous elevator that is used to lift semi-truck trailer rigs to the upper level of the ferry waited for us. Many of our friends have extolled the merits of a cruise vacation. I couldn't help wondering when they boarded, say, a Princess Cruise, if they had to walk through a smelly cargo hold and use an elevator meant for semi-truck trailer rigs.

The slick glossy brochure I was reading detailed our journey south: "It says here the route we're taking has one of the highest insurance premium rates in the shipping industry."

"Now is not the time to be telling me this," September said.

Katrina's Journal, April 3

Today we're leaving on a boat called the Navimag *that will take us to the southern tip of South America. Once we got on board we went to the common room and watched a movie of what to do if the ship started sinking. Mom said the background music that they played during the movie was about a sinking ship ["The wreck of the Edmund Fitzgerald"]. I thought that was pretty funny.*

My last act before boarding was to buy some motion sickness pills, because all September has to do to get seasick is look at a picture of a boat. Jordan is worse.

So why were we doing this? The short version is that it was all my idea. The long version is that I told September we would be in sheltered waters most of the trip and we would be asleep when the ship was in open sea. And I believed this. Really.

We got acquainted with many of our 60 or so fellow passengers and found that many were on journeys similar to ours; about half those on board were on around-the-world trips of six months or more. The *Navimag* seemed to be a magnet for the "around the world" demographic.

Our shipmates were college students, young couples just starting out in life together, and older couples who had waited for their children to leave the nest so they could strike out alone. As usual, we were the only family, and Katrina and Jordan were the only children. Most of the passengers were standard "traveling" European flavors—Dutch, German, Scandinavian, French, and English. The group also had the normal representation of young Australians and retired Canadians. We were the only Americans. For such a populous and affluent country, Americans just don't travel much. On the other hand, for such a little country, the Dutch are all over the place.

The afternoon of the first day the sailing was smooth as silk as we maneuvered through narrow, protected channels. That first night, however, the sea got very rough. By morning the waves had calmed down considerably.

"Rough night, huh?" I said to September when I saw her stirring the next morning.

"Yes, but I'm glad to get it over with. I was dreading it. Being able to lie down in the dark helped."

Our fellow shipmates stumbled into breakfast in a bleary-eyed stupor. Nobody had slept much the night before; most traded stories of the long hours lying down in the darkness, fighting seasickness.

The *Navimag* came with a chirpy, cheery liaison officer. She spoke English very well. Too well. Each time she introduced herself, she said her name so quickly that with her sexy Spanish accent I could never quite get it.

"Did you catch her name?" September asked.

"No. Ask her again. I've already asked her twice and I'm embarrassed to again."

"*I* asked twice," September said.

"I'm pretty sure it starts with an *M* and I think there is an *L* in there, too. She can be Mrs. Lady."

After breakfast, Mrs. Lady gave us our first official rundown of our route south and what to expect in the coming days. "During the night we passed through a channel that was opened to the sea somewhat and that was the source of the waves."

"So that was the rough passage I've heard about?" one of our fellow travelers asked.

Mrs. Lady's attempt at containing a laugh came out as a snort. "That was a mere dip in the pool for us," she said, composing herself. "Last night we were merely exposed to the open sea as we passed by the Golfo Corcovado. This afternoon we sail *into* the Golfo de Penas. It will take about twelve hours to cross the open water. If you are prone to seasickness," Mrs. Lady continued, "you should take a pill two hours before we enter the Golfo de Penas. I will make an announcement when the time comes. If you don't take the pill at least two hours in advance, the pill won't work." As an afterthought, as if for dramatic effect, she added, "If the boat rolls far over to the side, don't worry about the ship. It is built for these kinds of seas. It will not tip over."

That afternoon, right on schedule, the smooth sailing we had enjoyed inside the protection of the fjords started to give way to mild rolling.

At certain times of the day the passengers are allowed on the bridge of the ship to observe the captain and crew. I was admiring the geocompass, watching every turn of the boat reflected in its bearing.

Just then, Mrs. Lady's voice crackled over the loudspeaker. "It is time for everyone to take their seasickness pills. I repeat, take your pill now!" Her voice took on a slightly panicked tone. "Don't wait!"

The captain and crew on the bridge burst into laughter. "It's too late!" they all chortled. "We're twenty minutes away from the open sea!"

I ran down to our cabin to find September and Jordan already groaning in their bunks. This was not a good sign. The boat was rolling back and forth. It was only going to get worse.

I'd had a lot of boat experience, but this was new territory for me. Within the hour I joined September and Jordan moaning in bed. At moments it felt like we were in a free fall for one or two seconds from the top of a swell. To keep my mind occupied, I geeked out and calculated how high the swells would have to be if it took the boat one second to "fall" from the top to the bottom, and decided the swells were between 15 and 30 feet high. I found out later from the captain that the swells were actually 25 feet.

To summarize our state over the next several hours would be committing a TMI, but if you recall the restaurant scene from *The Meaning of Life* you have the gist of the situation. Katrina was the only one who wasn't hugging porcelain. In my misery, I lost track of time. Gradually, in the middle of the night, the waves subsided, the ship returned to calm waters, and the warm embrace of unconscious sleep overpowered us.

> *Katrina's Journal, April 5*
> *Dad showed me the bridge, which is where the steering wheel is, and the compass, and all the other things that tell you where you are, what the temperature is, how fast the boat's going, how fast the wind's blowing, and stuff like that. Dad really likes that stuff and I pretended to be interested. Then it started getting really, really wavy. It's supposed to stay wavy until about 2:00 in the morning. No one would go to dinner with me tonight.*

In the morning we all felt thoroughly thrashed, but it was over. Gradually, we pulled ourselves out of bed. Then it dawned on me.

"We aren't moving. The boat is at anchor."

"What do you think that means?" September asked.

"Dunno. I'll go find out."

When I got to the common room, rumors were flying. "The sea was so rough, we sought anchorage in a sheltered cove," was the collective opinion, but no one knew where we were.

We found out the sad reality after breakfast. "A few hours out at sea," Mrs. Lady explained, "the captain received a report from another boat heading in the opposite direction that the swells further south were thirteen meters high, five meters higher than we had been experiencing. He ordered a retreat to the shelter of the fjords. We will remain at anchor until conditions improve."

The puking of biblical proportions of the previous night was for naught. We were back at square one. 🌑

> *John's Journal, April 7*
>
> *We are on terra firma once again. The indigenous people [Kawesqar] of this area, now extinct, used to live virtually their entire lives in dugout canoes. They would build fires in their canoes to stay warm, and wore almost no clothes. Which is hard to believe as it's so cold. It is early autumn now and very nippy.*
>
> *The sky here is very big and different somehow. We watched the sun set and it seemed to take forever. The wind blows so very hard. We are on the edge of Drake's Passage, the only ring around the planet unbroken by land and infamous for its fierce wind and what it did to the early explorers.*

Weather delayed the *Navimag* two more days. When we arrived in Puerto Natales, our destination, we were a bit paler and thinner, but roughly in one piece. I said to September as we disembarked, "So, now what happens?"

September looked at me and I knew the answer immediately. "There is so much to do and see," she said. "A year just isn't long enough." We had arranged to meet September's father back in La Paz and had a flight the very next day.

Puerto Natales, Chile, is the gateway to the Torres del Paine National Park. Along with sticking our feet in the Straits of Magellan, seeing it was our *raison d'être* for coming south. But there wasn't time. The unplanned extra time on the *Navimag* had cost us our visit to Torres del Paine. I didn't say anything for a while. I was stoically rooted to the spot, trying not to get emotional. "We should've taken the bus."

"The key," Katrina reminded me, "is to not have any regrets. We'll just have to come back someday."

www.360degreeslongitude.com/concept3d/360degreeslongitude.kmz

On the "Mapa de Volcan Villarica Pelegro" (Map of Volcano Villarica Danger Zones), the bustling town of Pucon is set smack dab in the middle of the bright red "high danger" area. Hell-o! How smart is that?

25.

Aerobatic Maneuvers Not Permitted

April 9–April 20
Bolivia Again!

fter sticking our feet into the bitter cold waters of the Straits of Magellan, we said good-bye to the southern tip of South America and flew back to La Paz, Bolivia. In La Paz, we met up with September's father, P.

He has a real name, Dale, but everyone calls him "P." When the first grandchild came, rather than being called "Grandpa" he preferred "Aged Parent," in honor of a smelly, crotchety old man in a Dickens novel. "Aged Parent" was a bit tricky to pronounce for a two-year-old so it got shortened to "Aged P," which garnered a few stares so it was shortened to simply "P."

P is a techno junkie, and when September had asked me if I thought he would bring along his handheld GPS unit, I assured her he'd remember to bring his GPS before he'd remember to bring underwear.

Naturally, Katrina and Jordan greeted him at the airport by asking, "P, did you remember to bring any underwear?"

P looked a little perplexed. "I think so. At least I know I'm wearing some right now."

The tires on P's red-eye plane were still smoldering on the tarmac when we all hopped onto a single-engine plane to Rurrenabaque, in the northern Amazon region of Bolivia. One hour and more than eleven thousand feet lower in elevation, we were standing on a grass airstrip in one of the most untouched parts of the Amazon basin. From here we would start a six-day journey into the rain forest that would prove to be memorable not only for its beauty and remoteness but also for what we would learn about ourselves.

We checked into a small hotel in the tiny town of Rurrenabaque. The hotel courtyard sported a toucan and two macaws, and as Katrina and Jordan loved befriending the resident pets, all three birds immediately received more attention than they had in months.

To the kids' delight, P is a walking encyclopedia of animal knowledge. However, since after staying at Dolphin Bay in Panama, Katrina and Jordan had become toucan "experts," and were able to fill a void in P's knowledge.

"A toucan may have a really big beak, but it can't bite very hard, see?" Jordan demonstrated by sticking his finger out to let the toucan have a taste.

"But don't try that with a macaw," Katrina shot back. "It could take your finger off!" She tossed one of the macaws a large Brazil nut, which it cracked and opened with its beak as if the shell were no more than a candy wrapper.

The next morning we met our native guide, René, piled into a large canoe with an outboard motor, and began our journey into the rain forest. As I stood in the canoe, René tossed me an enormous propane tank as if it were a football. I staggered and nearly fell over the edge of the canoe into the water. "John-Rambo," René chuckled, "not too heavy for you, is it?"

The nickname John-Rambo stuck. Unfortunately, I don't think he referred to me as such because of my striking similarity to the movie character.

After loading our supplies, we puttered three hours up the Rio Beni, which is one of many tributaries to the mighty Rio Amazonas. P, who single-handedly keeps Duracell profitable by powering his small electronic gadgets, held his GPS unit toward the sky to receive satellite signals tracking our route. Our destination was a small jungle camp in Bolivia's Parque Nacional Madidi.

When we arrived at our camp in the rain forest, P immediately took a GPS reading and marked the location on the GPS's internal map. I gave him a glance with eyebrows raised.

"Just in case," P said.

"Just in case our guide has a heart attack?" I quipped. P begs for good-natured ribbing over his obsessive GPS data collection.

As we explored our small camp we were reminded that this region of Bolivia is relatively new to visitors. Had we chosen to visit the Amazon Basin in Peru or Brazil, we would have found a well-established jungle lodge complete with electricity and running water. In Bolivia, however, our camp consisted of a rough wooden hut with cots and lights powered by candlesticks. The camp did have a real toilet, although to flush it you had to dump a bucket of river water into the bowl.

Jordan's Journal, April 11

P brought us our books (instead of having them mailed to us). One of the books is Explorers Wanted! *about the Amazon Rain forest. Some of the animals that it talks about sound scary, but the scariest are the insects. There is one that bites you and then you just drop dead 20 years later. I like to read it to Mom because it grosses her out.*

I took to the camp hammocks immediately. When René found me lying in one he said, "John-Rambo, no nap time! Hike time!"

So almost immediately after arriving at our camp we took off on one of many hikes through the jungle. As we walked along, the tree canopy over our heads was so thick that it was almost dark, and insects buzzed constantly around our faces in the sweltering heat. We followed behind René as he hacked away at the overgrown trail with his machete.

René made a detour around what I considered a natural path. I didn't want to go out of the way to follow where he had walked, so I continued along my chosen path and blundered straight into a massive spider web. I didn't see the spider, but I'm sure the spider heard me.

"John-Rambo," René said patiently in his fractured English, "follow me. You don't want to scare spiders."

After that, I followed René's instructions exactly. We could be hiking along, passing all manner of flora and fauna, and suddenly René would state simply, "Don't touch that tree." Or, "Don't touch that plant." Sometimes his voice took on a bit more urgency as he would direct us to "run very quickly across these ants."

I'm not sure if he did that just to spook us. The kids were at an age where they were sure nothing in the world could harm them. September was a different story, and followed René's instructions precisely. Whenever René's voice took on a cautionary tone, P would say, "Oh my, yes. That's the flesh-eating (blank) of the Amazon. You wouldn't want to touch that!"

> *Katrina's Journal, April 12*
> *We saw a bunch of howler monkeys in the tops of the trees. They jump from branch to branch. René said that if one of them slipped and fell to the ground that they would be banished from that group and would have to find another group to live with. I thought that was really mean. Dad said, "The more things change, the more they stay the same." When I asked him what he meant, he said that after millions of years of evolution humans hadn't learned all that much, and then started muttering to himself like grown-ups do sometimes.*

As we trudged along, René pointed out animal tracks, but when he pointed out a set of jaguar tracks, September lost her cool. "What are we doing out here?" she cried. "Jaguars eat people!"

"Not you worry," René replied, "tracks are one week old."

This mollified September somewhat, until later that day when we found a fresh kill, which consisted of no more than a few feathers and something gizzardy. September gritted her teeth and trudged on.

During our jungle hikes we saw and heard lots of evidence of wildlife, but aside from various monkeys high in the treetops and a large herd of wild boar, we didn't see many mammals or reptiles in the jungle. There were just too many places to hide for an animal that didn't want to be seen.

After slogging through all manner of muck, hacking through dense undergrowth, and crossing streams and small rivers while balancing on the tiniest of log "bridges," René did manage to get more or less, um, disoriented. "A few weeks ago, a guide got lost," a red-faced René confessed. "He and his group had to sleep in the forest all night."

"Ha! Not to worry!" replied September. "We have a GPS device that will show us which way back to camp!" René had never heard of such a gizmo, which was just as well. The GPS didn't work.

"Well." (P tends to speak monosyllabically when on stage.) "It seems that my GPS unit can't pick up any satellites under the rain forest canopy."

Poetic justice. Ten billion dollars in satellite infrastructure rendered useless by about 50 feet of tree leaves! We did find our way back to camp using the low-tech method of retracing our steps, which was harder than it sounds.

René one, High Tech, zero.

The Amazon is insect heaven. Most strikingly, we constantly witnessed an immense kaleidoscope of colorful butterflies, and more ant varieties than we ever knew existed, such as the 24-hour ant.

Jordan, who had done extensive research in his *Explorers Wanted!* book, picked up one of the inch-long critters that was clinging to a stick. "Hey, Mom! If one of these stings you, it feels like you're on fire for 24 hours!"

September found the leaf-cutter ants more intriguing. To know September is to understand that she can't stand to see anyone, or any*thing*, mindlessly go along with the crowd. Which is why the leaf-cutter ants drove her mad. 🌐

Leaf-cutter ants are farmers. With one mind and one purpose they cut large bits of leaves off a particular variety of tree and carry the leaf fragments back to their colony. The leaves then decay and grow a fungus that feeds the colony.

In the rain forest we could see leaf-cutter ant highways everywhere. These paths were three to four inches wide and hundreds of yards long. The bumper-to-bumper traffic flowing in one direction was of empty-handed ants heading to the tree. Flowing the other direction was an endless procession of huge chunks of leaves, each being carried by a tiny ant. Each ant was working for the collective good of the colony, complaining about neither working conditions, nor the lack of days off, nor that the Internet connection is basic dial-up.

September took it as her personal mission to try to get an individual leaf-cutter ant to assert its own personality. She started by using a stick to pick up an ant that was heading back to the colony with its leaf.

"You don't have to do this!" she said to the ant. "The rest of the colony won't notice if you don't deliver your leaf! Take the rest of the day off and go to the beach."

With those simple instructions, she gave the ant a 180 degree about-face. In every case, the ant would figure out that it had been turned around and that it had to head back toward the colony and deliver its payload.

September has never given up easily. If she couldn't get one ant to take a mental health day, she would see if she could drive the entire column of ants off to ant Disneyland. She built an off-ramp from their little highway.

This started small—she placed just a single stick across their path. The empty-handed ants milled around, confused, on one side of the stick, and the leaf-carrying ants congregated on the other side. The ants ultimately prevailed and found a way around the stick. September's diversionary tactics grew until she had built a trench across their path several inches deep, lined with aluminum foil and filled with water.

It took the poor little critters quite a while to figure out what was going on, but eventually they were able to get around every diversion that September put in their way.

Her attempt at transforming a conformist ant into an individualist ant is the only thing I have known September to have failed at. That and getting me to like classical music. An ant is an ant, and will always be an ant.

Three days later we left our rain forest dwelling and made our way via canoe to the "pampas" region of the Bolivian Amazon, to the aptly named Mosquito Camp Number 3.

Mosquito Camp was not in the jungle, but in the grasslands on the edge of a slow-moving river, a tributary to the Rio Beni. We arrived at the very beginning of the dry season. The river was subsiding from its seasonal highs, but the water was still at the level of many of the tree-tops. Mosquito Camp was supposed to give us better wildlife viewing opportunities. It did just that, even before we arrived.

As René guided our canoe up the river, he maneuvered it next to a tree that had only its very topmost branches extending out of the water. In a few weeks the tree would be several yards away from the water's edge. The tree branches seemed to come alive. As if on cue, dozens of small, bright yellow monkeys came scurrying to the canoe. Clearly this wasn't René's first visit to this tree.

"John-Rambo, catch!" René threw an overripe banana to me as the monkeys came storming aboard. I broke it in half and gave the pieces to Katrina and Jordan. The monkeys swarmed all over Katrina and Jordan, jockeying into position to get a free handout.

An hour later, Mosquito Camp Number 3 came into view. René called out, "John-Rambo, hop out and pull the boat to shore and tie it up. Plastico, he may be lonely. Just scratch him behind the ears."

I had no idea what René was talking about, other than that he wanted me to tie up the canoe. Grabbing the rope that was fixed to the stern, I hopped into the water.

Something in the water moved. I saw a pair of eyes coming toward me. As the eyes came closer it was clear that they were attached to an eight-foot-long alligator.

I don't really know what happened next. Somehow I was hovering somewhere about four feet above the surface of the water looking down. "John-Rambo," René was laughing so hard he could hardly speak, "meet Plastico, the flesh-eating alligator of the Amazon. He just wants a scratch behind the ears. And maybe some spaghetti." I *was* four feet above the water, the hovering made possible by the balcony I was standing on; I just don't recall scrambling onto it.

Plastico was the resident alligator who had chosen to make Mosquito Camp Number 3 his home. We found over the next few days every camp in the area had its own resident alligator who hung out by the kitchen waiting for table scraps.

With the canoe tied up to one of the legs of the building, I called down to the kids, "An alligator can't climb up onto the balcony, so you'll be safe up here. Just step directly from the canoe to the balcony." After the kids scurried from the canoe to the balcony and were safe beside me, I continued, "as long as you're in one of the buildings or on the balcony, you're safe. You are to never come off the balcony without an adult."

This was the wrong thing to say. The kids are always drawn to a building's resident pets, such as the toucan and the macaws at our hotel in Rurrenabaque. Now that we had stumbled onto a resident alligator, they were immediately drawn to it.

It didn't help that René went up to the alligator and scratched the thing behind its . . . ears? Where does an alligator keep its ears? Anyway, you could tell by the way René moved that he respected Plastico, but was still comfortable approaching him, feeding him, and even scratching the thing behind the ears.

We had dinner a couple of hours later. Spaghetti. After dinner, René fed Plastico the table scraps. Somehow, Plastico didn't look as threatening with spaghetti dangling from his teeth. If it were possible, I became somewhat "adjusted" to life in camp with a resident alligator.

If Plastico had been a bear, he would have come right into the kitchen and torn the place apart, claiming every scrap of food for himself. But Plastico was content to sit outside the kitchen door with his mouth open, waiting for a handout. There he would sit, not moving or even, it would seem, breathing, for hours. Just waiting.

Now that we were in the pampas we went out on many sorties exploring and looking for wildlife. But unlike the jungle where our legs did the trekking, here we let the canoe take us on our expeditions.

We were looking for anacondas, piranhas, capybaras, pink river dolphins, and caimans, a kind of small crocodile. All these we found, in addition to a monkey for every branch. We even spotted a quetzal, a rare bird that symbolizes freedom throughout Latin America.

We went out looking for alligators that first night. We all piled into the canoe with our flashlights. After a few minutes, I couldn't help but think that this was futile. The river was so wide and black our puny flashlights were no match for the darkness. I shined my flashlight down river, but its light was swallowed by the blackness. As there was nothing to reflect back the light, all we could see were the fireflies dancing in the treetops.

René knew that was the point.

It took us about half an hour of searching before we found something that would reflect the light. In the distance, just breaking the surface of the water, a pair of glowing orange eyes shone in the blackness, waiting patiently—just like Plastico—for something to underestimate the blackness and venture within striking distance.

René had a genuine fondness for Plastico. But he kept several boat lengths between us and this pair of orange glowing eyes.

It was fitting that both Katrina and Jordan both asked about this later: why we didn't get any closer. "You need to know what is dangerous and keep your distance," P admonished. "And if you don't know, bring someone along who does." Useful advice for any jungle, concrete or otherwise.

• • •

"Today, we must catch our dinner!" René announced.

René passed out some loose fishing line and hooks, and prepared a small bowl with scraps of bloody raw beef. "Tonight we will be dining on the flesh-eating piranha of the Amazon."

We took the canoe to a promising spot, baited our hooks, and without benefit of poles, dropped our lines into the water. Immediately I could feel action on the end of my line, but when I tried to hook the fish, I missed. I pulled in the line and found just the bait dangling off the hook, looking forlorn.

From my database of playground folklore, my expectation was that I would pull my baited hook from the water and there would be a half dozen piranhas tearing at the bait like pit bulls.

René, on the other hand, *was* pulling in piranhas one after the other. The piranhas were tiny: Each would yield no more than a forkful. But the piranhas also had massive teeth for their size, and those teeth were very sharp.

"John-Rambo!" René was tweaking me again. "You no catch piranha? You need to learn first how they eat." He then demonstrated something that shocked me. He stuck his bare arm into the water.

"Unless the piranha smells blood," René blithely advised, "it will not feed. Don't try this with a cut on your arm."

I began to understand. The water is so black, the piranhas can't see their food. A piranha needs to smell blood in order to find its dinner.

"Got it, René. Don't slit my wrists and then stick my arm in piranha-infested waters. Important safety tip."

So how do you catch a piranha? You don't "hook" it, and then reel it in like a normal fish. When you feel it tearing at the bait you have to pull it into the boat with one quick yank. Before they know it, they's a-floppin' and a-twitchin' in the bottom of the boat.

We took the afternoon's piranha haul back to camp. As soon as Plastico heard the roar of the outboard motor, he climbed out of the water and onto shore. He stood patiently, mouth open, waiting for someone to throw something into it. Of course, Katrina and Jordan each wanted to feed Plastico a piranha.

"Oh, come on, Dad. Everyone else is doing it!" I had been dreading the day when Katrina would say this to me, but I always thought it would be about getting a navel ring or dying her hair flaming red.

I watched as the camp cook, the caretaker, and even René each threw Plastico a piranha. I heard a dramatic CHOMP! as the beast's jaws caught the offering. René stood close to Plastico, monitoring feeding time, presumably ready to manhandle the beast if things got out of hand.

And so it was that I demonstrated that when it comes to parenting, I have a backbone with all the structural integrity of well-cooked pasta.

I let Katrina feed a piranha to a wild alligator. Jordan, too. If someone had told me a year ago that I would be in the Amazon watching my kids feed a wild alligator several flesh-eating fish that they had caught just a few minutes before, I would have told them they were absolutely nuts. But here I was, watching the scene unfold before me, while I took out the digital camera and made an .mpg of it all. 🐚

· · ·

We had checked into our hotel room in the tiny Bolivian town of Rurrenabaque only ten minutes prior, but I was already showering off six days' worth of Amazon grime. September came bursting into the bathroom.

"Our return flight to La Paz tomorrow morning has been cancelled. We can either try to make a flight that leaves in 20 minutes or wait two more days."

Nineteen minutes later, without formalities such as tickets or security checks for derelict table forks, we were shoe-horned into a tiny Cessna. Two pilots emerged in military jumpsuits.

Our mighty steed was built for four adult passengers who knew one another very well, or who were about to get better acquainted. As our party was three adults and two children, we had to do some contortionist acts. I noted that there was an abundance of duct tape holding together the interior upholstery.

I was sitting behind the pilot of a tiny rubber band-powered Cessna that was looking down a short grass runway. I glanced over the pilot's shoulder to read a sticker on the instrument panel: AEROBATIC MANEU-VERS NOT PERMITTED. September leaned over and yelled in my ear so that she could overcome the roar of the propeller, "You didn't get all the shampoo out of your hair!"

Positioned right behind the pilots, I watched the youngest open what appeared to be a textbook in his lap. The senior pilot appeared to be giving his companion instructions. Our original plane tickets were with Amazonas Air, but there were no such markings on our plane. I tapped one of the pilots on the shoulder and confirmed my suspicions.

This was not a commercial flight. It was a military training flight, and our pilot was a new student, so would I please keep my questions to myself until we got airborne? They had a checklist to go through.

Pardonnez-moi, I thought to myself. The last thing I wanted to do was interrupt Junior and his checklist.

Soon we were airborne. The sky was clear and we had front-row seats to the green carpet of the Amazon basin below. As we climbed to the high Altiplano near La Paz, we watched the green turn to the browns of bare earth and the whites of the permanent snow cover of the higher elevations. Our Little Plane That Could couldn't quite get enough altitude to go over the mountain peaks, so we flew below and between them. 🔘 We could look out the window and see the sheer rock walls of the Andes only a few hundred yards away. The one-hour flight back to La Paz was thrilling, even without aerobatic maneuvers.

After landing at a Bolivian Air Force base near La Paz, we were escorted promptly out to the street so that we wouldn't observe that the entire military squadron was made up of Cessnas.

Typical Bolivia—spectacular, raw, rugged, and never a dull moment. For the adventurous, Bolivia is a thrill that must be experienced. Just don't expect a mint on your pillow.

I learned a lot about myself in Bolivia, and maybe something about human nature as well. It may not be possible to get a howler monkey to accept his own brother who fell out of a tree back into the tribe. It may not be possible to get a leaf-cutter ant to take a mental health day. But if I could get comfortable enough to let my children feed piranha to a wild alligator in the space of one day, given the right circumstances, people are capable of profound change.

www.360degreeslongitude.com/concept3d/360degreeslongitude.kmz

World's Most Dangerous Road. The primary road from La Paz to Brazil is acknowledged by *Guinness World Records* as the world's most dangerous. It is also the most fun you can have on a bicycle. Skip the return trip in the van, though.

26.

One Tough Kid

April 20–May 3
Peru

We were anticipating meeting Jessie, our guide for the Inca Trail, but at the moment I was focusing on making dinner at our Cuzco, Peru hostel. This was proving difficult because the burners on the stove were dominated by large cauldrons of a simmering green gelatinous liquid. A plaque on the wall above the stove hinted at the contents:

San Pedro is a sacred plant, a cactus, used in the Andes for healing purposes. Most people drink this medicine to heal on an emotional level, but it is also used to cure physical illness. San Pedro reconnects us to ourselves, and also to Mother Earth.

This plant is a Master Teacher, a great gift from Creator. It helps us to heal, to grow, to learn and awaken, and assists us to reach higher states of Truth and Consciousness.

When you hear this plant calling you, speak to Lesley.

I thought I had gotten used to the Andean extracurricular activities while we were in Bolivia. After reading the plaque, I glanced at the simmering liquid and listened. All I heard was gurgling so I didn't speak to Lesley.

Cuzco was the seat of Inca power in 1532 when the Spaniards appeared on the scene. The Spaniards found leading from Cuzco a series of roads that supported a Pony Express-like network used for sending communications throughout the empire, which extended down the western sides of the Andes from modern day Ecuador to Chile. One of those roads was to Machu Picchu, known today as the Inca Trail.

The Peruvian government limits the number of people on the Inca Trail to five hundred per day, and demand for hiking permits far outstrips supply so we had made our hiking arrangements several weeks in advance.

When Jessie, a native Quechuan young woman, arrived at the hostel to brief us on what to expect while hiking the trail, the smell of San Pedro simmering on the stove hung heavy in the air. Lesley, the 50-something Australian-born matriarch of our hostel, was guiding a fresh batch of 20-somethings on their journey to reconnect to Mother Earth in the next room. I heard giggling. I really did *not* want to know what that was all about. I tried to focus on what Jessie was trying to tell us.

"Since you elected to not have porters carry your personal belongings you will need good sturdy backpacks that are up to the task. If you don't have one of your own, you can rent one of ours."

Elect? I hadn't elected porters? My mind raced to understand this information. All I could think of was that I hadn't elected anyone since the last presidential election, and I couldn't even remember which candidate I'd chosen.

"Excuse me, Jessie," I found my voice. "I thought we *had* porters."

"There are porters to carry the food and tents," she replied, "but not your personal belongings such as clothes, sleeping bag, drinking water, camera, and so on. You can arrange to have a porter carry your personal belongings as well, but at additional cost."

This was starting to sound familiar. I now remembered thinking when I made our reservation, that I could carry my clothes—they weren't heavy—and then nixing the personal porter line item all those weeks ago. "Okay, we'll need to rent some backpacks."

September shot me a sideways glance, unleashing a death ray out of her left eye. Luckily, I narrowly escaped it. "Jessie," September asked, "how many hours of hiking can we expect each day?"

"The first day you will hike for eight hours," Jessie handed out a map of the trail, "then twelve on the second day, followed by ten on the third day. Depending on how far we get, there could be as many as four hours hiking on the fourth day."

September shot me another death ray, but this time I caught both barrels. I swear I had read that there were no more than four or five hours of hiking per day, which was the story I had told her when I booked the hike.

"What about the elevation profile?" continued September, as though she hadn't just mortally wounded her husband.

I didn't need to hear the answer. Looking at the map Jessie had handed out, it was clear that the second day was going to be the worst, when there would be 5,700 feet of ascent and 3,300 feet of descent. In Cuzco's thin air we were still struggling to get our breath just climbing a flight of stairs. This hike was going to push us to our limits. I wasn't looking forward to being alone with September, as this had been all my idea.

September then asked the $64,000 question. "Jessie, what age are the youngest children who have done the hike before?"

"Oh, this hike has been done by very young children, as young as twelve or thirteen years old, I think."

Nine-year-old Jordan beamed at the prospect of being the youngest to do the trail. Forty-five-year-old John was thinking of going into the next room and reconnecting with Mother Earth before September had a chance to unleash more death rays.

"We will pick you up at six in the morning!" was Jessie's parting, cheerful reply.

Our sole preparation for our hike had consisted of "being at altitude" for over a week. The entire length of the Inca Trail was so high that altitude sickness was a real concern. Now that we had a better idea of what to expect, I felt a little, shall we say, underprepared.

"You know, we don't have to do this," I told September after Jessie left. "There's a train that takes you from Cuzco to Aguas Caliente. From there you can take a shuttle to Machu Picchu."

I am the luckiest guy in the world because not only does my wife love me, but she puts up with me in spite of all my faults, such as being too clueless to grasp all the details of hiking the Inca Trail. Or boarding the *Navimag*. Or riding in the Unimog.

We briefly discussed forfeiting the hike and taking the train. Then she said, "Others have done this and we can, too. I'll bring some Armageddon Pills, though."

I smiled. I knew what she meant by that. Not that she was going to go out and buy a pack of M&M's, but that we both understood each other and knew that together we could overcome a lot of uncertainty and difficulty.

Early the next morning we met the other hikers in our group for the first time. There was our group of five (the four of us, plus P) and five others—an Israeli couple, another Israeli woman traveling alone, and two Dutch women traveling together—all in their twenties. The demographic reinforced our notion that the Dutch are the best-traveled group of people in the world.

Jessie was our leader, and supporting the ten hikers and one guide were twelve porters. Normally, the ratio is one porter per hiker, but the two Dutch girls were smart enough to pony up the cash to get a personal porter to carry their gear. By the time I was done packing for our hike, the weight of my backpack had ballooned to 25 pounds. P's backpack was probably 25 pounds just in Duracells. As I lifted my backpack onto the bus that would carry us to the trailhead, I was more than a little jealous of the two Dutch girls and their porter.

There were formalities involved before we could actually begin hiking. Each of the porters was required to weigh his massive load. They were limited to 25 kg (55 pounds) each. It seemed that in years past there had been some porter abuse so their loads are now regulated, but

I'm not so sure that the new and improved 55-pound limit still doesn't constitute abuse.

After the weigh-in, there was passport control. The Peruvian government takes the regulation of the trail seriously. I was glad we had extra pages put into our passports at the U.S. embassy before we left La Paz, as we were running out of places for stamp-happy officials to make their mark.

Once through passport control, we climbed for about an hour on a smooth and wide trail until we reached a broad plateau. The Urubamba River raged below us.

"We are all a family now," Jessie told us as she performed an Inca adoption ceremony. After blowing on some coca leaves and then burying them in the ground, it was official.

I would learn more information about the Incas over the next few days as we covered the distance to Machu Picchu, the most significant being that the Inca Trail is proof of an ancient civilization that was advanced enough to have arthroscopic knee replacement technologies, because otherwise they wouldn't have been able to go out on the blasted trail to begin with.

That first day of hiking was strenuous, but it was the second day that really tested us, and proved almost too much for Jordan. It started with a 5:00 a.m. wake-up call so we could have a good breakfast and hit the trail at first light. With twelve hours of hiking ahead of us and twelve hours of available daylight, we couldn't afford to waste any time.

Jordan simply refused to eat that early. I pleaded with him. "Little Dude, you need your strength to hike in this thin air. We'll be ascending 4,700 feet in the next six hours, and the lunch stop is over eight hours from now."

"I don't want anything!"

Yoda said that the mind of a child is a wonderful thing. Of course Jesus said almost the same thing. I doubt either had Jordan in mind, though, when they were being quoted.

As soon as we hit the trail Jordan's low blood sugar and the thin air packed a one-two punch. He quickly got physically ill and started throwing up despite his empty stomach. Moving very slowly, he required rest every 15 feet or so.

"There's no way he can make it like this," I whispered to September. September and I hadn't had a private conversation in almost eleven months and this was no exception. Whispering was the most reliable form of communication within our group.

"Don't whisper about me!" Jordan demanded.

Jordan simply *hates* to be treated like a little kid. I offered to carry his pack. I offered to carry him. Any offering of help served no other purpose than to remind him that he was little. I may as well have patted him on the head. It didn't help matters that every other adult on the trail showed equal concern. Every comment only served to increase his resolve that he was going to finish the hike, even if it killed him. ◓

Which, of course, was what I was worried about. Altitude sickness can be fatal. He had vomited several times and between dehydration and low blood sugar, I thought he might go into shock.

"Maybe we should just turn around," September reasoned, when I shared my concerns.

"There's just as much elevation gain behind us," I said, looking at our map, "as there is in front of us."

The part of the trail we were hiking had local entrepreneurs selling everything from food to shoe repair to porter services. It was Gatorade that saved the day. We bought some for roughly the equivalent of a small three-bedroom home in Silicon Valley.

"Drink this, Little Dude," I said, handing him the bottle.

"Ugh. I'll just throw it up. Don't make me."

"You got to have some, even if it's just enough to get the inside of your mouth wet. You have to drink some every time we stop to rest."

Katrina and P had gone on and were probably an hour or more ahead of us. Although P is a strong hiker, we had a good idea that Katrina would be running circles around him. With her boundless capacity for nonstop chatter, we also had a good idea that she would slowly be extracting energy from him, like a star orbiting a black hole.

September, Jordan, and I were in the back of the pack of the 500 hikers on the trail: only Jessie and a trail sweeper were behind us. Jessie carried oxygen and other medication for altitude sickness, but Jordan, who refused all of it, was starting to respond to the Gatorade therapy.

Mr. Trail Sweeper's job was to be sure no one got left behind. He carried a Peruvian pan flute and played a tune as he walked.

We were hiking along the side of a mountain that was part of a steep and narrow valley. The tune echoed beautifully across the gorge. I was huffing and puffing with all my might while Mr. Trail Sweeper played a tune as if he were on a street corner working for tips.

"He's playing an old Simon and Garfunkel tune," I said to September. I liked to annoy September with my knowledge of music from the '60s and '70s because she couldn't name anything that was less than 200 years old.

"Actually, it is a 300-year-old Peruvian tuned called 'El Condor Pasa' that Simon and Garfunkel put English lyrics to and made popular."

"Give me a break. You're making that up."

"Look it up, if you don't believe me."

"I can do better than that. I'll ask Mr. Trail Sweeper." Turning to the trail sweeper, I said, "That was nice. Do you know any other Simon and Garfunkel tunes?"

He looked at me as if I was from an alien planet. September has never said the words, "I told you so." I wish she would, just to get it over with.

Dead Woman's Pass, at 14,050 feet, is the highest point along the Inca Trail. Through sheer stubbornness, Jordan made it to the top. We found Katrina and P there waiting for us. Katrina was overflowing with energy, the excess coming out of her mouth as one long run-on sentence.

P congratulated Jordan for his tenacity in making it to the top. "Yes," I said, "stubbornness can be a good quality, so long as you don't have too much of it."

• • •

The day was far from over. Jordan even had some lunch at the top of Dead Woman's Pass. When we started again he was racing Katrina up and down the hills.

That is more than I can say for the adults.

At Dead Woman's Pass, the trail converged with the historical trail. The historical trail from Cuzco is judged to be to too treacherous and is thus closed to the public. We bid adieu to the broad, flat, hard-packed soil trail we had been following. Going forward the historical trail was uneven stone. Every step was a new opportunity for twisting an ankle or hyperextending a knee, requiring full concentration.

"I think I left my knees at the last stop," I said to September. "Going uphill merely made me tired. Going down makes me feel old." I acquired two walking sticks and was doing my best quadruped imitation. At the end of the day my triceps were as painful as my quadriceps.

"Would you like me to carry your pack?" September asked.

"You mock my pain? My ego is wounded enough as the porters fly past while I hobble along!" With a total of 500 people on the trail for any given day, about half are porters. They are the last to leave camp or to take a meal stop, and are the first to arrive at the next stop. So you are assured of having a gazillion porters passing in a blur two or three times a day. With these impossibly large loads tied to their backs with sashes of cloth and simple sandals on their feet, the porters *race* each other in a testosterone-fueled show of machismo.

"Don't mind the porters," September said. "Machismo doesn't turn the girls on like quoting π to the tenth decimal point. And the pack-carrying thing will be our little secret."

If we weren't already married, I'd propose all over again. With a rush of gratitude, I gave my pack to September. But only on the steepest of descents.

. . .

The ancient city of Machu Picchu is situated on a mountaintop with sheer cliffs all the way around, as if man finished the citadel that Mother Nature had started. One can hear the rapids of the Urubamba crashing in the canyon below, but the cliffs are so steep the river is well out of view.

When we arrived at Machu Picchu, we looked down on the tops of the clouds, which filled the canyon that defines the surrounding geography. To look down on the city emerging from the clouds gave a palpable sensation that this was more than a mere *place*. All over the world Switzerland seems to be the common standard for sheer, rugged, alpine beauty. Machu Picchu's setting is the only place I have ever been that is more stunning than Switzerland.

Crafted with intricate stonework, the city obviously wasn't built in a hurry. Machu Picchu is many things, not the least of which is a self-contained city with a temple, civic buildings, terraced, arable land where llamas still graze, and dwellings so fresh it is as if they are waiting for new move-ins.

I hadn't known anything about the Incas before I'd arrived, and once there, I couldn't learn enough about them. I was fascinated by anybody who could build a city with stone that fit together like a jigsaw puzzle and was so intricately cut that you couldn't slip a piece of paper between the pieces.

"Jessie," I asked our guide, "who lived here and where did they go?"

"No one knows. The Incas didn't have a written language. As such, they left no record. When Hiram Bingham discovered Machu Picchu in 1911 this is what he found. The inhabitants of this city remain a mystery to this day."

I didn't like that answer. The Incas may not have had a written language, but the Spaniards who wiped them out did.

. . .

Listening to the Urubamba River raging in a canyon 2,000 feet below, the only other sound I heard was September's labored breathing next to me. We were taking a well-deserved break. Physically, hiking the Inca Trail ranks as one of the hardest things we had ever done. Our legs screamed in pain.

After four days of hiking to Machu Picchu, a genuine hotel awaited us in Aguas Calientes, a 30-minute bus ride away. All of us were walking very stiffly, even the 20-somethings who made up the rest of our party of ten hikers. All of us, that is, except Katrina and Jordan.

I had been napping, lying in the grass, my bare feet dangling over the edge of one of Machu Picchu's stepped terraces. It felt good to have my toes out of my boots and in the crisp air and sunshine. Sitting up to look around for Katrina and Jordan, I let out a groan.

"Need some help, Dad?" Katrina was devilishly gleeful to assist me down a few steps.

"Yes. I carried you all over Europe. Now it's your turn to carry me." As we headed down the terrace, I let out a muffled groan with each step. "My legs just won't bend anymore."

"Then betcha can't do this." Katrina jumped a good two feet into the air, and while doing so kicked herself in the bottom with the heels of her feet. It hurt just to watch.

"Remember what Pa said in *Little House on the Prairie?* 'Children should be seen and not heard.'"

Jordan said, "Okay, then, just watch." And he and Katrina proceeded to jump up and down kicking themselves in the bottom with their own heels. All the adults in our group booed them.

Danielle, one of the Dutch women, looked at Katrina and, turning to me, said, "You carried Katrina all over Europe?"

"Yes. She suffered a broken leg in Switzerland. We had been cycling across Europe when a rock climbing accident left her in a cast on her leg, with a badly sprained wrist. I carried her on my shoulders much of our remaining time in Europe."

Danielle's gaze then turned to Jordan. "For a while, I didn't think he would make it! That's one tough kid."

Katrina and Jordan were paying no attention to the conversation. They continued to jump up and down, demonstrating their resilience. "Yes, I suppose he is. I practically begged him to let me carry him, but he was determined to make it on his own," I replied.

As the adults recuperated in Aguas Calientes (literally "hot waters") over the next day, it was easy to tell who had recently returned from hiking the Inca Trail. We passed each other in the street with a nod and a wink conveying much more than words could say. We all belonged to the elite brotherhood of Inca Trail hikers and walked proudly with the stride of one who had a severe case of diarrhea.

• • •

I had been both awestruck and bothered by Machu Picchu. Awestruck at the beauty of the surroundings and the complexity of the structures, and bothered by the apparent lack of information about the place and its inhabitants.

A few days later we were in Peru's capital, Lima to say good-bye to P and make preparations for the last leg of our journey. There, we were also able to find an alternate perspective on Machu Picchu. With the help of Google and Wikipedia, I learned the site was built in 1440 as a retreat for Inca royalty, like a modern-day Camp David, and Hiram Bingham was guided to it by locals who were quite aware of its presence.

"So why," I asked September, "do tour guides and books propagate the rubbish that no one knows?"

"I suppose if humankind could answer that one, we wouldn't be destined to repeat history."

www.360degreeslongitude.com/concept3d/360degreeslongitude.kmz

It isn't every day you see a guy towing an island with his rowboat. Once a month the inhabitants of the floating islands of Lake Titicaca add another layer of reeds to keep their island home above water—an admirable quality in any island.

27.

Kitchen Ballistics and the Cruisers of Paradise

May 3–June 1
Belize

There sure are a lot of 1968 VW Bugs in the developing world. It's a tribute to anyone that they can keep a single car running for nearly 40 years. Most of the Bugs don't look too spiffy, but they still do the job.

It never ceases to amaze me that you can give your credit card number to someone, hop on a plane, and within a few hours be in a place that is crawling with 40-year-old VW Bugs. It is a great life, even when the credit card company finally catches up with you.

Nonetheless, as our final hours in Peru ticked away I was sitting in a Lima hostel feeling sorry for myself.

"Be brave, little Piglet," September said. It was what Winnie-the-Pooh told Piglet when Piglet needed to rise beyond his full stature and accomplish a difficult task.

"But I don't want to go to the airport. It means we only have four weeks left on our trip." I had recently arranged for a new position at my former company, so at the end of those four weeks, a cubicle would be waiting for me in Silicon Valley. I could already feel its icy grip encircling me.

"We've already discussed this," September replied. "We agreed it's the right thing to do right now. We've got four weeks ahead of us on a tropical island, so let's make the best of it."

True. I knew there would be zero sympathy from friends and family because I was wallowing in self-pity at the prospect of spending a month on a tropical island.

We had discussed not returning home at all, and every time we did, the discussion focused on Bocas del Toro, Panama, and went something like this:

"Neil the Pirate said there was a great need for a boat mechanic on Bocas. We could sell the house, take a boat mechanic's course, and live a much more leisurely existence."

This was almost, but not always, me saying this. Over and over, we had to remind ourselves of two powerful lessons we learned on Bocas. The first is that things are not always as they seem: As much as we liked to fantasize about Gilligan's Island and the lifestyle of the marooned, the fact is we were not cut out for the island lifestyle. Relaxation is way overrated: After too much of it I feel like setting my teeth on fire. The second lesson takes more explaining.

On Bocas we observed the local children and the children of the Americans who had settled there. They seemed to be tropical transplants straight out of *The Adventures of Huckleberry Finn*. Bocas would be a fantastic place to be a kid, but it also seemed it would be a difficult place to make the transition to adulthood. Options were limited for all except the most ambitious, which is a polite way of saying we didn't see any future doctors or astronauts on Bocas. Returning home was the best way to give Karina and Jordan the same thing that September and I had had: the opportunity to do with our lives as we wanted.

. . .

Belize had been British Honduras until 1981, when the residents decided they wanted their independence. Britain was used to the "independence" thing by this time so, with no muskets fired and no tea being dumped into the bay, the keys of power were transferred to the locals.

We settled in on Ambergris Caye, a tiny island just fifteen miles from the mainland and protected by the world's second largest barrier reef. How we came to this place was quite simple. We were looking for a place like Bocas to spend our last month, but it had to have a real grocery store within walking distance and it had to be between South America and California.

Our goal for Ambergris Caye was to get such a powerful case of island fever we would be dancing around doing our Dorothy impressions, clicking our heels together and saying, "There's no place like home, there's no place like home . . ."

It's not that there was nothing to do on Ambergris Caye, nor is it like we did nothing during our four weeks there. We rented bikes and rode up and down the island several times. We went on a few snorkeling trips, fed eagle rays, and petted a shark. Those activities consumed a few days. Beyond that we mostly spent our days sitting by the pool or dangling our feet off the pier. Katrina also spent an awful lot of time in the kitchen of the condo we had rented. A day hardly went by that she didn't bake a cake, cinnamon rolls, cookies, or a pie.

Katrina and Jordan, who I previously would have thought could adapt to anything, were, for the first time, starting to count down the number of days until we went home.

During the first eleven months on our trip we rarely stayed more than three or four nights in a single place. We were always on the go, figuring out who the local people were, what the area's highlights were, where we should stay, and how we should get there. Until we stopped, it was difficult to realize how fast we had been moving.

After we arrived at our condo in Belize, I found myself thinking, "Gee, where are all the leaf-cutter ants?" Ambergris Caye seemed rather domesticated. In fact, it seemed a little too much like Maui; English was the official language, everything was clean, and there were no swarming insects to torment us. Not that there is anything wrong with Maui, but as far as an adventurous travel destination, it ranks right up there with Fresno.

As I contemplated the lack of leaf-cutter ants, I had to remind myself that we weren't there to partake of adventure, but to get bored and reflect on our year abroad.

So, what about that year? Did we learn anything? Well, I learned that foreign coins breed in suitcases. I don't know how many times I found a coin from, say, Turkey or Mauritius, in the bottom of my suitcase—countries we had left several months earlier.

We learned a lot of valuable things we wouldn't necessarily carry in our suitcases, such as we can get by with a lot less stuff than I would have guessed a year earlier. We learned a tiny bit about what the world is like, but also learned that there is way more that we don't know than we do know.

Ultimately, I concluded that not only would the lessons "we" learned be different depending on who was describing the lesson, but also when. Taking our kids around the world was a 20-year experiment in human behavior—to draw conclusions about "what we learned during our World-the-Round Trip" without the perspective of time would be too much like predicting the future.

. . .

Mr. and Mrs. Middle America were on Ambergris Caye in droves. Because there were almost no cars on the island, and zero rental cars, tourists tooled around in little golf carts. It was so different from the backpacker culture that had been present everywhere we went in Africa, Asia, and South America. The tourists were my demographic, but I identified with the backpackers, with their curiosity about other cultures and the natural environments found in out-of-the-way places around the globe.

Sitting by the pool at our condo, I listened to overstuffed Americans with gold chains around their necks brag about their cool toys back home—Jet Skis, snowmobiles, speedboats, and, of course, fast cars. Cooing over motorized toys seemed so trite, yet I heard myself in their voices, having the same conversation in a place not too far away, not too long ago. It seemed a lifetime had passed since I had lusted for mechanized gratification. Listening to such talk made me uncomfortable.

Katrina was a one-woman baking machine on Ambergris Caye. Jordan would eagerly wait outside the kitchen, just like Plastico. Though Jordan didn't stand outside the kitchen perfectly still with his mouth open for a treat, he didn't want to actually help with the baking or the cleaning process that followed, but was only too happy to eat the results.

One day when Katrina was making cinnamon rolls, Jordan came in from the swimming pool dripping wet.

"Hey, Katrina! Whatcha making?" Jordan inquired with a gleam in his eye.

"Cinnamon rolls. Want to help?"

"Nope. And I don't want cinnamon rolls. I want raspberry ribbon pie. Why don't you make a raspberry ribbon pie?"

"I made raspberry ribbon pie a couple of days ago, and I've already rolled out the dough for the cinnamon rolls. Besides, I don't have any cream cheese."

"I'll go to the store and buy cream cheese," he offered. Knowing that Katrina feared lighting the oven, he continued, "And I'll light the oven for your rolls." That clinched the deal. Jordan has potential in politics.

Later, when the rolls were ready to go into the oven, Jordan was eager to light it. He was of the age that anything to do with fire was cool, and so much the better if there was a chance it could blow up.

I happened to be standing by the oven and Jordan had his head halfway inside, ready to offer it a match. The next thing I knew there was a flash of heat on my legs, a tremendous BANG, and Jordan was flying across the kitchen toward the bathroom. He claimed he jumped backward, but I saw the incident with my own eyes, and I didn't think a human being could hurl himself backward that fast without some additional propulsion.

I gave Jordan a quick appraisal. Two eyes, one nose. That was good. No flash marks. That was good, too. The hair was all there, but I wasn't sure if that was a good thing or not. If I squinted hard, I thought I could see a singed eyebrow, but it might have been that Jordan had gone to seed a bit since we'd landed on the island.

The oven incident was one of those life lessons that will have a way of changing with the perspective of time. Now Jordan remembers to turn the gas on low and keep it on for only a moment before lighting the match. I hope that eventually the lesson will morph into something more along the lines of, "Just because you have done something many times, that doesn't mean you know all there is to know about it."

In the meantime, Jordan decided that lighting the oven is a job for Dad, who is still of the age that anything to do with fire is cool, and so much the better if there is a chance it can blow up.

---

www.360degreeslongitude.com/concept3d/360degreeslongitude.kmz

Science Moment—Entropy. A lab experiment in entropy to see what happens if one doesn't take a shower or comb his hair for a month. See?

During our stay on Ambergris Caye we rented bikes for the entire month. If there ever was a 1968 VW Bug of the bicycle world, these babies were it. When we went to the bike shop, I noted that every bike in the shop was the same: all built like locomotives and probably just as heavy, with only one speed and the kind of brakes where you have to press backward on the pedals and then hope that the bike actually slows down. Every bike, without exception, had deep patterns of salt corrosion. Before we could try one of the bikes, the shop owner ran a stiff wire brush over the chain to dislodge the larger chunks of rust.

Bicycles are a way of life on Ambergris Caye. Although the more affluent families on the island can afford golf carts, most of the population tools around on their one-speed rusty beach cruisers.

On our last day on the island, we packed some snacks and drinks into the wire basket mounted on the handlebars of my bike, filled the basket with ice to keep the foodstuffs cold, and then set out for a picnic at a pier at the end of the island.

As we pedaled down the sandy road on our 1968 VW Bug-bikes, I couldn't help but think about how far we had come during our year, both figuratively and literally. Our near-state-of-the-art tandems were waiting for us in storage at home. Most people in the world will never know the difference between a two-ton, single-speed beach cruiser with a wire basket mounted on the handlebars and a finely engineered modern bicycle, let alone a finely engineered modern car.

I knew the difference, though. Luckily, over the past year I had learned to be just as happy on a rusty beach cruiser, bouncing across potholes and sliding in the sand; I no longer saw my identity formed by where I lived, what I drove, or what I did for a living.

We arrived at the pier and ate our picnic. After we finished eating, no one moved. The sun was setting in the west and the four of us watched the horizon as it transitioned through the color spectrum from bright blue to deep red. "I can't help but think back on the sleepless nights before we left for Iceland, contemplating 'what if . . . ,'" September mused.

"Had we known Katrina would break her leg, or that we would get stranded, penniless, in Lushoto, would we have stepped on that first plane?" I responded.

Jordan stopped what he was doing and stared at me as if I had lobsters crawling out of my ears. "Why would that have stopped us?" he asked, incredulous.

"Before we left, we worried a lot about what could happen. A lot of the things we worried about actually did happen," September replied. "It's possible if we'd known all these things we may have simply stayed home."

That was true. Given the cold facts, September and I may have just chickened out. If I had learned anything though, it was that cold facts are just that. Cold. To understand something, someone, or someplace you can't simply analyze it intellectually and expect all the answers. To be understood, places, humanity, and culture have to be *felt*. To be lived.

"It's lucky you can't tell the future, then," Katrina responded. "Because everything turned out just fine."

REENTRY

John's Epilogue

After being away for more than 52 weeks, we landed at the San Jose, California airport at 11:00 p.m. on a Sunday night. I had to be at work for the first time in over a year at 9:00 the following morning.

When I arrived at work the next morning a colleague bumped into me in the hallway. He said, "Hey! I heard you were back. I, uh, expected you to be more suntanned."

He was looking for some sort of change in me. I *had* changed, but it wasn't visible. There was no real way to communicate that change, so I smiled and said, "A suntan is more than skin deep."

Later that evening a box full of mail was thrust into my hands. For twelve months, home had been "where our stuff was." Now I was holding mortgage statements, IRA statements, letters from the IRS, and property tax assessments. I hadn't opened a letter in more than a year. Why should I care about any of that stuff? Or any "stuff" at all?

"Stuff" just creates stress. Who's to say that *hakuna matata* isn't a better philosophy?

In the weeks that followed, I would find myself waiting in line at the grocery store, and a stranger would introduce himself (or herself) and tell me how much he (or she) enjoyed my e-mails and photos from our trip. "September's friend forwarded them to me!" Then came the standard follow-up question: "How is it being home?"

How is it being home? It took me months to sift through all of the conflicting feelings to formulate a good answer for that one.

It is good to be among friends again. It is indescribably wonderful to have a hot shower whenever I want one. We can also walk into a grocery store, buy fresh milk, and take it home and put it in the refrigerator where it will stay fresh.

But during our travels, "home" wasn't a place. It was a feeling of being together. Now that we have activities taking us in different directions, the hardest adjustment is that home once again has become a place. Capturing that same feeling of being together requires work.

Within a few months of reentry Katrina had entered a world of cell phones and chemically dependent hair. Jordan had become assimilated into a world of baseball and superhero comic books. September was once again doing hand-to-mouse combat with 1's and 0's and I was working on the next generation of satellites for satellite radio.

When we were traveling it felt natural that we would always be together. Now, our individual interests pulled us in different directions; if we wanted face time as a family, we had to schedule it on the calendar. So that's what we do.

"Movie night!" I exclaimed. "We're watching *Forrest Gump!*"

"Whatzit about?" Katrina and Jordan asked simultaneously.

"Doesn't matter. The four of us are going to cram onto the bed and pretend it's the Unimog and we're stranded in the middle of nowhere. There is a force field around us so nothing can get in or out until the movie is over. Cell phones off!"

An hour or so into the movie and the familiar "Life is like a box of chocolates" resonated as it never had before. In our year abroad, we found things are rarely what they seem. People are complex and are more than the sum of their experiences and our preconceptions. Seeing the WTO riots in Hong Kong left a much different impression than when I read about them in the *New York Times*. Being rescued by the humble people in the Usambara Mountains left a much different impression on me than if I'd read about those kind souls in *National Geographic*. As with chocolates, so with life. You may get chocolate-covered *dulce de leche* or a chocolate-covered prune; it might be a Horse Shit Ball special delivery from Switzerland or a tropical island-made bar that tastes like dirt. Or quite possibly M&M's on the Bolivian Altiplano.

But you'll never know until you take a bite.

Jordan's Epilogue

I wore my Tevas all the time when we were traveling. My first day back at school I was playing on the playground and one of the yard duty teachers said I couldn't stay on the playground because I was wearing sandals. She said I might stub my toe because they were open-toed shoes. What's up with that? I wanted to tell her that I had worn these shoes to search for lions in Africa and look for anacondas in the Amazon. But I thought that might be rude, so I didn't say anything.

I mostly don't talk about the trip to my friends because they don't really know where all of the places are. Sometimes when school gets a little bit boring I sit at my desk and remember things like feeding the alligator or riding on the elephant and I get a big smile on my face. When I get home I talk to Katrina about it and we laugh like we have a big secret!

Katrina's Epilogue

When I came home I was nervous about going back to school, since all we covered during our year away was math. But when I talked to my friends about it, they said I shouldn't worry because they didn't really learn anything in the sixth grade. At first it was difficult to adjust to all the homework we got in the seventh grade, but I found I wasn't behind my friends and they had to adjust to the homework, too.

Whenever adults ask me about how our trip changed me, I don't know how to answer. It is part of who I am. How would I know if I would be different if we hadn't gone? But I find myself thinking about our trip every single day, even though we've been home for over a year now. While Dad worked on his book he read us the chapters and I would remember things I hadn't thought of for a long time, like how a howler monkey would get kicked out of its family if it fell from a tree. Sometimes things he read didn't agree with how I remembered them.

One of the most memorable parts of the trip for me was reading books about people and places and then visiting those places. I'll never forget how bad I felt for the Japanese who were left in Korea at the end of World War II when I read *So Far from the Bamboo Grove*. But then reading the story of how badly the Japanese treated the Koreans in *Year of Impossible Goodbyes* made me realize that there can always be more to a story.

I want to take my own kids on an around-the-world trip.

September Gets the Last Word (You Expected Something Else?)

Now that we're home, holding onto the feelings of togetherness that we experienced on our trip has been like holding sand in our cupped hands. As we've gone about our suburban lives—registering the kids for school, moving back into our house, going back to work—some of that sand is slipping through our fingers. To counter that, we are now more careful about what individual activities we do so that we can continue to have time together as a family. It's a challenge. There are so many things competing for our family time—homework, church activities, sports, music lessons—that it takes constant prioritizing to make sure we carve out enough time to simply be together.

When we walked into our house for the first time, the kids exclaimed, "The house is way too big!" After spending twelve months rarely more than two feet from one another, even our small, three-bedroom house seemed like more space than anyone would ever need. The kids refused to sleep in separate bedrooms for several weeks. For me, I now delight more in simple things. I love my washer and dryer. I run out to my garden every morning to see if anything new has sprouted.

Many of our friends never expected to see us again. The consensus was that we would find some nice part of the world and just stay there. When we actually did return, our friends predicted that we would be too restless to endure suburban existence for long. The idea for the next big thing would materialize and we would vanish.

Tempting as it was to "just keep going," the reality was that our bank account had run dry. And beyond that, we had a reason to return home. Two reasons, actually: Katrina and Jordan.

Countless Sunday dinner conversations have been devoted to the topic of living an alternative lifestyle somewhere outside of the United States. The four of us agree that traveling the world enriched our lives so much and that we see the world through different eyes now than we did before we stepped on that first plane to Iceland. John and I agree that while there may be a place in our future for adventure and a romantic lifestyle on an island away from it all, that shouldn't be our focus. First we need to turn two kids into responsible adults who contribute to society. Along the way we want to find a way to make a contribution to the world that has given us so much.

We'll surely keep traveling. We still need to see huge chunks of the world—India, Australia, Russia, the Himalayas—but we'll have to squeeze future trips into the short spaces of time when the kids aren't in school. In the meantime, we're enjoying the things we missed while we were on the road—friends, extended family, neighborhood parties, refrigerators, supermarkets. As long as we can be together, life is mighty good.

APPENDIX OF
FAST FACTS

Cost for four people to travel around the world for a year. Includes everything from plane tickets to ice cream cones to storage costs for household items and a certain broken leg.*	$121,275.89
Countries "entered"	35
Countries "visited"	28
Number of places slept in	150
Average length of stay in one place	2.5 days

* For a more detailed cost breakdown, go to www.360degreeslongitude.com

Longest stay in any one place	28 days (Belize)
Types of accommodations/ number of nights	airplanes 5 trains 6 buses 5 boats/ferries 10 airport departure lounge 1 hostels 131 tents 43 caves 4 friends' places 6 guest houses 20 YMCAs 2 hotels 46 cabins 48 condos/apartments 38
Miles traveled	More than 67,000
Times we wished we were home	zero

APPENDIX OF
HOW TO

S o. You think you would like to do a year around the world with your family, but don't know where to start. You've come to the right place.

That said, no one book or person can tell you how to plan and execute a trip of this magnitude. Further, there is no way you can plan a trip like this in detail as you might a two-week vacation. Get used to the idea that trying to find accommodations at your next destination is your full-time job.

As with almost everything, the more you know about something, the more there is to know. By far the best advice is simply, "Don't panic."

How Much Does It Cost?

The number one question people have, but are often afraid to ask is, "How much does it cost to go around the world?" The quick and easy answer is that I don't see how twelve months on the road can be done for less than $30,000 per person.

Our *total* cash outlay was $121,275.89 for four people. Okay, so I'm a bit obsessive about numbers. Of that amount, $29,971.60 was spent before we even set a toe on a plane. Wow! That sure is a lot of money to spend before you even start! That's what we thought, too, but we had to take care of several up-front costs, such as plane tickets, equipment, clothing, vaccinations, storage, and medical insurance.

Thirty-thousand dollars per person per year seems like a lot of money, too. It is, but there is very little "air" that can be squeezed out of those figures. For example, we spent less than $100 on souvenir shopping for the entire year. For souvenirs we let the kids each get one item per continent, and collect every kind of coin they could find.

Methods to reduce costs would include:
• Reduce the number of countries visited, as getting from point A to point B was one of the biggest line items in our budget.
• Travel by bicycle for the same reason.
• Limit your itinerary to the developing world, as places like Switzerland are far more expensive than, say, Thailand.

We were very thrifty when it came to food and accommodations. Unless you can eat just bread and peanut butter and sleep outdoors full-time, it isn't possible to travel much cheaper than we did.

We were less thrifty when it came to activities; endeavors ranging from Wild Wadi to the Inca Trail do not come free. Our philosophy is, "Why travel at all if you can't partake of the local attractions?"

Equipment

There are a lot of equipment list suggestions available online. Some are okay, others less than helpful. I read one packing list online that boasted you could travel the world with only ten pounds of gear. The first entry at the top of that list was a three-pound computer. Rubbish.

In the weeks prior to our leaving, I think we became our local REI's favorite customers. The best investments by far were a new lightweight tent, tropical-weight sleeping bags, and silk sleep sacks. Even though they took up a lot of space in our luggage, we sure were glad we had them. When we were no longer camping, the sleeping bags and silk sleep sacks were still worth their weight in gold so we wouldn't have to sleep in fifty years of dust, as you might find in some of the bedding in less-than-elegant hostels.

Every time we considered purchasing something for our trip, we asked ourselves, "How would we feel if this were stolen?" We were careful not to overspend, because the reality of travel is that many people do have their backpacks or suitcases disappear. This was one reason we brought only a very small camera, no laptop, no GPS, and no satellite phone. On the Christmas before we left, I bought September a plain gold wedding band with the words World-the-Round Trip engraved inside so she could leave her diamond ring at home. Remarkably, we never had a single thing stolen on our entire trip, but that was not the case with many of the people we met on the road.

Before we left I had a long list of "stuff" that we had to buy that I thought I couldn't live without. When we were finally packing "for real" a lot of it got edited out and even more got left behind in various campgrounds during our first few weeks on the road. By the end of the year, other than some simple clothes, my silk sleep sack, and tropical-weight sleeping bag, the only thing I found that I was hoarding in my suitcase were my plastic eating utensils.

The lesson is you can get by with very little, and what you absolutely need, you can usually get on the road. And if you can't get what you absolutely need on the road, you will find you can do without that, too.

Books

Guidebooks are the single most important thing you will need to make your travel go smoothly. The problem is, you don't want to have to carry a year's worth of guidebooks with you all the time. They are really, really heavy! In many cases, we were able to find guidebooks along the way. Most big cities have at least one bookstore with a few books in English. In other cases, we had guidebooks sent to us from the United States along with our monthly shipment of books for the kids.

Typical guidebooks like *Lonely Planet* and *The Rough Guide* are good sources of information for a specific geographic region, but have no information for planning an expedition. One great source of practical information is *The Traveler's Handbook* (Globe Pequot Press). Now in its ninth edition, it has over nine hundred pages of information on topics ranging from how to respect local customs, to how to anticipate probable repairs for an overturned vehicle, to how to meet entry requirements for every country in the world. Some of the best information is about relative safety and general weather patterns per country.

If you will be traveling with children, and if your children like to read, keep in mind that there is *nothing* available in English for them overseas outside of a few obvious places, such as England, Australia, New Zealand, and South Africa. I take that back. You can find the *Harry Potter* series in English nearly everywhere, as it is popular among those trying to learn to read English. Other than that, you might be able to find *Moby Dick* in a bookstore in China, but trust me, your kids won't like it. Buy all of your children's and young adult literature before you go and arrange to have someone ship it to you. The good news is that nearly all juvenile literature is printed on cheap, porous paper, which happens to be fairly lightweight.

September purchased hundreds of dollars' worth of books for the kids before we left. She did a mountain of research and found historical fiction and other genres of literature that was set in the areas we were planning to visit. She separated the books into twelve piles, one pile for each month, roughly corresponding to the places we hoped we would be. Approximately once a month, we would send an e-mail to September's mother letting her know where we would be in a few days, and she would FedEx a package of books to us. Sometimes we would have her send the books to a friend of a friend who was living in a city we were planning to visit, and other times we would have the books sent to a hostel or campground where we were going to be staying. It was always complicated trying to figure out where we were going to be a few days in the future, but getting the package of books was always worth it.

I will say all the effort and money required to purchase and ship all those books was always worth the trouble. The impact on each of us from reading *Red Scarf Girl*, about the Chinese Cultural Revolution, was much greater when read in China than it would have been if read at home in Silicon Valley. As there can be l-o-o-o-ng stretches with nothing to do when traveling, I can't imagine going on such a trip with kids who couldn't entertain themselves with a good book.

How Do I Buy Plane Tickets?

There are dozens of companies that specialize in around-the-world plane tickets. We used AirTreks and highly recommend them. Googling the string "around the world plane tickets" will help you find many others.

There is a product called an "around-the-world ticket" that generally allows you to travel around the world in one direction, make a specific number of stops, and have flexible travel dates.

One problem we found with around-the-world tickets is that you cannot backtrack. For example, the itinerary we laid out for ourselves had us flying primarily east, but occasionally we had to fly west. This isn't allowed on a typical around-the-world ticket—those flight segments would have been simply out of pocket.

Another problem with around-the-world tickets is that they are generally all on one airline or airline alliance. For example, if you buy your around-the-world tickets on United, you can't fly to Mauritius.

After doing much research on the subject, we finally committed ourselves to what are known as open jaw segments. Open jaw segments are a series of one-way tickets strung together, connecting the dots on the globe you wish to visit. In the post-9/11 world, one-way tickets are hard to buy, so a good travel agent who specializes in around-the-world tickets is invaluable here.

With open jaw tickets you build your own itinerary, and the only limitations are your budget and your imagination. The drawback is that you fix your travel dates in advance.

How Do I Save for a Trip This Big?

The easiest thing would be to marry well or arrange to inherit a trust fund. Failing that, plan on saving for years.

We started saving for this trip about ten years before we left. In those ten years we bought less expensive cars than we could otherwise afford and a smaller house than we would have, and we put the difference into savings.

Our kids had heard us planning this trip since before they could talk. Our family mantra became, "Would we rather buy this, or go on our trip?" This applied even to minor expenditures such as clothing, not so much for the economic benefit as the psychological benefit that as a family, we were working toward our goal. Both kids became evangelical about cost cutting, sometimes to the point of being irksome, but it showed that we were united in our goal. In the end, it was worth being scolded by an eight-year-old for going to the occasional Giants game at AT&T Park.

It isn't as hard as you think. Funds for one backyard landscaping and a new minivan channeled into a different account would go a long way toward funding extended travel. The minivan will get old and the backyard will get overrun by weeds, but the memories you share as a family will last forever.

How Do I Carry Cash?

We didn't. Only very rarely did I carry more cash with me than I could tolerate losing if I were mugged. For example, when we were in Tanzania we had to pay our safari operator in cash; after I had concluded using the ATMs over several days wasn't going to work out, the tour operator arranged bodyguards to accompany me to the bank when I went for the cash advance on my Visa. The only other time I carried a lot of cash was in Bolivia when we took our Unimog adventure over the Andes. We had to pay for services along the way and there were no facilities for getting cash en route.

Nevertheless, when we found ourselves in certain places where we felt an elevated risk of pickpockets, such as the Covered Bazaar in Istanbul, we divided our cash and credit cards equally among the four of us.

How Do I Get Cash?

Mostly from ATMs. This worked great in Europe, Turkey, and the UAE. Unfortunately, this lulled us into a false sense of availability that backfired once we landed in Tanzania. After the Lushoto debacle, we learned to ask locally about ATM and bank availability before traveling into remote areas, because traveler's checks aren't universally accepted.

As noted above, relying on ATMs works well in Europe. It also works well in most parts of Asia, including China. We knew before going to Cambodia that there were no ATM services in the country, so we relied upon traveler's checks there.

One big surprise was Central and South America. While ATMs are plentiful, our Cirrus and Star system cards were almost universally rejected continentwide, even at machines specifically advertised to be on those networks. Slipping a credit card into the same machine, however, would almost always work—even though the credit card was also on the same network.

On the subject of credit cards, we carried three pairs of cards issued to both John and September, for a total of six cards. I would carry with me card "A" issued in my name. September's card "A" was kept with our passports. In a like manner, September carried card "B" with her, and my card "B" was with our passports. The rarely used pair of cards "C" was also with our passports.

We developed this strategy to minimize our risk in the case of lost or stolen cards, but also to protect ourselves if a bank decided to freeze our account due to "suspicious" charges.

Finally, we left letters on file with our bank and credit card companies with our rough itinerary and contact information.

How Do I Pay Bills?

I set up all my recurring bills for auto-payment, and then managed my accounts electronically over the Web. My mortgage holder, for example, never knew I was out of the country.

For nonrecurring bills, I used Checkfree, a bill-paying service that my bank worked with seamlessly. Everything was managed remotely using the Internet. September's mother handled our day-to-day mail and we kept in contact via e-mail for bills that might pop up.

All I needed to manage my finances remotely was an Internet café. The only country where I found it difficult to find an Internet café was in England. In fact, my experience was that the poorer the country, the more Internet cafes are available.

One Last Word about Money Matters

Before we left, I obtained a home equity line of credit, gave my mother-in-law power of attorney, and September and I each got our wills in order. Luckily, none of these were required although for the first few months after we returned, that home equity line of credit was mighty tempting.

How Do I Keep the Kids Entertained?

This is an important consideration for the mental health of the group. If the kids are bored, everyone suffers.

Kids aren't impressed by the same kinds of things adults are. Furthermore, you simply can't do something fun every minute or even every day. There were plenty of days where the only goal was to get the laundry done.

To combat boredom we deployed books. For this reason, I wouldn't recommend a trip of this type with children who are not yet good readers.

For an unusual insight into cultures that a typical traveler never sees, we also visited local amusement parks. The irony of a grim-faced Chinese man working the roller-coaster wasn't lost on the kids; neither was the smile we finally were able to coerce out of him. The contrast between Wild Wadi Water Park in Dubai versus the water park in Dar es Salaam, Tanzania was a good catalyst for a lesson on how people are the same, yet different.

What Would You Do Differently?

In retrospect, I wish we had spent less time in a few places, so that we could have spent more time in other places. But there is no way to know these kinds of things in advance; it is one of the frustrations about traveling that anyone with limited time, even if it is a year, has to accept.

For some folks there may be a clear advantage to liquidating all assets before embarking on a journey of this magnitude. There were many, many occasions when I was pulling my hair out trying to manage affairs at home from afar; the notice I received from the IRS asking questions about the previous tax year was one of the more choice frustrations.

I do regret not being more aggressive with taking pictures.

What Medications Should I Bring?

Our family doctor helped us out here. We simply asked him for his advice and he gave us prescriptions for several future and likely scenarios: Cipro, for diarrhea, was the only thing we actually used. It is straightforward to buy Cipro in most countries without a prescription.

What Immunizations Do I Need?

We scheduled a visit to our doctor a month before we left to get inoculated against yellow fever, hepatitis A, and typhoid as well as getting boosters for tetanus.

We also needed malaria pills because Tanzania was a malaria zone. Our doctor recommended the drug Malarone to us. It was $200 per person for a one month's supply. There were cheaper malaria medications, but they all sported nasty side effects.

On our doctor's advice we decided to wait and buy our malaria medication overseas, where he thought it was likely to be cheaper. We found that Malarone wasn't cheaper in Europe, and simply not available in Turkey or in the United Arab Emirates. So we picked up a supply of the inexpensive nasty side-effect kind of malaria pills before we left Dubai. Fortunately, we experienced none of those nasty side effects.

How Do I Stay Connected?

Being a geek, I agonized over this one. I *wanted* a computer. I *wanted* a satellite phone. Both would have been immensely useful. I brought neither.

It was a matter of bulk. The issue of bulk first reared its ugly head during one of our training rides. We had taken several long-distance, self-contained bike rides before we attempted to ride from London to Istanbul. One such ride was to circle the island of Maui. Anyone who has been on the backside of Maui knows how remote it is. Let's just say that we realized we couldn't eat a computer when we were tired and hungry and there were no stores around.

It was basically the same story for a satellite phone. I have a professional connection with one of the satellite phone services, and they offered a phone to me for our trip, but I had to decline because of size and weight. More than once I wished I had it, but we survived without it.

For a computer, I took a state-of-the-art PDA and a wireless keyboard. This was a fantastic solution and one I heartily recommend. The device I brought had Wi-Fi and Bluetooth connectivity. I used this "e.brain" for keeping a journal, playing chess, keeping documents handy, sending and receiving e-mail, Web browsing, and just about anything you can do with a computer.

For voice, I bought a simple "pay as you go" cell phone in London. I then bought a new GSM card for each local network as we made our way around the world. This solution worked okay. The obvious problem lay in the typical cell phone coverage issues. The not-so-obvious annoyance was arriving in a new place, needing to make phone calls for things like finding accommodations, but not being able to because the GSM card in my phone wouldn't roam on the new network.

My rule of thumb "Don't bring more than you want to carry, nor anything more expensive than you're willing to have stolen" applies to zippy electronics as much or more than any other equipment.

What about the Language Barrier?

You'll be surprised what you can accomplish with a smile and a credit card. Of course, that is of little help when you have to make a phone call. The best advice is to go over your phrase book before placing the call and hope for the best.

English, even if at only a rudimentary level, is spoken widely in the travel industry in much of the world. We found the exception to be China, but if we can stumble through, so can you.

An immense help is a universal picture dictionary. Don't leave home without one.

What Were Your Favorite Places?

That is a very hard question. I love Switzerland, and I would heartily recommend it to almost anyone. I also love Bolivia, and would recommend it to a select few.

The four of us have our own favorites, and for different reasons. The only country that is in each of our "top five" is Switzerland. A lot of places come close, but if you love the outdoors there is no substitute for Switzerland. The following rounds out the remainder of our top picks with a short summary of why:

John

1-Bolivia: Raw, action packed with a little bit of everything for the adventurous.

2-Thailand: Safe, easy to travel in, very affordable, lots of variety and activities to do in the great outdoors.

3-Cambodia: Be prepared to be humbled.

September

1-Turkey: We could afford to eat out in restaurants, people are friendly, and the country is exotic enough to let you know you are no longer in Kansas.

2-China: Just like interplanetary travel, but without the inconvenience of leaving Mother Earth. The overwhelming and pervasive entrepreneurial spirit is truly mind boggling.

Katrina

1-Tanzania: The Serengeti—there is no place on earth like Africa to see big game.

Jordan

1-Costa Rica: Vulcan Arenal, the rain forest, the river taxis— there is much to love about Costa Rica.

APPENDIX OF
STUPID FACTS

- Country with weirdest sayings on T-shirts: Japan
- Most ubiquitous fast-food restaurant: KFC
- Most ubiquitous food product: Pringles
- Most ubiquitous product advertisement: Coke
- Most counterfeited food product: Oreos (Okeos, Oleos . . . the list is endless)
- Worst food: England
- Best hot dogs: France
- Best ice cream (*ahem . . . gelato*): Italy
- Worst ice cream: Turkey
- Most ubiquitous product: Microsoft Windows
- Best postal system: Beijing, China
- Most mystifying postal service: Sweden, where there *are* no post offices

- Worst postal system: Czech Republic

- Most illiterate taxi drivers: China

- Most repulsive toilets: China, with (dis)honorable mention going to the "hotel" in Laguna Colorado, Bolivia

- Most elaborate toilets: Japan

- Best roller coaster: Thunder Dolphin, Tokyo

- Most shoe shine boys per square km: La Paz

- Most Internet cafés per square km: Tie, between Thailand and Bolivia

- Fewest Internet cafés per square km: England

- Best Internet cafés: Japan—wicked fast upload speeds!

- Most littered plastic bags per square foot: Tanzania

- Most Rolex dealers per square km: Zermatt, Switzerland

- Best water park: Wild Wadi in Dubai

- Most aggressive beggars and touts: Arusha, Tanzania

- Most bang for buck: Thailand

- Most stunning scenery: Switzerland, although Machu Picchu and the Lake District near San Carlos de Bariloche, Argentina are also fabulous

- Best chocolate: Forget Switzerland. San Carlos de Bariloche, Argentina. Go for the chocolate and stay for the scenery.

- Most appalling gutters: Dar es Salaam

- Most colorful hair on old ladies: Japan

- Most aggressive carpet salesmen: Turkey

- Most helpful people: England

- Most friendly people: France—surprised? Of course, we found friendly people everywhere we went.

- Best children's parks above the tree line: Switzerland

- Best public swimming facilities: Germany

- Prettiest big city: Stockholm
- Most dazzling big city: Hong Kong
- Hardest to travel in: China, as the language barrier is huge
- Most pickpocket attempts per hour: Rome
- Most obnoxious coins: Sweden and Costa Rica (tie); forget stuffing them in your pocket. You need a wheelbarrow to cart them around they are so huge.
- Most on-time trains: Tie between Switzerland and Japan
- Hardest place to lunch: Dubai during Ramadan
- Coolest over-the-counter fireworks: Mauritius
- Most complicated bathing ritual: Japan
- Most blatant product counterfeiting: China, although Bolivia is a very close second
- Noisiest country: Tie between United Arab Emirates and China
- Noisiest city: Panama City with their freaking buses
- Nicest subway: Hong Kong
- Most confusing subway: Paris
- Most elaborate subway: London
- Mean time for solicitation in Bangkok: Twenty minutes
- Worst traffic: Phnom Penh, Cambodia
- Worst drivers: Istanbul
- Most perplexing economy: Thailand. How can things be so cheap?
- Strangest question asked at a restaurant: "Do you want gas or no gas?"
- Worst pencils: Tanzania—the lead breaks if you dare write anything
- Most dangerous thing we did: cross the street
- Most traveled citizens: Dutch. They are everywhere. Twenty-year-old Israelis are a close second.

- Worst Fanta flavor: Belize. We think it is aspirin flavor.
- The most enduring U.S. personality worldwide: Monica Lewinsky
- Most bizarre law: Kids under eighteen can't use the Internet in China

GOOGLE EARTH!

Google Earth is the perfect backdrop for telling the story of *360 Degrees Longitude*. This book has a Google Earth companion on the Web that will enhance the story as it unfolds. Google Earth is free, but it does require a broadband Internet connection to run properly.

Verify that you have a computer, with any modern Internet browser.

Check that you have a broadband Internet connection. This usually means a cable modem or DSL. Sorry, but a dial-up connection will result in little more than frustration. Google Earth is made up of terabytes of data, and while you don't need to access all of that data at once, you will need to process a couple of megabytes per second to enjoy all there is to offer.

Download Google Earth, at http://earth.google.com

Get the *360 Degrees Longitude* Google Earth companion file at http://www.360degreeslongitude.com/concept3d/360degreeslongitude.kmz and save it.

Throughout the book you will see the Google Earth logo 🌐 when there is more information for you to find online. Want to visit the pampas where Katrina and Jordan fed piranha to Plastico the pet alligator? Fire up Google Earth, spin the digital globe to Bolivia, and drill down to Rurrenabaque and click the icon. That will pull up additional information about Rurrenabaque, along with photos and video taken in the area.

If you are unfamiliar with Google Earth, here are a few basic steps that will help you get started.

Google Earth comes with several "layers" that you can turn on and off. There is a layer for international borders, a layer for populated places, a layer for bus stops, one for ATMs, and so on. The *360 Degrees Longitude* companion file is simply another layer.

If you turn on all the layers simultaneously, the digital globe can quickly become overwhelmed, so explore the different layers that come with Google Earth to familiarize yourself with what's available so you can turn them on and off as you see fit. One of my favorite layers is the terrain layer. With the terrain layer enabled you can see the texture of the surface of the earth when you zoom in and tilt the horizon.

Once you have the feel for how Google Earth behaves, download the layer for *360 Degrees Longitude*. After the download is complete, Google Earth will automatically open and you should see something like this:

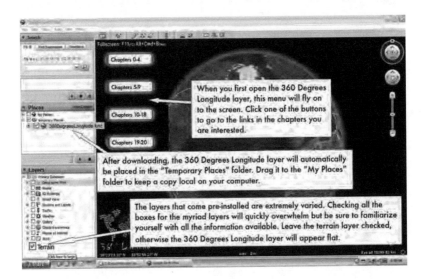

Clicking on one of the "Chapters" menu buttons (see above) opens a list of all the links from the book. Clicking on one of the links will open a dialogue box with photos, video, and text that describe events in that part of the world. For example, clicking on Chapters 0–4, then "Pingvellir" under Chapter 1 will open the dialogue box shown in below.

There are more features in the *360 Degrees Longitude* layer explained in the online tutorial at http://www.360degreeslongitude.com/ge/ge_how2.pdf. If you have a question that isn't covered in the online tutorial, send me an e-mail at john@360degreeslongitude.com. Enjoy!

Google™ and the Google Earth icon 🌐 are registered trademarks of the Google corporation. Used by permission.

ABOUT THE AUTHOR

After completing his graduate degree in aerospace engineering, John Higham moved to the San Francisco Bay Area where he started his career and accumulated ten U.S. patents for various aspects of satellite design. Although he arrived in the Bay Area single, it wasn't long before he met September and they became inseparable. John, September, and their two children, Katrina and Jordan, still live in the San Francisco Bay Area where John continues to design satellites to keep the mortgage current.

When he was about three years old, John used to enthusiastically jump up and down on the bench seat of his family's Ford station wagon, chanting, "Go on a long-long bye-bye!" as the car motored down the highway. Although the days of jumping up and down in a moving car are over, he still gets just as excited at the prospect of going somewhere new.

ACKNOWLEDGMENTS

I am the luckiest guy in the world. Not just because I was able to travel around the world with my family and live to write a book about it, but also because of the people who helped along the way. Words cannot express the gratitude I feel for the many people who contributed to making this book a reality.

I'd like to start with Chris MacAskill. If it hadn't been for his enthusiasm and great connections the train never would have left the station.

A heart-felt thank you goes to my friends at Google, Mark Fuchs, John Hanke, and Melissa Crounse, for their support and encouragement of this project. A big *muchas gracias* also goes to the talent at Concept3D! Oliver Davis and Matt Brown took the odds and ends that made up all my *Google Earth* placemarks and turned them into a true work of art.

To Linda Cashdan, who read an early version of this manuscript and gave me encouragement at a critical time, thank you for your kind words and for giving me the drive I needed.

More than any one person, Larry Habegger helped me take what was essentially a pile of e-mails and journal entries and turn it into a book. His assessments were always accurate, insightful, and invaluable. Thanks for your friendship and help in making this project a reality.

If a writer ever needed a friend in the world, it would be his agent. It is impossible to describe how much Jason Ashlock did for this project. I can't imagine going through this process without his guidance and friendship. I especially want to thank Richard Fumosa for recognizing the potential of this project.

I also owe a debt of gratitude to September's parents, Dale and Marie Blanchard, for looking after our domestic affairs while we were on the road.

Thanks to the legions of people who helped us find our way around the world. There are simply too many to mention, and many whose names I simply do not know. We will take all the generosity we received during our year on the road and pay it forward.

Most important, thanks to my lovely wife, September. Without her, this book would have never happened. Not only because she let me off the hook for my half of the laundry and dishes all those months I was writing this book, but also because when I asked, "remind me why I'm doing this again?" she knew just what to say to keep me at the keyboard when I really wanted to be riding my bike. It is because of her that I truly am the luckiest guy in the world.